The Making of Mexican Modernist Architecture

This book presents the making of Mexican Modernist architecture through five power structures – academic, social status, economic/political, gender, and postcolonial – and by interviews and analysis of 13 key Mexican architects. These include Luis Barragán, José Villagrán García, Juan O'Gorman, Pedro Ramírez Vázquez, Agustín Hernández, Abraham Zabludovsky, Carlos Mijares, Ricardo Legorreta, Juan José Díaz Infante, Enrique Norten, Alberto Kalach, Javier Sordo Madaleno and Clara de Buen.

Although the five power structures framed what was built, the testimony of these Mexican architects helps us to recognize and discover subtleties and nuances. Their views thereby shed light on what contributed to making Mexican Modernist architecture so distinctive globally. Even if these architects were not always aware of the power structures, their projects nonetheless supported discrimination, marginalization and subjugation. In that sense the book also reveals the extent to which these power structures are still present today.

The Making of Mexican Modernist Architecture's uniqueness lies in uncovering the remarkable buildings that arose amid the five power structures while at the same time questioning their validity. It also voices the urgent need today for a new kind of architecture outside these boundaries. The book is essential reading for anyone studying Mexican and Latin American architecture.

Celia Esther Arredondo Zambrano was born in Monterrey, Mexico. She graduated from Tecnológico de Monterrey with a degree in Architecture, and has a master's degree in Landscape Architecture from Texas A&M University and a master's degree in Urban Design from Oxford Brookes University in England, where she later obtained her PhD in Architecture. She is Emeritus Professor at Tecnológico de Monterrey, Mexico and her areas of expertise are theory, history and cultural studies in architecture, as well as sustainable architecture and urban design. She has numerous publications in the fields of architecture, both in Spanish and in English. She was the first female president of the National Academy of Architecture, Chapter Monterrey, and was granted the status of Academic Emeritus, the highest distinction awarded by the National Academy of Architecture of the Mexican Architects Society.

THE MAKING OF MEXICAN MODERNIST ARCHITECTURE

Celia Esther Arredondo Zambrano

LONDON AND NEW YORK

Designed cover: Front and back cover images by Carsten Krohn.

First published 2023
by Routledge
4 Park Square, Milton Park, Abingdon, Oxon OX14 4RN

and by Routledge
605 Third Avenue, New York, NY 10158

Routledge is an imprint of the Taylor & Francis Group, an informa business

© 2023 Celia Esther Arredondo Zambrano

The right of Celia Esther Arredondo Zambrano to be identified as author of this work has been asserted in accordance with sections 77 and 78 of the Copyright, Designs and Patents Act 1988.

All rights reserved. No part of this book may be reprinted or reproduced or utilised in any form or by any electronic, mechanical, or other means, now known or hereafter invented, including photocopying and recording, or in any information storage or retrieval system, without permission in writing from the publishers.

Trademark notice: Product or corporate names may be trademarks or registered trademarks, and are used only for identification and explanation without intent to infringe.

British Library Cataloguing-in-Publication Data
A catalogue record for this book is available from the British Library

Library of Congress Cataloging-in-Publication Data
Names: Arredondo Zambrano, Celia Esther, author.
Title: The making of Mexican modernist architecture / Celia Esther
 Arredondo Zambrano.
Description: Abingdon, Oxon : Routledge, 2023. | Includes bibliographical
 references and index. |
Identifiers: LCCN 2022047411 (print) | LCCN 2022047412 (ebook) |
 ISBN 9781032332772 (hardback) | ISBN 9781032332741
 (paperback) | ISBN 9781003318934 (ebook)
Subjects: LCSH: Modern movement (Architecture)—Mexico. |
 Architecture and society—Mexico—History--20th century. |
 Architects—Mexico—Attitudes.
Classification: LCC NA755.5.M63 A77 2023 (print) | LCC NA755.5.M63
 (ebook) | DDC 720.972/0904—dc23/eng/20221026
LC record available at https://lccn.loc.gov/2022047411
LC ebook record available at https://lccn.loc.gov/2022047412

ISBN: 978-1-032-33277-2 (hbk)
ISBN: 978-1-032-33274-1 (pbk)
ISBN: 978-1-003-31893-4 (ebk)

DOI: 10.4324/9781003318934

Typeset in News Gothic
by Apex CoVantage, LLC

Printed in the UK by Severn, Gloucester on responsibly sourced paper

To my father

CONTENTS

Foreword	*ix*
Murray Fraser	
Introduction	**1**
1 Mexican Architecture as an Academic Discipline	**13**
Academic Discourse	14
Architectural Schools	16
Architectural Practice	20
The Role of Architectural Guilds and Associations	25
Architecture as a System of Meaning	26
Written Architecture	27
Architectural Classification Systems	30
Architectural Treatises	36
Photographed Architecture	41
Architects and Their Authorship	48
The First Generation (1900–14)	49
José Villagrán García (1901–82)	49
Luis Barragán (1902–88)	50
Juan O'Gorman (1905–82)	52
The Second Generation (1915–29)	53
Pedro Ramírez Vázquez (1919–2013)	54
Abraham Zabludovsky (1924–2003)	55
Agustín Hernández (1924–2022)	56
The Third Generation (1930–44)	58
Ricardo Legorreta (1931–2011)	58
Carlos Mijares (1930–2015)	60
Juan José Díaz Infante (1936–2012)	61
The Fourth Generation (1945–60)	62
Enrique Norten (1951–)	62
Clara de Buen (1954–)	63
Alberto Kalach (1960–)	64
Javier Sordo Madaleno (1956–)	66
2 Mexican Architecture and Economic and Political Power	**73**
Architecture and Power	74
Main Power Groups in Mexico	76
Twentieth-Century Mexican Economic Models	77
Influence of Economic Models on Twentieth-Century Mexican Architecture	79
Power in Twentieth-Century Architectural Modernism in Mexico	83
Hospitals	83

Contents

Museums	86
Hotels	92
Transportation Buildings	95
Banks	98
State Buildings	102
Private and Public Office Buildings	105
Public and Private Schools	112
Religious Architecture	116

3 Mexican Architecture as Social Status in a System of Consumption — **125**

Mexican Architecture and Consumption	126
Mexican Architecture as a Sign Within the Consumption Cycle	130
The Image of Mexican Architects	136
Mexican Architects and Their Social Status	145
Mexican Architects and Their Social Image	150
Spatial and Social Marginalization in Mexico City	154

4 Mexican Architecture and Gender — **171**

Mexican Architecture as a Gendered Discipline	172
Architecture as an Artefact of Gender Differentiation	180
Women's Place in Mexican Architecture	181
Men's Place in Mexican Architecture	197

5 Mexican Architecture and Postcolonialism — **217**

Mexico's Postcolonial Identity	218
Mimicry and Dissimulation	226
Hybridity and Simulation	241
Emotional Architecture or Magical Realism	248

Epilogue — **261**

Acknowledgements — **273**

Illustration Credits — **277**

Bibliography — **289**

Index — **297**

FOREWORD

Professor Murray Fraser,
Bartlett School of Architecture, University College London, UK
September 2022

Mexican Modernist architecture was once among the most eagerly anticipated and studied in the world, yet today it is nowhere nearly so well known. Why should this be the case when we are, after all, living in what is an increasingly globalized world?

In this fascinating book, Celia Arredondo explains the causes full well. European-inspired Modernism established itself quickly and firmly in Mexican architecture during the 1920s, through figures like José Villagrán García and Juan O'Gorman, and then, in the very capable hands of those such as Luis Barragán, it grew to encompass the whole discipline to such an extent that Pedro Ramírez Vázquez in the 1990s could still be declaring his adherence to 'functionalism' long after that concept had become totally discredited elsewhere. Even the efforts of a few famous figures who attempted to flirt with Postmodernism, such as Ricardo Legorreta, had done very little to alter the course of Mexican architecture.

The idea of Modernist architecture as becoming an almost-religious orthodoxy within Mexico, while undoubtedly impressive, also came with major consequences, as Arredondo makes very clear. In a riveting series of chapters, she shows how Modernism took over the scene: it became the only approach taught in Mexico's architectural schools; it was adopted by the upper classes as a badge of elitism that separated them from their servants; it was incorporated into the various economic plans of successive Mexican governments; it was used as a means to reinforce the prevailing macho attitudes towards woman; plus, it fed into dreamlike postcolonial fantasies about the country's cultural uniqueness. Arredondo characterizes these strands in terms of five power structures which in effect framed the production of architecture in Mexico, and which adhered to the broader social norms of that era.

Arredondo's book really comes alive to us because she interviewed ten of the important Mexican architects who form the basis of the book's analysis (the other three architects having died prior to her starting upon her research). By hearing the voices of those architects involved, we are given a real sense of how they thought about their design projects, and to what extent they were (or were not) aware of the five dominant power structures. Arredondo does superbly in allowing

Foreword

these architects to speak for themselves, not requiring them to answer directly about the power structures she is hoping to investigate, yet subtly letting their values and ideologies come across in what they are saying.

In the final section of the book, Arredondo calls for a broadening of Mexican architecture today, thereby extending the important contributions of figures like Clara de Buen, who was the only female architect of note in twentieth-century Mexico. Now, thankfully, there is a confident and growing body of women architects in the country that includes Tatiana Bilbao, Fernanda Canales and Frida Escobedo, each of which is also gaining a lot of international attention. It is highly tempting to wish for a resurgence of global acclaim for Mexican architecture, yet this time based on female architects who are embracing a more inclusive and nuanced architectural approach within an age of hyper-modernism – one that is clearly far more relevant today than that of their celebrated male predecessors in the previous century. In this regard, for all its critical precision, Celia Arredondo's book also offers much hope for the future of architecture in Mexico.

Introduction

DOI: 10.4324/9781003318934-1

Introduction

Mexican Modernist architecture came into its own during the twentieth century. Due to opportune conditions and strongly held convictions by many architects and clients, it soon enough evolved into a mature and confident movement. These circumstances and beliefs were produced in a country that was then experiencing a tremendous transformation from a rural into an urban nation, as part of the wider process of modernization/westernization. For the first time, Mexican architects were able to increase their participation in the production of new buildings, and as such became recognized both nationally and internationally. Major developments sprung up in Mexico's cities that introduced new cultural patterns and contributed widely to the making of Mexican Modernism.[1] What is also especially notable is the relative homogeneity of Mexican Modernist architectural discourse across the decades, when compared to the critiques of Modernism that arose in Western countries from the 1960s onwards and which fed into counter-movements such as Postmodernism, Deconstructivism and the like. Instead, once it had been accepted in Mexico, Modernism effectively prevailed thereafter. Indeed, the influence of Mexican Modernist architecture as established in the twentieth century is still alive and well today, shaping the production of current architecture and being embedded in the country's twenty-first century lifestyles, values and ideals. Now, with Modernist architecture celebrating 100 years since its initial introduction to Mexico, it seems a pertinent time to examine the elements underlying it.

Modernist architecture in Mexico was always very much a product of its cultural settings, taking hold during a century of enormous changes that were epitomized by the Mexican Revolution from 1910–20. This sole event triggered a radical transformation that aimed to unite a country which was culturally and ethnically diverse, indeed divided, by creating new government institutions to deal with healthcare, housing and education as a national project; these initiatives embraced both modernity and a new sense of national identity. It meant that the 'national project' consisted of two apparently opposite concepts: one was to create a modernized and westernized country capable of being an active part of the international scene, while the second was of a country which possessed a strong national character, rich in tradition, imagery, legend and colour. Politically and economically, Mexico shifted from a rural feudal system under the dictatorship of Porfirio Díaz, who ruled the country up until 1911, to an increasingly industrial capitalist system governed by a democratic, constitutional republic. After the Mexican Revolution, therefore, Mexico's overriding aim was to achieve economic competitiveness and therefore worldwide recognition. Artistically speaking, this impetus produced the celebrated muralist movement,

Introduction

which contained such notable figures as Diego Rivera, José Clemente Orozco and David Alfaro Siqueiros, and which aimed at a revival of Mexico's cultural past fuelled by new social and political overtones. Architecturally speaking, after briefly implementing various eclectic styles, the leading architects in the country openly adopted Modernism following the lead of several Western architects, like Walter Gropius and Le Corbusier, and tried to apply their functionalist principles in buildings that would help to celebrate a condition of modernity and provide suitable settings for newly established institutions. This kind of 'national project' was most vividly, and epically, displayed in the 1968 Mexican Olympic Games, which were explicitly framed to show the world the country's progress, drive and character.[2]

As Mexico evolved into a modernized nation, it also experienced an astonishing increase in population, rising from around 14 million in 1910 to nearly 100 million by the end of that century. This exponential growth became especially acute in the late-twentieth century, and along with an internal migration of people from the land, as also seen in many other nations, this meant that the population explosion was concentrated mainly in cities that were now being built on Modernist principles. Octavio Paz, the famous Mexican poet and diplomat, once stated memorably that 'Architecture is the incorruptible witness of history'. However, in this case, Mexican Modernist architecture was more than a mere witness: it was created as an active protagonist and ally in the construction of the Mexican modern nation. Even when the perceived need to express a national identity began to dwindle towards the end of the twentieth century, architecture continues to play an important role by transforming itself, to a large extent, into a mechanism for real-estate investment, as part of the nation's switch towards a neoliberal economic system deriving from the USA. This process has been especially fuelled by the North American Free Trade Agreement (NAFTA), a trilateral trading bloc as signed in 1994 between Canada, Mexico and the United States. Thus, like in many countries, the adoption of Modernist architecture in Mexico was and still is culturally driven, yet what has made it so unique is that it has been able to transform this design approach into a genuinely expressive Mexican form that has gained, at least for a while, a powerful international reputation. In this sense, the situation can be seen as parallel to other celebrated examples of the 'International Style', such as Brazil and Japan. However, very much unlike Brazil and Japan, it can be argued that Mexican Modernist architecture has endured virtually unchanged throughout the course of the twentieth century and into the first decades of this century, experiencing relatively little deflection from other later, rival architectural movements.

Introduction

In this manner, Mexican Modernist architecture responded and contributed to the changes taking place during this period, and therefore it was by no means an autonomous phenomenon but was welded into the process of modernization/westernization. What, then, were the main factors that intervened so decisively in terms of making Mexican Modernism? It is the aim of this book to identify the key drivers, referred to by me as the 'power structures', which established and framed Mexico's architecture in the twentieth century and up till now. These power structures thus form the central interest of this book, since they were responsible for the creation of Mexican Modernist architecture as a consequence of Mexico's modernization/westernization process – and, more recently, in the new condition of globalization. The power structures that I have identified are five-fold: namely, academic; economic/political; social status; gender; and postcolonial. While there were, of course, many other power structures at work, I have chosen to focus only on these five, since they were the most important. To explain why, it is worth briefly spelling out their definitions and premises.

Firstly, 'the academic power structure' refers to the systems and processes which present architecture as a learned discipline and as a mode of practice. As such, it exerts its greatest control through schools of architecture, professional publications and other similarly institutionalized formats. The main premise for looking at it here is to establish how this power structure has contributed to the discourse and practice of Mexican Modernism by defining and controlling its classification systems, paradigms, archetypes, models, journals, monographs, etc.

Secondly, 'the economic/political power structure' regards the production of buildings as being controlled predominantly by three groups: public sector/governmental agencies, private enterprises/corporations and religious organizations. Together, they constituted Mexico's twentieth-century hegemonic elite and it was they who sponsored the new architecture by enforcing specific policies through the successive economic/political models introduced in Mexico. These models defined the production of a Mexican architecture that was seen as economically feasible and politically correct by introducing, maintaining or eliminating the relevant architectural typologies, technologies and patterns. What is essential, therefore, is to understand how these three power groups shaped Mexican architecture and how they exercised their power through built form.

Thirdly, the social status power structure saw architecture transformed into a symbol of power and an interchangeable object that was immersed in Mexico's acceptance of the capitalist consumption cycle rooted in modernization and westernization. As such, architecture came to be produced by and for an elite social group which possessed sufficient access to architectural discourse to be able to sustain their privileged social status. Key here is to examine how Mexican Modernist architecture was defined intellectually and culturally, and thus, what meanings it was endorsing or rejecting in order to be part of the consumption cycle.

Fourthly, the gender power structure established architecture as a deeply gendered profession, predominantly governed by males, as well as a means of maintaining specific gender patterns and behaviours. With female marginalization still clearly widespread in Mexico, the book will focus on how architectural practice and architectural space and form came to be defined and transformed into a gendered profession and be used as a gendering artifact to maintain gender inequality.

Fifthly, the postcolonial power structure portrayed Mexican architecture as a postcolonial construct that was non-western, yet, at the same time, a willing subordinate to Western paradigms. Hence, due to Mexican architecture's essentially postcolonial condition, it came to be classified both in terms of its 'Mexican-ness', or 'otherness', and its role in enabling the introduction of Western values and ideals. The aim here is not merely to recognize that this contradictory situation existed, but also to study how Mexican architecture was defined and even romanticized as 'other' through new activities, typologies, spaces and forms that were associated with modernization and westernization.

Each of these power structures will be addressed in five separate chapters, yet this book shows that, while Mexican twentieth-century architecture was defined by each of them, they also worked together as interrelated power structures that constituted and determined Mexican culture in general – and thus were determinant for its Modernist architecture. To examine how, when, where and to what end architecture was defined by cultural ideas and values through these five main power structures, I adopted a cultural studies approach that borrows freely theories and methods from other disciplines such as philosophy, linguistics and psychoanalysis, albeit concentrating mainly upon semiology,[3] discourse analysis,[4] and deconstruction.[5] The methodology offered by cultural studies thus provides the tools necessary to reveal the making of Mexican twentieth-century architecture more broadly. I have thus adopted a deliberately eclectic methodology when combining these theories. For instance, a semiotic approach is used to establish how Mexican Modernist architecture communicates to society through the forms of its key buildings, and to show also that it creates a system of signification which denotes and connotes meaning via its academic teaching and the classification systems used by the discipline.

Discourse analysis is also part of my methodology, and as such is used to reveal the relation of power and knowledge within architecture discourse. It is also

Introduction

applied in relation to architectural space to identify, by looking at floor plans and sections, the interplay between human relations and interior spaces, as well as the presence of disciplinary mechanisms like exclusion, confinement and surveillance that are imposed by social hierarchies. For this purpose, discourse analysis is applied combined with some aspects of Kim Dovey's critical method[6] and of Space Syntax[7] via spatial diagrams which identify the socio-spatial patterns in the key buildings that I am discussing – thereby revealing the control exerted within those buildings by power, status and gender. Deconstruction methodology is also applied to uncover the layers of constructed meanings and is mixed here with discourse analysis to examine architectural space in relation to gender, class, identity, economic and political power, as well as status. It is particularly useful in gender discourse to reveal the role of the privileged male, and this can also be extended to postcolonial discourse to identify the ways whereby Western cultural patterns shaped Mexican architecture. Deconstruction, along with the postcolonial methodology introduced by Homi Bhabha[8], is hence used to identify the cultural ambivalences and power struggles found in architectural patterns and elements.

This mix of methodologies thus provides the tools necessary to understand Mexican Modernist architecture. The underlying purpose of the study is to expose and explain the power structures that created this key architectural manifestation of the twentieth century. It means that there is less emphasis in this book on describing architectural features, or design methods and representational techniques, and far more on identifying the cultural beliefs and values embedded within Mexican Modernism. To be able to examine this subject, however, it is essential to be able to select a sample of architects and buildings which can define the scope of analysis. This then leads to the question of how best to choose which architects, what buildings and what reference materials should be investigated.

Clearly, the extent of Mexican twentieth-century architecture is vast; hence, more than 250 books about Mexican architecture were reviewed as potential reference sources. From these, I selected 36 key texts (see list in Chapter 1) and, using their indexes, a list of the Mexican architects mentioned were identified and ranked accordingly as suggested by American Architecture Professor Roxanne Williamson.[9] Still, the number of architects was immense, so, to decide on the sample of Mexican architects to study, I took note of Colombian architect Silvia Arango[10] and, based on her analysis, I divided Mexican Modernist architects into generations. To define the necessary timescale of each generation, I turned to the principle set by the famous author, José Ortega y Gasset, who argues that, in regard to the sociology of knowledge, the vital cycle of each major phase of

Introduction

thinking lasts for approximately 60 years; with this, then, I divided the list of Mexican architects into four generations of roughly 15-year intervals.[11] The first of these generations tends to invent and propose the new order of knowledge; the second generation consolidates and institutionalizes it; the third one criticizes it; and the fourth, and last, tends to reject or break away from it, leading thereby onto the next cycle of thought. In the case of Mexican Modernists, I selected a total of 13 from the list of architects most mentioned and featured in the 36 key publications. Thus, based on Ortega y Gasset's schema, this sample of Mexican architects were organized into four generations (i.e. birthdates from 1901–15, 1916–30, 1931–46, 1947–60). As a result, the following grouping of selected architects was established: from the first generation, Luis Barragán, José Villagrán García and Juan O'Gorman; from the second generation, Pedro Ramírez Vázquez, Agustín Hernández and Abraham Zabludovsky; from the third generation, Carlos Mijares, Ricardo Legorreta and Juan José Díaz Infante; and from the fourth generation, Enrique Norten, Alberto Kalach, Javier Sordo Madaleno and Clara de Buen. Interestingly, these 13 major architects all lived and worked – or indeed some still live and work – in Mexico City, revealing just how metropolitan-based architectural culture was in Mexico in the twentieth century, and still is.

Once this sample of 13 Mexican Modernist architects was selected, an investigation was conducted to draw up a comprehensive list of buildings they designed, mainly for analysis in Chapter 3. Further research was conducted to select some key buildings by each of these architects to start the process of obtaining relevant photographs, floor plans, spatial diagrams and site locations, with this information then being used as examples within each chapter in this book. To this basic source information, I was able to add in first-hand knowledge from a series of in-person interviews which I had undertaken as a research project back in the early 2000s. Hence, a crucial part of this book's investigations centres on these now-archival interviews. Ten personal interviews thus cover the work and thoughts of Pedro Ramírez Vázquez, Agustín Hernández, Abraham Zabludovsky, Carlos Mijares, Ricardo Legorreta, Juan José Díaz Infante, Enrique Norten, Alberto Kalach, Javier Sordo Madaleno and Clara de Buen. These interviews served as an even more important part of my ongoing research because six of these architects have, sadly, since passed away, making their interview testimony invaluable. Regrettably, I never had the opportunity to meet or interview those architects from the first generation of Mexican Modernism, which, in terms of the sample used for this book, means Luis Barragán, José Villagrán García and Juan O'Gorman. To compensate, I turned instead to the helpful publication of interviews with these three pioneering architects in the book, *Testimonios Vivos: Veinte Arquitectos*

Introduction

(Cuadernos de Arquitectura y Conservación del Patrimonio Artístico). Furthermore, a fascinating recorded interview with Luis Barragán by Alejandro Ramírez Ugarte was also very useful for my analysis. Key quotes from all the interviews are hence inserted into the text here to accentuate an argument, explain a concept or give specific information through the words of the architects themselves.

Although this book focussed on these 13 key architects, it is not intended to be a book about them; instead, they are featured here to give an overview of twentieth-century developments in Mexican architecture. Other sources of information were gathered and used, such as that relating to architectural teaching or economic models, for instance, where it could help with the examination of how Mexican Modern architecture was influenced by, and indeed defined by, the five main power structures mentioned above. Evidence is thus provided by the verbal testimonies and personal experiences of the selected architects, and by the analysis of the spatial and built forms of their major buildings. Modernist architecture is shown as the product of academic institutions, agencies of power, social status symbols, gendered practices and Western paradigms, each participating in the creation of Mexican cultural patterns during this period. Unfortunately, most of these practices and parameters are alive and well today, still directing and controlling Mexican architecture. Therefore, the analysis of Mexican Modernism in this book is not simply intended to unpick or undo it as an act of historical destruction, but rather as a dissection of a live organism, in hope that, by challenging the core of the professional institution in Mexico, in terms of its foundations and boundaries, a process of intellectual and cultural change can now begin that will encourage novel ideas and raise provocative questions, while also suggesting further issues for research.

However, what motivates this book most goes beyond the need to reveal the making of Mexican Modernist architecture. Indeed, it interconnects with a personal concern of mine that is inspired by a story, *The Circular Ruins*, written in 1940 by Jorge Luis Borges. When I first read this tale, I was quite shaken at the end when the main character discovers that he is, in fact, not real but is instead just the product of someone else's dream. I was particularly stunned when reading the words: 'With relief, with humiliation, with terror, he understood that he too was a mere appearance, dreamt by another'.[12] This thought horrified me, particularly this sudden realization of not being 'real'. What if I myself was not real? What if everything that I had previously thought was real was not real, either?

The more that I thought about this story and the way that Borges had meticulously described the work required to construct a dream, it started to dawn on me that I was indeed the dream of others. In some sense, we all are. We are

Introduction

each the dream of our parents, for one thing. Furthermore, I, as a Mexican, am also the dream of those who founded my country. As a woman, I am likewise the dream of those women who came before me. After reading Borges's tale, I also came to realize that I had known all of this instinctively all along, and that I knew that I would have – at some point in my life – to stand up to claim my own autonomy. Indeed, to some degree, we all need to stand up to assert ourselves in this way. I was also aware of my unavoidable accountability in the construction of others, or in dreaming up future generations, particularly through my role as an architecture professor, an activity to which I dedicated almost 40 years of my life. As a result, this book came ever more to focus upon the questioning of our belief systems – particularly that of Mexico's twentieth-century architecture – and of the construction of these beliefs, by trying to work out how we have come to believe what we believe. This critical intention is part of the need to question all our thinking and to challenge the paradigms of our lifestyles, in which architecture clearly plays an important role, so that we can produce new ones. With this notion in mind, the first chapter will therefore examine the formation of Mexican Modernist architecture as part of academic discourse, with all of the positives and negatives entailed.

NOTES

1 There is no definitive definition of 'Modernism', but rather various differing interpretations. Therefore, the usage of this term in this book derives from the one given by American philosopher and writer Marshall Berman, which is that 'Modernism' was the specific response by avant-garde architects/artists to the everyday experiences of people living in a new condition of Modernity – with the latter being the result of emerging socio-economic processes generally referred to as Modernization (e.g. capitalism, industrialization, mass urbanization, etc). Although there are other interpretations – for instance, some scholars have talked of concepts such as 'multiple modernities' and such like – this widely understood idea of 'Modernism' – hence also of 'Modernist' architecture – will be used in this book. For further reading see, Berman, Marshall. *All That Is Solid Melts into Air: The Experience of Modernity*. New York, NY, USA, Penguin Books, 1988.
2 See Castañeda, Luis M. *Spectacular Mexico: Design, Propaganda, and the 1968 Olympics*. México, Grupo Financiero Banamex, 2014.
3 Semiology, as the study of signs, is applied here mainly by drawing on the work of two noted French philosophers and cultural theorists, Roland Barthes and Jean Baudrillard. The semiotic approach treats architecture as a sign and system of signification that both denotes and connotes meaning. See: Barthes, Roland. *Elements of Semiology*. Translated by Annette Lavers and Colin Smith, New York, Hill & Wang, 1973 and Barthes,

Introduction

Roland. *The Fashion System*. London, Jonathan Cape Ltd., The Trinity Press, 1985, also Baudrillard, Jean. *The System of Objects*. Translated by James Benedict, London, Verso, 2006, and Baudrillard, Jean. *Jean Baudrillard selected writings*. Edited by Mark Poster, London, Polity Press, 1998.

4 Discourse analysis was largely created by the French philosopher and historian, Michel Foucault, and is the most common method used in cultural studies. It examines architecture as a discourse in order to assess its relationship to power and knowledge and also its relationship to space. In terms of the former, architecture is conceived as a normative discipline that establishes and legitimates its own ethos and ethical values, while, in terms of the latter, it helps to identify, through the use of floor plans, the interplay between human society and built space, where the presence of disciplinary mechanisms like exclusion, confinement and surveillance, as well as the social hierarchies, are at work within architecture. For this purpose, this book builds upon the work of Beatriz Colomina, and Kim Dovey. See: Foucault, Michel. *The Archaeology of Knowledge and the Discourse on Language*. Translated by A. M. Sheridan Smith, New York, Pantheon books, 1970 and Foucault, Michel. *Power/Knowledge, Selected Interviews and Other Writings 1972–1977*. Edited by Colin Gordon, Brighton, The Harvester Press, 1980. Also, Colomina, Beatriz (ed.). *Sexuality and Space*. New York, Princeton Architectural Press, 1992.

5 Deconstruction theory, as conceived by Jacques Derrida, another renowned French philosopher, ruptures the logocentrism of Western philosophy and is helpful in uncovering the layers of constructed meanings within all forms of discourse. This book combines Foucauldian discourse analysis with Derridean deconstruction, to analyse space and its relationship to gender, class, identity, economic and political power, as well as status. It is also used here to analyse the gender power structure to reveal the privileged male position. See: Derrida, Jacques. *Writing and Difference*. Translated by Alan Bass, Chicago, University of Chicago Press, 1978, and Derrida, Jacques. *On Grammatology*. Translated by Gayatri Chakravoty, John Hopkins University Press, Baltimore, 2016.

6 Kim Dovey is an Australian architectural and urban critic and professor of Architecture and Urban Design. He develops a methodology in his book *Framing Places* to explore, through case studies, his theories of place as mediators of power. See: Dovey, Kim. *Framing Places Mediating Power in Built Form*. London, Routledge, 1999.

7 Hillier, Bill. *Space Is the Machine*. Cambridge, University Press, 1999.

8 Bhabha, Homi. *Location of Culture*. London, Routledge, 1994. Bhabha is an Indian critical theorist, who developed a postcolonial methodology to identify the ambivalence present in architectural patterns using concepts like hybridity and mimicry, present in the postcolonial power structure.

9 For more information, see Williamson, Roxanne Kuter. *American Architects and the Mechanics of Fame*. Austin, University of Texas Press, 1991.

10 Arango Cardinal, Silvia. *Ciudad y Arquitectura. Seis Generaciones que Construyeron La América Latina Moderna*. México, Fondo de Cultura Económica, 2012.

11 Whether this periodization of thought is totally correct, or not, is not important; for this scheme will be used here as a tool to establish the different periods or generations of

Mexican Modernist architects. See: Ortega y Gasset, José. *El Tema de Nuestro Tiempo*. Madrid, Espasa-Calpe, 1975.

12 Borges, Jorge Luis. 'The Circular Ruins' (1940). In Luis Donald A. Yates and James I. Irby (eds.), *Labyrinths, Selected Stories and Other Writings*. London, Penguin Books, 1964, pp. 72–77.

1

Mexican Architecture as an Academic Discipline

DOI: 10.4324/9781003318934-2

Mexican Architecture as an Academic Discipline

The discipline of architecture in Mexico was created as an academic system following the patterns and principles of Western architecture and Western institutions, from the eighteenth-century rationalist Enlightenment principles through to the greater degree of intellectual plurality common in the late-twentieth century. To establish its contribution in the making of Mexican Modernist architecture, this chapter will address its discourse, structure and rules, adopting Michel Foucault's ideas regarding discourse analysis. It will also refer to Roland Barthes' study of fashion, to look into how Mexican Modernist architecture communicates as a system of signification that denotes and connotes meaning. These theories and methodologies will help to explain the academic concepts, patterns and principles that make up Mexican academic discipline, its 'power-knowledge nexus' and its inner logic and truth. They will also reveal how this architectural discipline, its academic discourse, its training process and its publications have contributed to the production of Mexican architecture.

Therefore, this chapter will analyse the theory and practice of Mexican architecture through a study of the main architectural schools in Mexico and their ethos. It will also analyse the main publications, both Mexican and foreign, dedicated to twentieth-century Mexican architecture with the purpose of identifying how it constructs symbolic meanings and classifications. It will also use the verbal testimonies of the 13 selected Mexican architects, their professional careers and their main buildings. The intention is not to describe the 'official' history of Mexican twentieth-century architecture and its various styles or trends, but to show the relationship between the architectural academic system and the production and construction of Mexican architecture. Therefore, this chapter will examine Mexican architecture in terms of its academic system and the power within it, to address much wider cultural issues looking deeply into the architecture produced during the past century from the vantage point of the twenty-first century.

ACADEMIC DISCOURSE

Architecture as a discourse is part of a linguistic system defined by writings about architecture. Yet it must be seen as an institutionalized practice and a licensed profession. As such, architecture is determined by implicit rules within the architectural discourse that establish or delineate what is considered to be architecture. Hence, architectural discourse defines the thoughts, representations, images, themes and preoccupations within this discourse, as well as the rules that define its practice. Any discourse requires, for it to sustain itself, a surface of emergence,

Mexican Architecture as an Academic Discipline

the existence of an authority of limitation and a grid of specification.[1] Therefore, in architecture it requires, firstly, an elite community that supplies the architects and perpetuates its existence through its patronage; secondly, architectural schools and guilds that provide control, order and validation to the profession; and thirdly, the architectural history and theory that creates the ethos and the value systems for evaluation, analysis, organization and classification of this discipline. Architectural discourse also requires its own internal system of 'government' that shapes, guides and affects the conduct of individuals or groups, and which is exerted through power structures and their 'rituals of truth'.[2]

In architectural circles, the individuals considered to be the experts are either architectural practitioners, architectural critics, or qualified academics who can claim to possess the 'knowledge' necessary to command what can be termed 'governmentality' within architectural discourse.[3] The institutions that are considered the official centres of knowledge are the schools of architecture and the various architectural associations and professional guilds. Due to the influence and authority of these institutions and associations, a process of 'normalization' is achieved by the shaping and moulding of individual architects. As a result, these combined institutions, associations and individuals are not only submitted to a series of rules, but they also subscribe to an established and shared 'truth' that sustains architectural discourse. Hence, in architecture, this 'truth' emerges only within certain sets of rules set by these institutions, as we will see later on.

According to the US architectural theorist, Dana Cuff, the primary provider of this truth as professional knowledge, both tacit and explicit, are the architecture schools; for it is there where 'future professionals are trained, acculturated, regulated, and socialized'.[4] Therefore, architectural schools provide the truth and ethos through an apparatus of knowledge and tacit or unspoken assumptions, at times more important than the skills themselves, contributing to architecture's indeterminacy and its secretive and mysterious body of knowledge.[5] Consequently, the truth that supports architectural discourse as an academic institution is established through the theory and the practice of this discipline, as the ethos that is inscribed in its everyday activities, as well as in its deepest abstract notions.

Unfortunately, the link between education and practice in Western countries seems to have lost its original purpose, since architectural theory now serves only as inspiration; there appears to be no relation between the architectural ethos instilled at school and the actual pressures of architectural practice.[6] Hence, the majority of architectural practitioners hold academic degrees mainly because the academically trained will be more likely than those without degrees to be socially recognised and to head their own architectural firms.[7] As a result, 'the primary

Mexican Architecture as an Academic Discipline

role of professional schools is its socialization process but not its training'.[8] This is also true in Mexico during the twentieth century, and indeed in most parts of the world. As a consequence, most Mexican architects prefer to adopt a creative, empirical and anti-theoretical attitude towards their designs. This is true for instance of Luis Barragán, who mentioned in an interview the crucial difference between a theoretical approach towards architecture and an empirical or intuitive approach, such as his. He made his point obvious in declining to explain his own interpretation of architectural aesthetics:

> I would have to make those concepts on beauty and style clear to me first. I have not asked myself those questions. It would be very interesting if I had time, to study them and analyse them, but I have never done this in all of my life. I feel sure when I see a building or an artistic expression that I have the sense not to understand it, but to feel it, like many other intuitive people. What happens is that it is impossible for someone who has no theoretical studies or methods to give any answer that would be satisfactory. I confess to be one of those incapables of giving an idea about the concept of beauty, even though I think I have felt it many times in my life, even in poetry in which I am interested, but I cannot analyse it. All of this is the work of a lifetime, in the analysis and theory of beauty in architecture and everything. I have never entered this analysis because I have a very active lifestyle, and I have tried to develop my sensibility without an analysis and without depth.[9]

This does not mean, as will be seen through the verbal testimony of the selected Mexican architects, that architects underestimate the theoretical fundamentals of the academic discipline. What it means is that they recognize that a key role of schools of architecture is to provide environments where individuals can learn the architect's social skills and are acculturated. Therefore, it is important to analyse the main architecture schools and architectural institutions that have contributed to Mexican architecture discipline during the past century.

Architectural Schools

By the early decades of the twenty-first century, there were over 122 registered architectural schools in Mexico, which, alongside professional guilds and associations, were working together to create the country's architectural discourse, as well as ensuring its 'governmentality'. Mexican schools of architecture have

Mexican Architecture as an Academic Discipline

followed the academic patterns and stylistic trends of Western architecture ever since the colonial origins in 1783 of the Real Academia de San Carlos – the country's first training establishment for architects, as a part of the Real Academia de Bellas Artes de San Fernando back in Spain. This school was subsequently incorporated in 1929 into Mexico's public higher education system via the Universidad Nacional Autónoma de México (UNAM), and later on became the Facultad de Arquitectura that was part of the newly designed CU, or Ciudad Universitaria Campus from the 1950s. Also in the mid-twentieth century, other architectural schools, both private and public, began to flourish. By the end of the century, the most prosperous Mexican schools had established links with prestigious foreign universities and started an accreditation process in order to achieve international recognition. These architectural schools also introduced the latest innovations in digital technology similar to the most prominent universities abroad. Thus, through international accreditation, state-of-the-art technology and an ideology of internationalization, these leading Mexican architecture schools continued to subscribe to Western paradigms, and as such were largely responsible for the trends, theories and styles incorporated to the architecture practice in Mexico. Thereby, these schools were also contributing directly to the urban imagery of Mexican cities and to the accultured tastes of those cities' inhabitants. Shown in Chart 1.1

University and School of Architecture	Foundation	Location
Real Academia de San Carlos Universidad Nacional Autónoma de México	1791	Mexico City
Instituto Politécnico Nacional Escuela de Arquitectura	1936	Tecamachalco
Tec de Monterrey Departamento de Arquitectura Campus Monterrey	1946	Monterrey
Universidad Autónoma de Nuevo León Facultad de Arquitectura	1946	Monterrey
Universidad Autónoma de Guadalajara Escuela de Arquitectura	1948	Guadalajara
Benemérita Universidad Autónoma de Puebla Escuela de Arquitectura	1954	Puebla
Universidad Iberoamericana	1955	Mexico City
Instituto Tecnológico y de Estudios Superiores de Occidente Escuela de Arquitectura	1963	Guadalajara
Universidad de Guanajuato Escuela de Arquitectura	1959	Guanajuato
Universidad La Salle Facultad de Arquitectura	1962	Mexico City
Universidad Anáhuac del Sur Escuela de Arquitectura	1967	Mexico City
Universidad de Las Américas Escuela de Arquitectura	1968	Puebla
Universidad de Monterrey, UDEM	1972	Monterrey
Universidad Autónoma Metropolitana Escuela de Arquitectura	1974	Azcapotzalco, Edo de México
Universidad Autónoma de Veracruz Escuela de Arquitectura	1987	Boca de Rio

Chart 1.1 Main Schools of Architecture in Mexico During the Twentieth Century

Mexican Architecture as an Academic Discipline

is a list of the leading 15 schools of architecture in Mexico during the twentieth century arranged in relation to their date of establishment.

The existence of an authority of limitation for the architectural profession in Mexico has been, and continues to be, imparted primarily by its schools of architecture. These have also instilled in their students certain 'truths' that contribute to notions of architectural theory and practice. By far the most important and radical theoretical – indeed ideological – change that these schools experienced during the past century was the introduction of functionalism in the 1920s by the first generation of Mexican Modernist architects. This European-style functionalism was initiated mainly by José Villagrán García's lecture course at the Real Academia de San Carlos, and the changes went on to have strong repercussions for the second generation of modern Mexican architects, such as Agustin Hernández, who was a student at that time. When asked if he had been aware of the changes at the time, he replied, 'Well, not really. We really were not doing it consciously'.[10] This was mainly due to the Real Academia's eclectic mixture of methodologies and ideologies. However, Carlos Mijares, an architect from the third generation, says that he witnessed how the traditional Neoclassical academic techniques, such as the use of *relèves*, were altered dramatically at the end of the 1940s in order to embrace an anti-historical functionalism now explicitly based on the work of Le Corbusier and Mies van der Rohe. Mijares recalls: 'It was a very radical change but very appropriate for that time. There was no interest in historical architecture because repetition was prohibited. It was not valid since it was against the principles of functionalism'.[11]

Following the successful, and radical, introduction of the functionalist approach by Mexican architects, it is telling that no later transformation of such importance has taken place since then. The only slight variant that occurred in many schools from the late-1950s until the 1970s was the introduction of far more contextual and human-centred responses in students' design projects. This corresponded to the introduction to students worldwide of the work of Alvar Aalto and Frank Lloyd Wright by the Italian historian, Bruno Zevi, as part of what he called 'Organic Architecture'.[12] It explains why architects of the third generation in Mexico, like Mijares, came to be inspired more by the work of Alvar Aalto and Frank Lloyd Wright – and likewise, by the work of Louis Kahn, Eero Saarinen and Jørn Utzon.[13] This was in no way considered to be contrary to the principles of functionalism, but was rather a partial response to the latter's cold rationalism. This new sensibility and concern for context was passed from the architects of the third generation to the students of the fourth generation. Clara de Buen, one of the fourth generation, recalls this influence as part of the methodologies used in the school at Universidad Iberoamericana, commonly known just as Ibero:

> When I was studying, all the other courses were focused on the design studios (which were) very concerned with context. We would make enormous models of the site, and we would travel to historical locations where we would insert our projects. We would travel and map the area and then design the different projects.[14]

Javier Sordo, also from this fourth generation and from Ibero, similarly explained his commitment to the idea of urban context:

> Well, I believe that one of the responsibilities of an architect is not to be selfish about his buildings, creating a precious thing on its own. There are some places in the city where you can do this, but I think that in Mexico City, what is most gratifying is what the buildings give. So, I try to design buildings that give something to the city.[15]

According to such testimonies, the ideologies being imparted in Mexican schools of architecture were still almost exclusively the product of Western influence from Le Corbusier and Frank Lloyd Wright to Alvar Aalto and later figures. Despite following westernized values and knowledge, however, these schools did not reproduce every single trend. For instance, none seemed to emulate the Postmodernist trend of the 1980s seen in the USA and some European countries, refusing to join in critiques of their functionalist predecessors. To this day, there remains a distinct respect for Modernist architecture in Mexico, based on the belief that it is still always original and fitting both to its time and its place. Consequently, the Mexican schools of architecture in the last decades of the twentieth century have continued to train their students in essentially the same Modernist tradition, particularly in terms of their design courses.[16]

In analyzing the curricula of the widely acknowledged top 15 schools of architecture in Mexico, it is clear how much emphasis they place on teaching both construction and design, as shown in Graph 1.1. This emphasis, again, reveals the persisting influence of the Modernist functional tradition. Design courses, which constitute the main part of the curriculum in these schools, remain based upon the Bauhaus studio tradition, using an analytical architectural brief or programme rather than looking at a speculative theoretical or cultural issue as the starting point of each design project. Antonio Toca, a well-known Mexican critic and architect, has written that the teaching methods used in these design

Mexican Architecture as an Academic Discipline

Graph 1.1

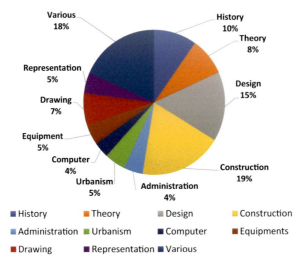

studios consist essentially of successive corrections of a student's project, as part of a trial-and-error process, thus creating a linear series of design approximations through which the student eventually arrives at the 'right' design solution.[17] Therefore, these practical design skills, rather than theoretical concepts, are the main elements that have shaped Mexican architectural academia and practice during the past century.

Architectural Practice

It is no surprise, therefore, that architectural practice in Mexico tends to overlook theoretical aspects, since architects in practice are so strongly influenced by their professional context and their everyday activities. Few of them are ever encouraged to develop a theoretical position or to write about their architectural ideas. Some tend to romanticize their role as designers as a way of reinforcing the myth and mystique behind their methodology. Consequently, the professional ethos that is predicated in Mexican schools somehow pales in comparison with the social skills and the professional network that architects establish, even while they are still students. It is, for example, through the connections established in schools that most Mexican architects obtain their first work opportunity in an

Mexican Architecture as an Academic Discipline

architectural firm. Network maps that show the relationship between the selected architects and their teachers, classmates, employers and partners were created using the information gathered through their interviews. These network charts clearly show that the relationships between specific students and teachers, or between students and fellow students, later develop into professional relationships in terms employer/employee or forming a partnership. This was certainly the experience of Abraham Zabludovsky, as his network map shows, in that he first worked for his teacher, Mario Pani, and later became partners with Teodoro González de León, his classmate at the Academia de San Carlos. Zabludovsky recalls:

> I believe we were a fortunate group of architects, with brilliant teachers who also had a very successful professional career. This group of teachers took it as a personal thing to make their most distinguished students part of their team in their private practice.[18]

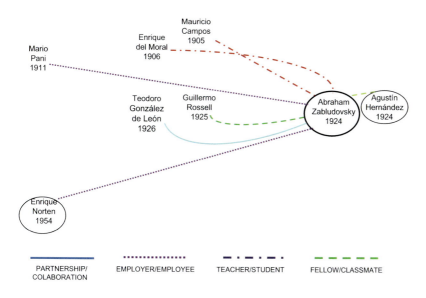

Map 1.1 The Network Map of Abraham Zabludovsky

If we carefully study the network map of each architect, it is evident that the connections established at architectural schools were extremely important. Ricardo Legorreta, for instance, also began his professional experience by working for his teacher José Villagrán García, which he sees as a vital relationship. Legorreta

Mexican Architecture as an Academic Discipline

explains, 'Of all of my teachers, on top of the list is Villagrán García, who besides being my teacher was also my boss since I worked in his office for many years'.[19]

Map 1.2 The Network Map of Ricardo Legorreta

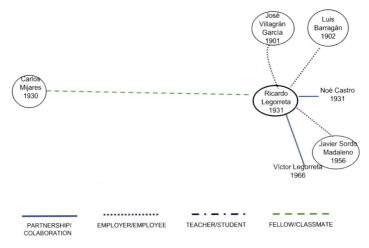

The Network Map of Ricardo Legorreta

The only successful Mexican architect who appears to have been disconnected from his teachers professionally is Luis Barragán, as his network map shows. This is understandable, given that Barragán did not, in fact, study architecture; instead, he had studied civil engineering in Guadalajara, a city where there were no architectural schools at that time.

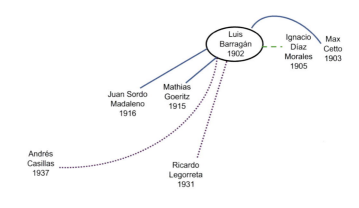

Map 1.3 The Network Map of Luis Barragán

The Network Map of Luis Barragán

Mexican Architecture as an Academic Discipline

In general, the associations made in architectural schools were most likely to develop into clear professional connections, as can be seen also in the case of Clara de Buen, who went on to work with her teachers, Carlos Mijares and Aurelio Nuño. Ultimately, she went on to become a partner with Nuño and one of her fellow classmates, Carlos Mac Gregor.

It is interesting to note that the school of architecture at the Universidad Autónoma de México (UNAM) was the one that produced the majority of the first, second and third generation of leading Mexican architects, but that the most important architects of the fourth generation studied at Universidad Iberoamericana. This is a significant change, because the schools provide, as the network maps demonstrate, the essential initial connections between teachers and students and fellow classmates that are likely to feed into subsequent practice. Indeed, the combined network map of all the 13 key Mexican architects indicates just how closely knit is the architecture community in Mexico.

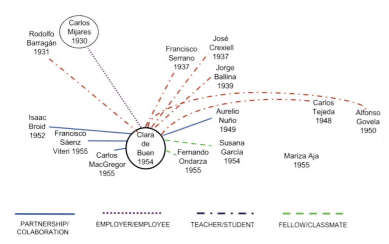

The Network Map of Clara de Buen

Map 1.4 The Network Map of Clara de Buen

Mexican Architecture as an Academic Discipline

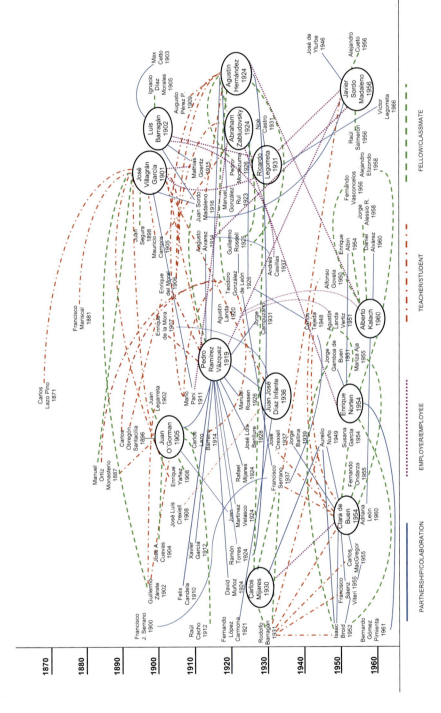

Map 1.5 The Network Map of All 13 Key Mexican Architects

The Role of Architectural Guilds and Associations

It is not just the architectural schools that have entrenched discourse in Mexico. Mexican architectural guilds and associations, such as the Academia Nacional de Arquitectura or the Colegio de Arquitectos, also experienced increasing power in every state across the country. Although the power within these guilds and associations is relatively weak in comparison to architectural schools, the strongest ones are those located in Mexico City. Mexican architectural guilds and associations again follow the trends and activities of their Western counterparts, organizing exhibitions and conferences, and giving awards and offering recognition to the most distinguished designers and built projects. They are relatively well respected amongst the architectural community, albeit they are always eclipsed by their bigger counterparts in Europe or the United States, as Abraham Zabludovsky explains:

> The buildings that we have done have been publicised, they have achieved recognition, have been given awards (nationally), but we have also presented many in architectural exhibitions, like the [Venice] Biennale. I call these festivals because they are architectural celebrations. These international festivals promote architecture and allow you to establish relationships with certain people abroad.[20]

Acknowledgement from these Mexican architectural guilds and associations guarantees the designers with the publicity that they need to increase the possibility of securing future assignments, as well as perhaps higher architectural fees. The system also guarantees the appearance of these architects in the most important periodicals and publications. Mexican architects thus recognize the importance of these guilds and associations, while often being critical of how they are performing. Clara de Buen, for one, believes that they bear the responsibility of providing Mexican society with a more accurate image of the architecture profession, when she states:

> It is not very clear what we do, or indeed if we really do anything. I believe that this has been in part the result of bad public relations from our associations and schools of architecture, because, for example, engineers and other professions do have a certain prestige here. I do not know if it is the same outside Mexico City, but here our association of architects is not good, and it has not managed to promote a good image of what we do in society.[21]

Yet, despite the connections forged in schools of architecture, and the efforts of architectural guilds and associations, Mexican Modernist architects found themselves unable to achieve proper academic recognition until their work was documented in the form of written reviews and photographed buildings. To understand this important factor in the equation, it is first necessary to address architecture as a system of communication and meaning.

ARCHITECTURE AS A SYSTEM OF MEANING

The architectural discourse of twentieth-century Mexican architecture as a system of meaning is centred on recognizing this discipline as a system of signs. Hence, it is based on publications written on Mexican architecture during this period. Here, words are used to refer to architecture and architectural features that already in themselves constitute an architectural system of signification. As such, it represents the architectural codes and classifications assigned to the architectural manifestations of Mexican Modernist architecture. These codes and classifications are always 'written', given that academic architecture needs to be written about and codified if it is to have any meaning at all. Using Roland Barthes' *The Fashion System*, it is possible to understand the 'translation' of architecture into a system of signs.[22] Hence, architecture, like fashion, also uses words profusely, with an economic intention that will be explored in the following chapters, but which acts ultimately to constitute an academic discipline and discourse. This means that the words used to name or classify creates the architectural manifestation. For it is the written recognition of the architectural object in publications and by architectural academics and critics that seals its validation as an academic manifestation.

Academic architecture, as outlined through publications using written words and photographs, generates three categories of building for each actual project. Firstly, there is the 'real' or actual building that becomes the model which is being written about; secondly, there is then the resulting 'written' building, which consists of various descriptions of the 'real' building; and thirdly, there are the photographs of the 'real' building, which constitute its primary route for visual representation. These three categories have different structures and substances. The first is made up of forms, lines, surfaces, colours, materials and space. The second, which is made up of words and their relationships, is thus syntactic. The third refers to the image of the building that conforms to a specific formal language, with its own vocabulary and syntax.[23] The written-building and the photographed-building are both derived from the actual-building, and so are equivalent but never identical. The actual-building, based on technological elements and a construction process, serves as a model or as the mother-tongue from which the two others are 'translations'. In architecture, representation via drawings is also very important in depicting the actual-building, given that they follow a specific set of rules and conventions that isolates certain details and in doing so emphasises certain values and principles.

Therefore, the architectural discipline tends to have a normative nature in which every word in a publication goes beyond the everyday regular words to constitute a specific system of significations. In this system, signs can be visible and distinct, such as the term 'apartment block' that refers to a building's visible use. Or it can be a specific attribute that conforms to a set of architectural values and ideologies, like the terms 'modern' or 'functional'. The written-building involves two main systems of information: one that is specifically related to the linguistic system, or language, and another that is related to the larger 'architectonic' system. These two systems are, however, not unconnected; in fact, they operate at two different levels: the level of expression and the level of content. The level of expression corresponds to denotation, while the level of content corresponds to connotation, as will be discussed more later. For instance, the word 'Mexican' in the term 'Mexican architecture' denotes its place of origin, while also simultaneously it connotes a certain style. In the architectural system, signs remain relatively arbitrary, since these are mainly assigned by architectural individuals or groups and perhaps by architecture publications as in the case of classifications. For this reason, an architectural sign is created by decree, by those involved in creating the discourse, and not by collective consensus.

Written Architecture

Mexican Modernist architecture in its built sense has been translated into written and photographed architecture in the publications that have documented it as part of the academic discipline. These publications decide who and what are considered to be the best examples of Mexican architecture during the twentieth century. In addition, these publications are also dedicated to presenting and producing the body of knowledge, as well as to assigning the meaning of the discipline by establishing classifications, denotations and connotations. The following graphs were developed by considering only 253 books written between 1920 to the year 2000. These books constituted the primary media through which Mexican twentieth-century architecture was constructed both in Mexico and abroad, and so their analysis enables us to see the ways in which Mexican architecture was constructed, perceived and presented during the past century. For instance, Graph 1.2 shows that 30% of these key books were written in the 1980s, and a further 39% in the 1990s. This corresponds to the sizeable increase in the number of architectural students and schools of architecture in Mexico at that time. Understandably, the relative decrease in publications during the 1940s is the result of the Second World War.

Graph 1.2 indicates the different types of architectural publications on Mexican twentieth-century architecture that range from texts on architectural history, theory, practice monographs, catalogues, typological studies, conservation projects and urban issues. It is interesting to note that monographs are the most common type of publication on Mexican architecture, at some 38% of the total, mainly due to their obvious use as self-promotion by the practices that are featured. Architectural history books are also important, amounting to 28% of the selected sample, their main purpose being to document the key events and to portray the best designs of their period. Books about buildings and specific typologies occupy only 16% and tend to concentrate simply on illustrative architecture examples. Regrettably, only 9% of these selected publications deal to any degree with theoretical issues, which seems to confirm the general lack of interest in and investigation of such topics by Mexican architects.

Also notably, Graph 1.3 shows that 78% of these books were published in Mexico itself, with another 12% stemming from the USA and 5% of from Britain, revealing that, after the great publicity given internationally to Mexican architecture in the mid-twentieth century, this has since largely disappeared. Graph 1.3 confirms that 80% of the books were thus published in Spanish and only 18% in English (with 2% published in other languages). This situation effectively limits knowledge about Mexican Modernism to a solely Spanish-speaking audience, clearly a problem today when otherwise architectural knowledge is becoming much more globalized in scope.

Mexican Architecture as an Academic Discipline

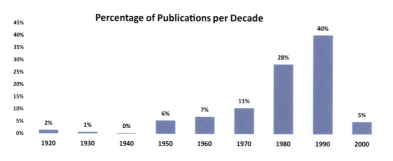

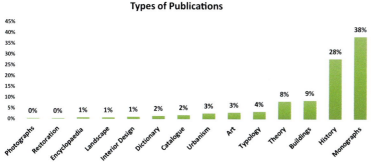

Graph 1.2 Statistics for the main architectural texts about Mexican Modernist architecture written from 1920–2000

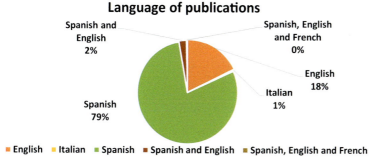

Graph 1.3 Locations/languages for the main architectural texts about Mexican Modernist architecture written from 1920–2000

Mexican Architecture as an Academic Discipline

Architectural Classification Systems

Architectural discourse is achieved in part though classification, as a means of achieving order and a set unit or arranged rationale which thus can be used to create a grid or framework. Classification sets the boundaries determined by the theory or the concepts that order architecture, which tend to follow the cultural codes or values and morals of the dominant social group. This process is essentially a tentative or empirical process, an arbitrary task that reveals the criteria of assigned values established by a group of individuals that determine the categories and parameters of what is being classified. Architectural classification systems thus attempt to convey a logical and rational order to a practice that is usually considered empirical and creative. Consequently, it is no surprise that architectural classifications tend to lack theoretical or scientific explanation, again emphasizing their empirical character, as well as their inherent partiality.

Architectural classifications are established primarily through writings. Therefore, it is important to analyse the classifications assigned to Mexican twentieth-century architecture in the 36 selected publications shown in Chart 1.2. By analysing each of these books, it is possible to trace the classifications and denotations and connotations applied to the buildings and key architects featured in each text. Some of the writings explicitly use Mexican architecture to fit their particular theory, such as Christian Fernandez Cox's concept of 'post-rational' architecture or Kenneth Frampton's notion of 'critical regionalism'. Other authors, like Israel Katzman and Enrique X. de Anda, attempt to apply more precise classifications to describe the otherwise-diverse manifestations of Mexican twentieth-century architecture. It is interesting to observe that the classifications given to Mexican Modernist architecture by most of the publications in Mexico are centred on the principles of functionalism, whereas the classifications in the foreign publications describe Mexican architecture as emotional and colourful, or even as Surrealist, in the case of Carranza and Lara's book. This dichotomy of functional and emotional classifications creates a real sense of ambivalence as to whether Mexican twentieth-century architects were tasked with producing an emotional identity for the country's people or were applying an international functionalist approach adapted from architects abroad.

All of the classifications and denotations and connotations in the 36 selected books on Mexican twentieth-century architecture are identified in Chart 1.3. Despite the diversity of these architectural terms, it is obvious from this chart that

Mexican Architecture as an Academic Discipline

the most frequent descriptions were 'functional', 'modern', 'international' and 'rational', which corresponds to the fact that these terms were preferred by the Mexican writers who were predominant in the selected sample, whereas it was the (fewer) overseas writers who tended to apply words such as 'emotional'. The common use of the former kind of terms parallels also the dominant discourse in Mexican schools of architecture. Chart 1.4 is based mainly upon Enrique Xavier de Anda's book, in which he identifies 15 classificatory terms. The chart arranges them in their chronological position from when they first appeared to when they began to fade out. It seems remarkable that, although 'functional', 'international', 'modern' and 'rational' were first used in Mexico back in the late-1920s, these same terms continued to carry great importance throughout the decades to such an extent that they were still being mentioned uncritically in the publications of the 1990s. Significantly, virtually all of the terms listed in de Anda's book are from Western architectural classifications that became Mexican architectural trends, with the only term that refers to a trend beginning in Mexico being 'emotional', as first introduced by Mathias Goeritz[24] – a German/Polish émigré painter and sculptor – and which was later used to classify Barragán's architecture. Barragán himself recalls:

> Now we talk about emotional architecture but then the term was not known. The only term that was known was functional, which appeared in the 1930s more or less; the emotional part, although it was known, was not discussed as such. Mathias Goeritz later established the need to do emotional architecture.[25]

In this quote, we find a term being generated by Goeritz and recognized by Barragán, although the latter never himself used it to refer to his own architecture. Such reluctance was certainly not the case for words like 'modern' and 'functional', both of which were abundantly used to denote a sense of usefulness, as well as connoting the Modernist style. The number of times that the terms 'modern' and 'functional' are used in publications clearly establishes their enduring presence within Mexican architecture, due to the ongoing influence of functionalist ideas. Although Mexican architects in general recognize and respect the academic part of the architectural discipline, most tend to disagree with the writings of architectural critics – especially when it comes the established systems of classification. These reservations are shared by practically every Mexican architect. For instance, Ricardo Legorreta, although he admits his work is inspired

Mexican Architecture as an Academic Discipline

List of 36 Key Books

1. Myers, I.E. *Mexico's Modern Architecture*. New York, Cornwell Press, 1952.
2. Obregón Santacilia, Carlos. *Cincuenta Años de Arquitectura Mexicana (1900-1950)*. Mexico City, Editorial Patria, 1952.
3. Fernández, Justino. *Arte Moderno Contemporáneo*. Mexico City, Ed. UNAM, 1952.
4. Hitchcock, Henry-Russell. *Latin American Architecture since 1945*. New York, ED. MOMA, 1955.
5. Cetto, Max. *Modern Architecture in Mexico*. New York, Praeger, 1961.
6. Villagrán, García. *Panorama de 62 Años de Arquitectura Mexicana Contemporánea*. Mexico City, Cuadernos de Arquitectura, 1963.
7. Katzman, Israel. *La arquitectura contemporánea mexicana: Precedentes y desarrollo*. México, INAH, 1963.
8. Bullrich, Francisco. *Nuevos Caminos de la Arquitectura Latinoamericana*. Barcelona, Ed. Blume, 1969.
9. Benévolo, Leonardo. Historia de la Arquitectura Moderna. Barcelona, Gustavo Gili, 5th edición, 1982.
10. Frampton, Kenneth. *Modern Architecture a Critical History*. London, Thames &Hudson, 1992.
11. Placzek, Adolf K. *Macmillan Encyclopedia of Architects*, New York, 1982.
12. Salvat, Juan, José Luis Rosas, et al. *Historia del arte mexicano: Arte contemporáneo*. vols. 13-16, México, Editorial Salvat,1986.
13. Cruickshank, Dan. (ed.), Sir Banister Fletcher's A History of Architecture (20th Edition). Architectural Press/RIBA, London. 1996.
14. Browne, Enrique. *La Otra Arquitectura en Latinoamericana*. México, Ed. Gustavo Gili, 1988.
15. Jencks, Charles. *Architecture Today*. London: Academy Editors, 1988.
16. Noelle, Louise. *Arquitectos Contemporáneos de México*. México, Ed. Trillas, 1989.
17. Toca, Antonio y Figueroa. *México Nueva Arquitectura*. México, Ed. Gustavo Gili, 1991-1995.
18. Noelle, Louise & Carlos Tejeda. *Catálogo Guía de Arquitectura Contemporánea*. Mexico, Ed. Fomento Cultural Banamex. 1993.
19. González Gortázar, Fernando. La arquitectura mexicana del siglo XX. México, CONACULTA, 1994.
20. de Anda X, Enrique. *Historia de la Arquitectura Mexicana*. Barcelona, Ed.Gustavo Gili, 1995
21. Adria, Miguel. *Mexico 90s A Contemporary Architecture*. México, Gustavo Gili, 1996.
22. Ferguson, Russell. *At the End of the Century One Hundred Years of Architecture*. London, Abrams Pub, 1998.
23. Fleming, John. Hugh Honour, & Nikolaus Pevsner. *The Penguin Dictionary of Architecture and Landscape Architecture*. London, Penguin Books. 5th Edition, 1998.
24. Fernández Cox, Christian. *América Latina: Nueva Arquitectura una Modernidad posracionalista*. Mexico, Ed. Gustavo Gili, 1998.
25. *Enciclopedia de México*. In CD Rom. Copyright. Sabeca International Investment Corporation.1998
26. Gutiérrez, Ramón, Eladio Dieste and Graciela María Viñuales. *Arquitectura Latinoamericana en el Siglo XX*. Barcelona, Lunwerg Editores, 1998.
27. Toppelson, Sara. *50 Años de Arquitectura en Mexicana*. México, Ed. Plazola, 1999.
28. Fraser, Valerie. *Building the New World: Studies in the Modern Architecture of Latin America 1930–1960*. London, Verso, 2000.
29. Olsen,Patrice. *Artifacts of Revolution: Architecture, Society, and Politics in Mexico City, 1920-1940*. Lanham, Maryland, Rowman & Littlefield Publishers, 2008.
30. Hernández, Felipe. *Beyond Modernist Masters: Contemporary Architecture in Latin America*. Berlin and New York, Birkhäuser, 2009.
31. Canales, Fernanda. *Architecture in Mexico, 1900-2010: The Construction of Modernity Works, Design, Art, and Thought*. Mexico City, Grupo Financiero Banamex, 2013.
32. Castañeda, Luis. Spectacular Mexico: Design, Propaganda, and the 1968 Olympics Minneapolis, University of Minnesota Press, 2014.
33. Bergdoll, Barry, Carlos Eduardo Comas, Jorge Francisco Liernur and Patricio del Real. *Latin America in Construction: Architecture 1955–1980*. New York, Museum of Modern Art, 2015.
34. Carranza, Luis E., and Fernando Lara. *Modern Architecture in Latin America: Art, Technology, and Utopia*. Austin, University of Texas Press, 2015.
35. O'Rourke, Kathryn. *Modern Architecture in Mexico City: History, Representation, and the Shaping of a Capital*, Pittsburgh, University of Pittsburgh Press, 2017
36. Hernández, Felipe. 'Central and South America, 1920–Present Day'. In Murray Fraser (ed.) *Sir Banister Fletcher's Global History of Architecture (21st Edition)*. London, Bloomsbury, 2020, pp.1228–1263.

Chart 1.2

Mexican Architecture as an Academic Discipline

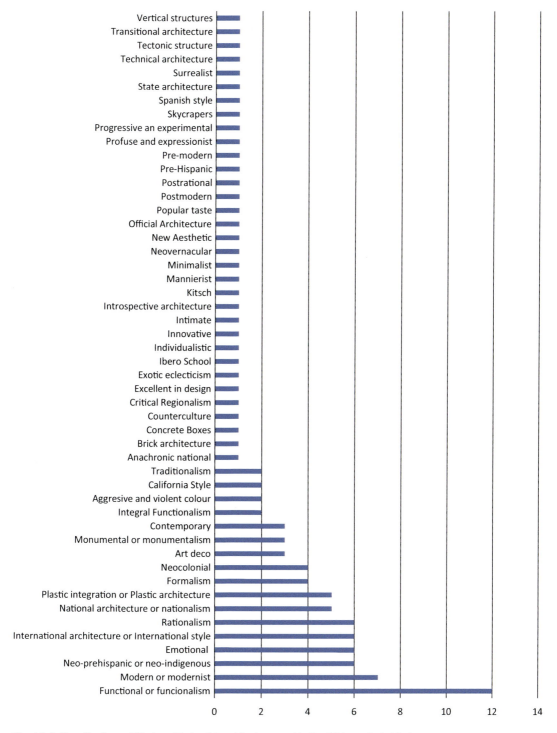

Chart 1.3 Classifications of Mexican Modernist architecture used in the 36 key selected texts

Mexican Architecture as an Academic Discipline

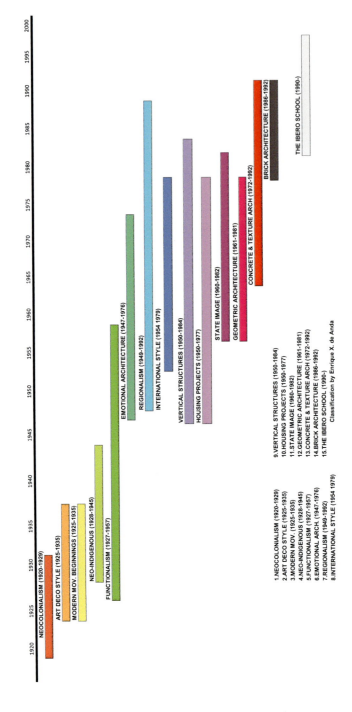

Chart 1.4 Chronology of descriptions of Mexican Modernist architecture identified by Enrique X. de Anda

by vernacular colours and elements, disagrees with words like 'vernacular' and 'emotional' architecture being ascribed to his designs. He states:

> I have a lot of problems with classifications. I find it sort of a North American obsession for classification. I do not consider (my work) to be vernacular architecture. But it all depends on what you understand by vernacular architecture . . . So, if you use simple wall finishes and colours that is only a language. The real philosophy and the real depth of architecture is its emotional part, the part that uses light and space more than materials.[26]

Carlos Mijares feels precisely the same way about the way in which his architecture is sometimes described as 'Critical Regionalism'. Mijares shows he is aware of the dangers of cataloguing when declaring:

> Well, I think that I have never liked classifications, and in general terms I do not like them because it is simply a comfortable way to box or pigeonhole someone . . . I believe that an architect makes architecture and that architecture is a language . . . That is why I believe that it makes no sense to define it or classify it as a manner or a style, because you use a different language to try to define another one.[27]

The four architects from the fourth generation, as noted, all Ibero graduates. As such, de Anda writes about them being exponents of the so-called 'Ibero School'. In his view, they all share in common an emphasis on constructional features, or what he calls 'architectural jewellery', due to the care they each give to these details.[28] This classification is, however, bewildering to each of the architects concerned, none of whom agree in the slightest bit with de Anda's interpretation. Clara de Buen instead argues that:

> I do not doubt that there are people from Ibero who are very much interested in (designing) details. But I believe that our architecture does not go in that direction. For me details are a necessary evil, which we must solve. We must solve them so that you do not get water inside the building; this is the way I see it.[29]

Javier Sordo Madaleno is also reluctant to agree with this taxonomy when stating:

> In part this could describe my work, but I definitely believe that it is not only that. I consider my work in general to be an evolution from my father's work, and also part of Luis Barragán's work, and of all those architects who have influenced me. But it has become mine with its own expression, because my architecture is very different.[30]

Mexican Architecture as an Academic Discipline

Alberto Kalach interprets de Anda's classification of design details as referring to an excessive use of ornamentation, and thus being overly designed. In protest, he explains:

> I do not believe that I am inclined towards details. In fact, I believe that many of the buildings that we have made are very primitive in terms of concerning their details . . . The details are only the ones that need to be there; there is no over-design . . . we do not work in this manner. We do simple details that are more austere than those of a welder, but above all, because I do not like to put up with little things that take up lots of time. Otherwise, they take time away from the main ideas.[31]

There is little doubt that Mexican architects recognize the importance of establishing an academic discipline, yet they are openly aware of the subjective, empirical nature of the classification systems and so declare a preference not to be labelled. This is perhaps also responsible to the fact that Mexican architects are not prone to theorizing about their work or their design methodology, and hence, have contributed very little to written discourse. This does not mean that theory is more important than practice or vice versa, or even that both should be equally balanced. The fact remains that this is the general tendency among Mexican architects. Yet, in spite of this, there are nonetheless two important architects from the selected sample who developed and published their own architectural theory, and which ought to be noted here.

Architectural Treatises

Architectural theory also constitutes part of the written discourse; for it can be passed on in architecture schools or can be published to establish the grid of specification within the architecture discipline; hence, it is also present in Mexican Modernist architecture. Taking a lead from the ideas of French architectural and urban historian and theorist Françoise Choay about the relationship in architecture between the design 'rule' and the 'model',[32] two contributions of Mexican architects were identified in this manner. These theories were published amid a plethora of books about Mexican Modernist architecture; the authors correspond to two of the key architects selected for this book: they are José Villagrán García, with his book, *Teoría de la Arquitectura*; and Juan José Díaz

Infante, who wrote the book called *Del Dolmen a la Kalikosmia*. These two texts develop a theoretical approach that is largely derived from Western architectural treatises but applied to respond to Mexico's particular architectural problems, yet in no way do they challenge the preestablished Western academic discourse. Choay distinguishes within architectural theory two mechanisms, the 'rule' and the 'model', the first taken from written treatises and the second, from projected utopias. These two mechanisms somehow also correspond to these two texts. For instance, Villagrán's functionalist theory corresponds to the rule and is taken from Le Corbusier and Julian Guadet. Accordingly, it was introduced by Villagrán as functionalism in the wake of the Mexican Revolution. Díaz Infante's theory, on the other hand, corresponds to a projected utopia, modelled on the work of Buckminster Fuller, the Japanese Metabolists, and Britain's Archigram group. Infante argued, for example, that prefabrication alongside more efficient construction techniques was the best route to solving Mexico's housing deficit in the 1960s.

José Villagrán's functionalist text was an outcome of a renowned theory course that he taught at the Real Academia de San Carlos from 1926 onwards. Those lectures were never officially written down until 1964, when a version was created by using notes taken by his students. Subsequently, a more comprehensive text that unifies Villagrán's theoretical work and teachings under the title of *Teoría de la Arquitectura* was published in 1988 by the Universidad Nacional Autónoma de México. Villagrán's functionalist ideals were also very much put to the test in his buildings, principally in his hospital projects. These buildings offered archetypical examples of his theory in their abandonment of overt decoration, their pioneering of specific formal innovations and their initiation of the language of functionalism in Mexico.[33] Perhaps the best example is the Hospital Manuel Gea González, with its shockingly stark external appearance, which, in 2013, was remodelled by Elegant Embellishments Studio with a depolluting yet ornamental façade.

Villagrán's book was essentially an argument against Beaux-Arts theory, being focussed instead on the concept of the building programme. He defines the four core values of architecture as follows: the useful, the logical, the aesthetic and the social. Villagrán regarded the term 'useful' as the structural function; the second term, 'logical', was related to the truthful use of materials, construction and form; the third term, 'aesthetic', represented unity, clarity, contrast, symmetry, character, style and proportion; whereas, fourthly, the term 'social' dealt with the tricky relationship between architecture and society. Villagrán's theory, despite being heavily based on Le

Mexican Architecture as an Academic Discipline

Corbusier's celebrated 1923 treatise, *Vers Une Architecture (Towards a New Architecture)*, was also inflected by Beaux-Arts architectural ideas due to the way that Villagrán had himself been trained.[34] According to Alberto Pérez-Gómez, a noted Mexican architectural historian and theorist, Villagrán failed to discuss the diverse interpretations of the theoretical issues he was raising in his book – and thus Villagrán's theory should be seen as the applied science of functionalist discourse.[35] As a result, Mexican architects tended thereafter to regard Modernist architecture simply as the resolution of programmatic questions in order that form might 'follow'.[36] This limited viewpoint was instilled in every one of Villagrán's students, and then the students of his students, as can be seen in his network map; thus, it constitutes the dominant theoretical ethos of Mexican Modernism throughout the twentieth century. Villagrán's theory in effect became established dogma; its permanence long outlasted the original author and the academic institutions that had created it.

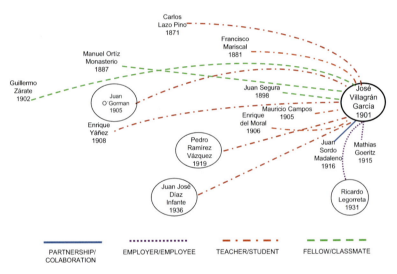

Map 1.6 The Network Map of José Villagrán García

The Network Map of José Villagrán García

In contrast, Juan José Díaz Infante sought to introduce a theory based upon the idea of the architecture of tomorrow and today, which he did through his designs for a utopian fictional world called 'Kalikosmia'. 'Kali (or 'Calli') means 'house' in Nahuatl, and 'cosmia' means 'cosmos', and Díaz Infante later explained how he had been inspired to come up with this theoretical proposal back in 1968:

> It was a search for less matter and more space. The design for the plastic house was based on my observations of architecture's evolution, beginning with Santa

Sofia (Hagia Sophia), which was built in five years, and had a dome that was considered to be a contribution towards a New Jerusalem. So, if Santa Sofia could be built in five years with a dome that was 42 meters in diameter, that is with less matter and more space, through this analysis I realized that there was less matter being used, and more velocity or speed in construction which was more economical. So, from there I extrapolated this idea to the present. [37]

Díaz Infante's main aim was to build with less mass more internal space, thereby creating a perfect design that would have the right equilibrium between the amount of built matter used in relation to the space being created. He traces a route from Stonehenge to the Pyramids in Egypt, to the Parthenon, to the typical Gothic church, to the Eiffel Tower, right through to the relative 'lightness' of modern-day skyscrapers, as support for his 'Kalikosmia' theory. Díaz Infante believed that architecture, if interpreted in such terms, would become a never-ending process in which humankind would participate in an entirely ethical manner. He explained his ideas always in a poetic fashion:

Live daily in space, the created space that is lived, inhabited, discovered, and designed . . . Await in hope the forgiveness of the forgiven, and the love of a God who loves and waits to be loved, in a cosmos that is tired and damaged, that begs and cries to be changed into a recycled space, into an ordered disorder, towards a unified chaos. [38]

This, then, is the spirit of 'Kalikosmia', and according to Díaz Infante, an architect should always present to his/her client a favourable project in which all of these variables are balanced, ordered and efficient. [39] In his view, it is imperative to apply this approach to every building design or else humankind would be in trouble. As he stated:

It is important because it should not stay only as a theory. It means that with less matter and more velocity, you can make more space in less time, and in the end this is economical. This means less matter was taken from the Earth in less time, using less money, to make more space. So, you pay less money, you use the building sooner, you make people happier. [40]

Diaz Infante believed the igloo to be the perfect example of a structure whose relationship between space and matter is ideal. He claimed to have applied this direct and simplistic relation between space and matter to some of his own buildings,

Mexican Architecture as an Academic Discipline

such as his own house on Amsterdam Street in Mexico City or the TAPO (Terminal de Autobuses de Oriente) bus station in Mexico City, wherein the space and form correspond perfectly to the use of a dome. La Bolsa Mexicana de Valores, or Mexican Stock Market building, is also an excellent example of his ideas on optimal design, as he explained in an interview: 'The bottom part is a concrete structure, followed by a steel structure, and on the top, there is a spatial structure corresponding to the equation: less matter, more space. The same thing goes for the dome; it is very light'.[41]

Díaz Infante's theoretical contributions can thus best be described as speculative and utopian. The words used by Díaz Infante are meant to be poetic and prophetic, as are the photographs that give his book a futuristic feel. In stark contrast to Villagrán's functionalist treatise, however, 'Kalikosmia' is known by very few people either in Mexico or beyond. In fact, the publication of the book in 1965, under its original title of *Del Domen a la Kalikosmia*, and then in its newer version by Cecilia Ortiz and María Rosenberg as *Las Pieles del Espacio* (*Space, Speed and Skin*), were both actually published and financed by Díaz Infante himself. The diffusion of his theory thus remains low, in spite of his extensive teaching work in architectural schools at Ibero and Universidad Anáhuac. This remoteness can be seen and explained by Infante's network map, where it is evident his lack of influence on students and employees.

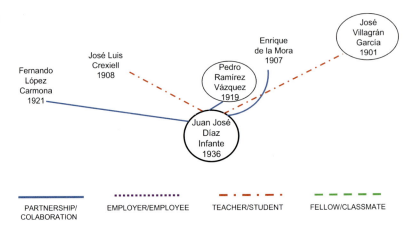

Map 1.7 The Network Map of Juan José Díaz Infante

In these two contrasting theoretical texts, Western architectural theories provided the original source. It is also possible to trace, by examining the language being used and the photographic evidence that was presented, the canon of domination that is inscribed within both of them. In addition, it is interesting to

Mexican Architecture as an Academic Discipline

see how these two theories try to insert their concepts into the Mexican context as if they were naturally derived from it. For example, Villagrán often compares Mexican architecture with Western architectural models to support his ideas, whereas Díaz Infante attempts to make his book more 'Mexican' by assigning it with an indigenous, Nahuatl-language title.

Photographed Architecture

Mexican twentieth-century architecture as an academic discipline and a system of meaning relies heavily on written-buildings and photographed-buildings, as mentioned previously, although there is also a clear understanding neither constitutes the actual-buildings. For instance, Carlos Mijares argues that an emphasis on representation is particularly dangerous when teaching architecture, precisely because of the lack of any direct involvement with real-world architectural production:

> Maybe a meaningful and good example that illustrates the confusion in things related to architecture, and its systematisation, is given by Rene Magritte's painting. You probably know it, the pipe with a text that reads: 'This is not a pipe'. Of course, it is not a pipe, but people think that it is, and get confused and say that it is a pipe. This same thing happens with the presentation and definition of architecture: that should not be regarded as architecture. It is, at best, a few phrases, a definition, a criterion, a system, call it what you may, about architecture. But it is not architecture. Like Magritte's painting, it is not a pipe, because it cannot be lit, it cannot be smoked. It is only a representation of a pipe. I think that this has happened in architecture. They have forgotten that architecture is a building that you can walk through, that has spaces, shapes, walls, columns, floors, roofs, etc, something that is located in a particular place, with a particular scale, and that must be experienced. The rest is only make-believe, or a story.
>
> I believe that this is why the schools of architecture are the way they are because they rely on theoretical conditions instead of experiencing architecture . . . Architectural teaching has focused on these things for a long time, especially ever since the academy was structured as such. These institutionalised teachings have distanced us more and more from the actual experience not only of making architecture, but also of enabling students to be able to make architecture. Despite all its limitations, students must always be in close contact with architecture. This

Mexican Architecture as an Academic Discipline

> fact has been forgotten, and it has now become a grave mistake that I believe will
> have terrible consequences. [42]

This issue is also of particular concern to Pedro Ramírez Vázquez, especially in regard to the portrayal of architecture created by academics and others through photography. He states:

> I believe that architecture is what is built because architecture always has to be
> made. It is not what is in plans and exhibitions. That is speculation. Architecture
> is what is built and what survives . . . Time is architecture's best judge, not the
> formal result that is usually the shared merit of a photographer and an architect.
> Architecture tends to be judged, like people, by their physical appearance, and
> not by what they are and what they contribute. Architecture needs to be lived
> and used. It should not be judged by photographs since these are totally false
> and staged. [43]

Yet, in spite of such arguments, photographed architecture clearly possesses the power to establish values and principles as part of architectural discourse. Perhaps one of the best examples of the way that photographed-buildings have affected Mexican twentieth-century architecture is in the case of Luis Barragán. Marc Treib has observed that the photography of Armando Salas Portugal, Luis Barragán's favourite photographer, was largely responsible for the dissemination of Barragán's work and the portrayal of his ideals. [44] Less known, perhaps, is the assessment by José Villagrán García, who describes Barragán's photography as a 'dangerous example for impressionable young architects and students who might suppose that an individual path . . . can be converted into a universal orientation'. [45] But perhaps the strongest demonstration of the power of photography comes from Keith Eggener, who points out that most of the members of the Pritzker Prize jury, which selected Barragán in 1980, refused to comment publicly on how they had reached their verdict. Only Cesar Pelli would admit that 'most members of the Pritzker jury were familiar with Barragán's architecture, but primarily though photographs . . . And Barragán's work was extremely photogenic'. [46] This clearly proves the power of photography in shaping people's perceptions and understanding of architectural values and principles.

Photography – and the associated image it creates of certain Mexican twentieth-century buildings – has thus strongly contributed to the academic discipline.

Mexican Architecture as an Academic Discipline

Rank	No. of Citations	Top Ten Most Photographed Buildings	Architect	Generation
1	14	Museo Nacional de Antropología	Pedro Ramírez Vázquez	2
2	13	Biblioteca UNAM	Juan O´Gorman	1
3	10	Casa Estudio Diego Rivera	Juan O´Gorman	1
4	10	Torres de Satélite	Luis Barragán	1
5	10	Casa Estudio Tacubaya	Luis Barragán	1
6	9	Sanatoria para Tuberculosos de Huipulco	José Villagrán García	1
7	9	Jardines del Pedregal	Luis Barragán	1
8	8	Hotel Camino Real México	Ricardo Legorreta	3
9	6	Hotel Camino Real Ixtapa	Ricardo Legorreta	3
10	6	Heroico Colegio Militar México CDMX	Agustín Hernández	2

Through photography, many publications have, knowingly or unknowingly, created icons as a way of constituting our understanding of Mexican Modernism. By analysing the selected 36 key books, I was able to count the most photographed buildings in these architectural publications (Chart 1.5). This reveals the list of buildings that have become emblems of Mexican twentieth-century architecture, and which have thus established its stereotypical image. Foremost on the list is the Museo Nacional de Antropología (Figure 1.1) by Pedro Ramírez Vázquez, followed by the Biblioteca Central of the Universidad Nacional Autónoma de México (UNAM) by Juan O'Gorman (Figure 1.2) and Barragán's own house, or Casa Estudio Tacubaya (Figure 1.3). Even the Torres de Satélite (Figure 1.4), which is essentially just urban sculpture devised by Barragán and Goeritz, was one of the images most frequently found in books on Mexican Modernist architecture.

Chart 1.5 Top Ten Most Photographed Buildings in the Selected 36 Books

43

Mexican Architecture as an Academic Discipline

Figure 1.1 Pedro Ramírez Vázquez: The Museo Nacional de Antropología, Main Façade, Mexico City, 1964.

Mexican Architecture as an Academic Discipline

Figure 1.2 Juan O'Gorman: Biblioteca Central UNAM, Mexico City, 1952.

Mexican Architecture as an Academic Discipline

Figure 1.3 Luis Barragán: Casa Estudio Tacubaya, Mexico City, 1948.

Mexican Architecture as an Academic Discipline

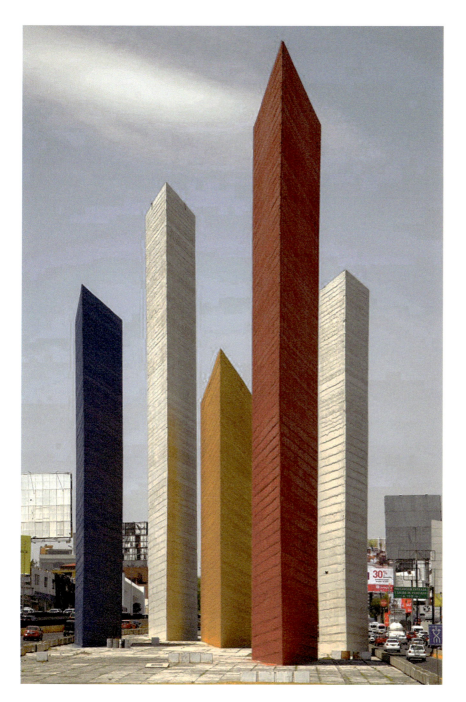

Figure 1.4 Luis Barragán and Mathias Goeritz: The Torres de Satélite, Mexico City, 1957.

Mexican Architecture as an Academic Discipline

ARCHITECTS AND THEIR AUTHORSHIP

Architectural discipline, through its theories and methodologies imparted in schools and publications, has established the academic concepts, patterns and principles that make up Mexican twentieth-century architecture discourse. Yet this discourse could not be possible without the participation of Mexican architects through their thoughts and their architectural production. Therefore, it is also crucial to consider key Mexican architects and their contribution. Here, the concept by Michel Foucault of 'author-function' can usefully be applied to architectural texts and designs.[47] Therefore, the architect, as an author, should not be regarded as a genius or creator but as the person that through his or her work creates a wealth of significations and the necessary delimitation of the architectural discourse. As such, there are two types of authors: the trans-discursive author, who is not only the creator of buildings but also the author of a wider architectural theory, tradition or discipline; or else, the discursive author, who is simply the creator of buildings that simply reproduce an already-established discourse.[48] Hence, the value of trans-discursive architects is their radical contribution to architectural discourse and architectural practice, making them more than just ordinary 'authors', and their work more than the outputs of the usual 'author-function'.

The importance that the architect as an author carries in his or her contribution to the power-knowledge network sustains architectural discourse via their built body of work. But it cannot be just any architect and not just any building that is regarded as constituting an essential part of architectural discourse and practice. Hence, for this book, the 13 selected architects and their buildings will serve as a sample and a representation of the production of the architectural discourse in twentieth-century Mexico. They are: José Villagrán García, Luis Barragán and Juan O'Gorman from the first generation; Pedro Ramírez Vázquez, Agustín Hernández and Abraham Zabludovsky from the second; Carlos Mijares, Ricardo Legorreta and Juan José Díaz Infante from the third; and finally, Enrique Norten, Clara de Buen, Alberto Kalach and Javier Sordo Madaleno from the fourth generation. Through the work of these eminent architects the dominant architectural canon in twentieth-century Mexican architecture can be recognised, as can their contribution to both Mexican and international architectural discourse. It is worth now explaining more about each of these four generations.

Mexican Architecture as an Academic Discipline

The First Generation (1900–14)

This generation is responsible for having introduced the 'Modern Movement' to Mexico, in spite of their neoclassical upbringing. They were keenly aware of the historical conditions generated after the Mexican Revolution, and as such, bravely accepted the challenge of creating a new architecture incorporating a Mexican identity. As initiators, they were responsible for providing the theoretical foundation to this new architectural movement stemming from Western architectural discourse. Their built work lasted from the late-1920s until the 1970s, creating the patterns and models followed by the next generations.

Figure 1.5 First Generation, from Left to Right: José Villagrán García, Luis Barragán and Juan O'Gorman.

José Villagrán García (1901–82)

Villagrán (Figure 1.5) is generally considered as the 'Father of Mexican Rationalism'.[49] He fearlessly pursued the ideals of European functionalism at a time when Historicism was still prevalent in Mexico, and so other influences like Art Deco, Mexican Colonial and neo-pre-Hispanic styles were being experimented with. As mentioned, he was the foremost teacher of Mexican Modernism,[50] and as such, has directly or indirectly influenced virtually every Mexican architect since, with his functionalist writings becoming the main theoretical treatises in Mexico. Villagrán openly confirmed his intention to make an original contribution to Mexican architecture:

> I graduated in 1923, and by 1924 I was the professor of my first group (of architecture students), as I mentioned before. I had just finished school and I made it my purpose to follow the advice given by that great French teacher (Julien Guadet): 'one must receive from schools everything that they can give us'. So,

Mexican Architecture as an Academic Discipline

I told myself: 'first I must receive everything they can give me, and as soon as I graduate, I should start to develop my own thoughts'.[51]

Yet, the importance of Villagrán resides not merely in his theory and teaching, but also in his architectural practice. Although there is no written anthology about his buildings in the same way that there is of his theoretical ideas, the buildings that have been published as his *oeuvre* are principally his hospital projects at the Sanatorio para Tuberculosos en Huipulco and the Instituto Nacional de Cardiología. Little, if anything, has been said of his earlier buildings in the 1920s that were not in the Modernist functional style. Although Villagrán continued to design and build until the late-1960s, his later projects, such as the Oficinas de ICA (Ingenieros Civiles Asociados) in 1969, were deemed by critics to be much less successful than his earlier work.[52] José Villagrán García's contribution can be defined as being trans-discursive in Foucault's terms, since it was instrumental in establishing the ground rules of an objective and rational Modernist discipline in Mexico, in which the role of the architect is that of a professional expert, as opposed to seeming to be a whimsical and superfluous artist.

Luis Barragán (1902–88)

Barragán is without doubt the most mythical figure in Mexican architecture, and certainly the best-known within its international context.[53] He is the only Mexican architect ever to be awarded architecture's most prestigious award, the Pritzker Prize. Barragán (Figure. 1.5) is widely described as one of architecture's most respected and refined designers, and his architecture should be seen as a sublime act of a poetic imagination, according to Emilio Ambasz.[54] Barragán has thus gained universal recognition, and his architecture continues to be seen as a unique and quintessentially Modernist style.

Publications usually portray Barragán's work by selecting the most colourful and supposedly 'emotional' examples, such as his own house and studio in Tacubaya. Very few books on twentieth-century Mexican architecture include his more rational designs, like his Melchor Ocampo #38 apartment building, which he designed as a coherent Modernist housing model.[55] Due to the huge admiration for Barragán, and indeed his mythical status, there are now publications that painstakingly document everything that he designed, even those projects that were previously discarded from the canon. Most of his buildings, however,

Mexican Architecture as an Academic Discipline

are usually classified as being regional, introspective and emotionally charged designs that convey an architecture that is based on a vernacular way of building, yet which was also highly sophisticated in its simplicity.[56] Barragán is often acclaimed for architectural projects that go beyond the international norm to produce examples regarded as expressive and poetic in their 'Mexican-ness'. The buildings that form the most iconic images of his work are Casa Estudio Tacubaya, Cuadra San Cristobal and Casa Gilardi, as well as Jardines del Pedregal neighbourhood. Casa Gilardi is considered in itself to be an anthology of all of his work, one that 'presents with few elements the height of Barragán's metaphysical concerns in the use of sky, sun, water and colour'.[57] Barragán considered his work as that of a traditionalist architect and gives his own particular definition of the term:

> *I am going to see if I can explain the incorrect use of the term 'traditionalist architect'. It is generally used to label an architect that resorts to the architecture of a style that belongs to another era, but of the same place. Philosophically, this should not be considered as traditional since the style that he is copying is not contemporary with his time. This means that a true traditionalist consists of doing an architecture that is contemporary. For example, if the colonials had made Mayan architecture, they would not have been traditionalists, and the same thing if the Mayan had copied a preceding architecture, and so on indefinitely. I do not know if I have explained this clearly. Tradition is to do with the architecture of our time according to our life and era and corresponding to the culture of that period.[58]*

Luis Barragán can thus also be defined as a trans-discursive author, since he is the creator of an architectural language that continues to be imitated by many others. Although his architecture is personal, he created a colourful and emotional language, in contrast to, or even in protest against, the modern commercial world and its dehumanizing processes.[59] Although Barragán did not establish a clearly articulated theory, he was not against theorization per se, as we have already seen. Due to his own highly intuitive nature, he attempted instead to inspire in others a personal attitude towards architectural design. He did not consider himself to be an artist, a hero, or an expert. Instead, he saw himself as an apprentice who was continually trying out new things. His formal language, awkwardly often classified as 'emotional', was, in fact, clearly influenced by both the abstract simplicity of Modernism along with the directness of the colours, textures and sounds of Mexican tradition.

Mexican Architecture as an Academic Discipline

Figure 1.6 Juan O'Gorman, Diego Rivera, Ruth Rivera Marín and Heriberto Pagelson: Museo Anahuacalli, Mexico City, 1955.

Juan O'Gorman (1905–82)

Known both for his controversial character and his passionate temperament, Juan O'Gorman (Figure 1.5) was perhaps one of the most interesting personalities within Mexican Modernism generally. He is not only famous for his architectural work but also widely known as a talented painter. Initially, his buildings were so violently functionalist that they produced an uproar that even antagonized his teacher, José Villagrán, since he rejected any artistic intention at all in his designs. The best example, and the most publicised one, is the house and studio that he designed for the artists Diego Rivera and Frida Kahlo. Juan O'Gorman changed radically, however, from being a strict functionalist after he became disillusioned with communism and its idealization of technology; instead, he returned to painting, resorting also to a highly decorative architecture that used murals and

Mexican Architecture as an Academic Discipline

pre-Hispanic influences. He alleged that this change came about mainly due to maturity:

> Ah . . . the wisdom that comes from old age!! You see, it is not a question of learning from a book. Any foolish person could do that if he read and learned. But the hard thing is to gain knowledge from life. That is what is difficult. Wisdom consists in being able to understand others and oneself a little bit more.[60]

Examples of O'Gorman's later period are his grotto house, or Casa-Cueva in San Angel, and his participation in the Anahuacalli (Figure 1.6), a museum built to hold Diego Rivera's pre-Hispanic treasures. Yet what has proved to be his most important work, and which became a shining symbol of Mexican Modernist architecture, is the Biblioteca Central of the Universidad Nacional Autónoma de México (UNAM) on Ciudad Universitaria (CU) campus in Mexico City. This building is considered to be by far the most convincing and successful of O'Gorman's work.[61] Indeed, its bold integration of murals and architecture are regularly cited as a superb example of syncretism and formalism.[62]

Despite this dramatic design shift, the participation of Juan O'Gorman in Mexican architecture has to be seen as simply discursive, since he was working with the possibilities of pre-existing architectural discourses in both his use of the rational language of Modernism and the decorative language of pre-Hispanic elements. O'Gorman's novelty in applying these languages might be confused with that of a trans-discursive author, but his own shift from one language to another openly denotes his discursive intentions. His authorship transcends stylistic trends and was determined more by the passion and the content of his projects than in the coherence of any particular style or of any architectural expression.

The Second Generation (1915–29)

This generation is considered to be the one that institutionalized Modernist architecture as both a Mexican and an international mode of expression. Their buildings, alongside those of the first generation, exemplify what is generally known as Mexican twentieth-century architecture, spanning for more than 50 years from the 1950s into the beginning of the twenty-first century. Hence, this generation has created the most prolific body-of-work and thus contributed the greatest to the making of Modern Mexican architecture.

Mexican Architecture as an Academic Discipline

Figure 1.7 Second Generation, from Left to Right: Pedro Ramírez Vazquez, Abraham Zabludovsky and Agustín Hernandez.

Pedro Ramírez Vázquez (1919–2013)

Perhaps no single architect personifies the ideals of Mexico's internationally minded architecture better than Pedro Ramírez Vázquez (Figure 1.7). His design philosophy is based on that which can be built, rather than focussing on formal attributes or stylistic trends. He believes in the universality of Modernist architecture, and of functionalist principles, and thus is a loyal follower of Villagrán's ideas, which he has devoted to the service of Mexico and its people. His oeuvre is so diverse that it ranges from prefabricated rural classrooms through to museums, churches and basilicas, to corporate offices, exhibitions and political embassies. He also built widely abroad, including other parts of Latin America, the United States, Europe and Africa.[63] When asked why his buildings were so diverse in style, Ramírez Vázquez explains:

> *I have never been interested in being recognized as the author of any of my buildings. I am interested in expressing the destiny of each building and trying to make them comfortable. I do not limit myself, because if I wanted my buildings to be recognized formally, I would get myself into very serious problems. How would I manage to make a basilica like a stadium? There are architects who think this way. They believe that architecture is poetry, like the extraordinary work of Luis Barragán. But how would Barragán have done a poetic stadium? Barragán's architecture is very intimate and pleasant, full of ambience, but he never tackled complex functional buildings. This is justifiable. We all use different formal languages. An architect is only a translator. He translates the users' requirements into a construction language, and as in literature, each author has his own interpretation and way of expressing himself.*[64]

Ramírez Vázquez is considered in Mexico as a truly national and political figure that became one of Mexico's most honoured architects. He is known best for the 'official' architecture that represented the presidency of Adolfo López Mateos, with buildings such as the Museo Nacional de Antropología, through to the presidency of Carlos Salinas de Gortari, with the Mexican exhibition building, or Pabellón de México, at the Seville Exposition in 1992. The Museo Nacional de Antropología is perhaps Ramírez Vázquez's most esteemed building, along, perhaps, with the Museo del Templo Mayor, both of which express Mexico's past through an international Modernist language that also carefully uses the proportions of pre-Hispanic examples.[65] Ramírez Vázquez has thus contributed to Mexican architecture as a discursive author by producing new alternatives within an accepted international discourse. His presence as an author is strong, despite the variety of his design typologies, ranging from skyscrapers like the Torre de Mexicana de Aviación to football stadiums like Estadio Azteca. The authorship of Ramírez's work is always present in the way he manipulates the meaning of his architecture and the response of its occupants. He does not claim or even want to be a form-giver, hero, or artist. Instead, he claimed to be a professional service-provider, arguing that his design expertise was based solely on the objective and rational disciplinary basis of Mexican architecture.

Abraham Zabludovsky (1924–2003)

Zabludovsky is regarded as another of Mexico's most prolific architects, due to his long professional career in Mexico and in foreign countries. His projects vary from apartment blocks, commercial buildings, banks, public buildings, museums, cultural centres and auditoriums designed either in his own independent practice or along with Teodoro González de León. Zabludovsky (Figure 1.7) is foremost a constructor and an administrator, with his projects expressing clear solutions and simple concepts. His careful use of materials and technology, chosen in order to reduce maintenance,[66] went, however, beyond his stated interest in functionalism to begin to suggest a clear formal expression. By frequently using exposed reinforced-concrete, Zabludovsky was able to develop his own style with a strong personality that emphasized horizontality and long dimensions. His architecture can easily be identified by the simplicity of its volumes, its use of durable materials, the limited areas of glass and a continuous search for new kinds of surface texture. He wanted his work to respond to the context and the features of each site, and so his projects are also characterized by the use of courtyards and porticos that relate the buildings to their urban surroundings, as an attempt to encourage public interaction and equally be reminiscent of traditional Mexican architecture.

These design features can be seen in his entire body of work, but perhaps particularly in the most recognised public buildings, such as the Museo Tamayo, Delegación Cuauhtémoc and Universidad Pedagógica Nacional, as well as private buildings like the Centro Financiero Banamex and Colegio de México. Zabludovsky's architecture has not only been described as an architecture that endures through time[67] and which weathers well,[68] but is considered as bold, tectonic Expressionism due to its monumentality, plasticity and texture.[69] It might even be classified as Brutalism, although no-one has ever described it as such. Yet it is evident that Zabludovsky is a discursive author, since his architecture is based on the existing discourses of previous formal languages. He nevertheless does not create an architecture analogous to International Modernism, but instead is motivated by the search for a more formal and contextual expression, more akin to Brutalism. Zabludovsky, likewise, does not assume the role of a form-giver, but instead adopts a professional position as the refiner of formal solutions and construction techniques, as seen in this following statement:

> *The only thing I know is that since I started my first job, and up to the last one I have done, I have had the same enthusiasm and the same will to portray with absolute sincerity my thoughts of what I believed to be the adequate solution at that particular moment. The most important thing in my work is the way it has portrayed the different periods of our country, as well as the way it has ventured in our society and in the structure of its history.[70]*

Agustín Hernández (1924–2022)

One of the most creative Mexican architects of the second generation is Agustín Hernández (Figure 1.7), who has recently died at the age of 98. Although also influenced by Villagrán, he credits his teacher, Augusto Pérez Palacio, for his over-riding interest in construction technology. Hernandez's ideas thus respond to his functionalist training and his belief in an architecture that needs to balance structure, form and function.[71] Hernández's designs are all based on geometry as part of his pursuit of a sculptural architecture that tries to challenge technology and engineering solutions. He emphasizes the importance of history and of producing an architecture that expresses a Mexican identity by combining bold, tectonic forms with traditional symbolism. This is evident in his most renowned building, the Heroico Colegio Militar, in which he resorts to Nahuatl cosmology to design a monumental complex with a harmonic tension of solids and voids, as if the elements are in search of equilibrium.[72] Yet perhaps his most daring designs are for his own house and studio, both of which were widely publicised and photographed.

Hernández is clearly a discursive author, one who bases his work chiefly on the Modernist architectural language and on developing construction technology. His architecture denotes his authorship by its persistent search for innovation in both spatial solutions, as well as formal expressions with iconic shapes, as can be seen in the Calakmul building (Figure 1.8), also popularly known as 'the washing machine'. Hernández believes his buildings speak for themselves:

Figure 1.8 Agustín Hernández: Calakmul, Mexico City, 1997.

You see, creativity works in the subconscious mind rather than in the conscious mind. Many times, when you are looking for rhythm, you try to use a module, but rhythm really comes out instinctively. I do not believe in styles. I believe that each building has to have a different style, determined by its structure, its materials and its entire architectural programme.[73]

Paradoxically, however, he disrupts the functionalist discourse through bold designs that rely upon inventive technological feats. His work could perhaps be classified as Late-Modernist, or even High-Tech, although he is not interested in acknowledging such terms. Instead, he claims that technology and construction are the inherent generators of his creativity.

Mexican Architecture as an Academic Discipline

The Third Generation (1930–44)

This generation of Mexican architects openly questioned the prevailing Modernist architectural discourse of the previous generations. Instead, they followed closely the social and architectural disruptions that appeared during the 1960s in the USA and Europe, and as such introduced the novel concepts generated by Western architects which criticized Functionalist Modernism. Their projects stretched from the 1960s into the first decades of the twenty-first century. But, although they questioned the key principles of Mexican Modernism, it is important to note that they did not abandon them completely, nor did they abandon the pursuit of a specifically Mexican mode of architectural expression.

Figure 1.9 Third Generation, from Left to Right: Ricardo Legorreta, Carlos Mijares and Juan José Díaz Infante.

Ricardo Legorreta (1931–2011)

Legorreta (Figure 1.9) is undoubtedly the most internationally renowned and successful Mexican twentieth-century architect, after Luis Barragán. He achieved extensive recognition from Mexican and international critics and architects, well into the first decade of the twenty-first century. As an architect and as a Mexican, he felt the need to exalt his country's values through his buildings, each intended to express a sense of traditional Mexican architecture. Historians and critics have variously described his architecture as Regionalist or Neo-Vernacular, or indeed as a multi-coloured architecture with a sense of mystery, surprise, humour, drama and sensual richness that was nurtured both by Mexican culture and by his personal experiences. Legorreta's entire body of work remained loyal to his particular approach. One of his most famous buildings is the Hotel Camino Real in Mexico City. It was one the first projects in which he attempted to capture Mexican expression and an emotional style through the use of its monumental scale and bright, colourful design. His emotional style did not waver after his son joined as a partner in 1991, nor in his last projects – some of which he did not see completed, such as the Torre BBVA (Figure 1.10), designed in collaboration with Richard Rogers and not finished until 2016.

Figure 1.10 Legorreta + Legorreta and Rogers Stirk Harbour + Partners: Torre BBVA, Mexico City, 2016.

Mexican Architecture as an Academic Discipline

Ricardo Legorreta's contribution can be said to be that of a discursive author, since his architecture was based so clearly on Barragán's original trans-discursive discourse. Despite this, Legorreta definitely pioneered his own architectural language via the use of monumental scale and of elements of surprise. He appeared at times to challenge the huge influence from Barragán's architecture, altering the latter's introspective qualities by exalting, instead, human emotions and by creating a sense of awe and amazement. Legorreta's authorship clearly evolved during his career, and this was particularly evident in his use of emotional and cultural factors identifiable by locals and foreigners alike. He admitted to his desire to be seen as a hero and form-giver, as an artist who sacrifices his personal life in the name of a noble profession, while also admitting that a leading role can only be played by a person who has the support of other fellow architects and colleagues:

> I must insist that happiness in life is not achieved through public recognition. I have a partner that very few people know. In fact, he does not want to be known. It really bothers him when I acknowledge him publicly. His name is Noé Castro. He once told me: 'You are becoming very important . . . you appear in magazines and people interview and recognize you. But I do not know which one of us is happier. I control my life and you do not'. So, I think I would also tell young architects that they should search for their happiness, and not be deceived by the glitter of fame.[74]

Carlos Mijares (1930–2015)

Although Carlos Mijares (Figure 1.9) designed relatively few buildings, he represented a departure from Modernist paradigms by pursuing an architectural alternative that was rooted in local materials, traditional labour, the use of natural daylight and a sense of integration into the landscape. His contribution to Mexican architecture is not limited to his buildings, since he also devoted his career to teaching in several schools of architecture. Mijares achieved much academic recognition due to his strong convictions and architectural principles that were centred on an architecture that could be experienced directly:

> I believe that architecture (again according to the limitations of each case) is either good or bad . . . Good architecture should enrich everyone that comes in contact with it, or that happens to live in it. It must contribute to our everyday life and our intellectual life in its poetic perception; and this experience should not wear off, at least not soon. This is not a definition since it is impossible to do this.

Mexican Architecture as an Academic Discipline

This is a reality that needs to be perceived, but for which we must have or develop certain ability. It is like wine tasters. What makes a good wine? Well, in order to determine this one must learn to taste wine, and this cannot be described, you need to savour it. This is also true in architecture. One must experience it.[75]

Mijares integrated contextual elements, the participation of the user and the construction worker to produce a sensorial and perceptual approach to architectural design. His projects, often loosely classified as 'Critical Regionalism', integrate traditional materials with modern elements in a search for a local identity through traditional materials and construction systems. The extensive use of brickwork, which identifies the authorship of Mijares in his buildings, can be seen in the Iglesia del Perpetuo Socorro, Capilla del Panteón and Christ Church in Mexico City. Mijares is another discursive author, inspired by the architectural discourse of trans-discursive architects like Alvar Aalto, Louis Kahn or even Mies van der Rohe. Despite such influences, Mijares preferred not to get caught up in issues of architectural form or style. Instead, he surrendered his position of author in favour of the site context, the skills of the construction workers and the needs of the client. He saw his role very much as that of a service-provider, one who remains open to different architectural experiences.

Juan José Díaz Infante (1936–2012)

As mentioned earlier, Díaz Infante (Figure 1.9) was an innovator determined to discover new alternatives for design solutions, influenced greatly by Buckminster Fuller, the Japanese Metabolists and Archigram. These precedents, alongside his experiences as a designer, inspired him to develop his 'Kalikosmia' theory. As a theory, it remained entirely abstract, so its aim was not to produce a new architectural language but to inspire a condition of continuous experimentation.[76] This is witnessed in Díaz Infante's own house in Amsterdam Street, the Buffet Industrial offices, La Bolsa Mexicana building and the TAPO bus station. Although stylistically these buildings are very different, they all share the same concept of seeking the most effective use of time and energy.[77] Díaz Infante was a discursive author who rethought previous architectural principles to create his experimental designs as a perpetual innovator in continuous search for revolutionary solutions. He preferred to remain anonymous, declaring that:

I believe that it would be better to be forgotten. Because when you are remembered, you are going to get someone stuck. Whereas if someone forgets you,

61

Mexican Architecture as an Academic Discipline

they will advance. I would like people to say: 'I do not know who designed this building, but it has values.' Lastly, the best music is anonymous, like Jesusita en Chihuahua, Las Mañanitas, and inventions like the clip, the pin and the hammer. All the great discoveries are anonymous. I would like to be anonymous and to be analysed as one who contributed with a grain of sand to produce a change, but no imitations. It would sadden me greatly if they would imitate me; that would be my greatest failure.[78]

The Fourth Generation (1945–60)

This generation of Mexican architects, although considered a breakaway generation, do not disapprove of Modernism nor Functionalism; instead, they seem to want to break free from a constant preoccupation with asserting their Mexican identity. These architects all started working in the 1980s, and therefore their work had barely got going during the twentieth century and instead can be best be seen in the first two decades of the twenty-first century. As such, they are still going strong, working on projects both domestic and abroad, and bravely competing with their international counterparts in an ever-more globalized condition.

Figure 1.11 Fourth Generation, from Left to Right: Enrique Norten, Clara de Buen, Alberto Kalach and Javier Sordo Madaleno.

Enrique Norten (1951–)

He is generally considered to be an avant-garde architect due to his use of 'High-Tech' techniques and materials. Richard Ingersoll, the US architecture critic, labels Enrique Norten (Figure 1.11) as trans-cultural because of his partial education at Cornell, along with his 'high technology aspirations with an architecture that aspires to reach an artistic status, like all Mexicans'.[79] Hence, Norten's interest in 'Mexican-ness' is believed to reside in a faith in the functionalist tradition as a reaction against the previous architectural generation. In this vein, Norten has also been called a 'Mex-Tech Creole', one who belongs to two worlds without betraying either.[80] Ingersoll says that Norten's architecture 'says yes to modernity and function through the use of technology. Since for him, form follows the method that produced it'.[81]

Perhaps the best-known buildings at the beginning of Norten's career were the Televisa mixed-use building and the Escuela Nacional de Arte Teatral in Mexico City. In both examples, Norten shows that he is partial to the use of light materials and technical innovations in order to produce all-encompassing, cylindrical metal-roof forms that have since become urban icons. Nowadays, his workload is increasingly international, having an office both in Mexico City and in New York City, where he has designed important projects like the Mercedes House and the BAM South Site, or 300 Ashland. Enrique Norten must be considered a discursive author who resorts to the current international architectural trends, relying upon his position as an author to impart an innovative, avant-garde feel to his buildings. As he notes:

> In order to be an architect, one must be very much in love with the profession, without a doubt. Within our social value scale, architecture is not a good solution if one looks at economic remuneration. In our society, what you earn is what you are worth, and this does not only apply to our discipline. So, you must truly have a great passion and a great love, and a great faith that is almost religious. In order to find values that are not present in our society, one must work tremendously. This is to have the discipline that commands you to wake up every day and every day to create architecture.[82]

Clara de Buen (1954–)

The buildings by de Buen are specifically designed so that they do not require very much maintenance. In this goal, they depict her passion for the honest use of materials and constructional systems, as well as her interest in the context of the site. Clara de Buen (Figure 1.11) admits to being strongly influenced by her mentors, who include Carlos Mijares, Francisco Serrano and Aurelio Nuño. She is often not recognised individually as a designer, given that her work is the result of the teamwork of Nuño, Mac Gregor and de Buen. These three Ibero graduates continue to uphold their conviction in teamwork and shared responsibilities, which is rare enough in a profession filled with would-be prima donnas. Colegio Alemán Alexander Von Humboldt was perhaps one of the first projects that gave de Buen and her practice a degree of fame amongst her peers. Although their manner of designing is rare in twentieth-century Mexico, the firm's architectural contribution is still only discursive, since it resorts to a pre-existing architectural discourse established by their mentors. This is particularly noticeable in projects like the Museo de Arte e Historia de Guanajuato, completed in 2008, where the design team remained faithful to the use of raw reinforced concrete to create massive structural elements.

The work of de Buen has thus abandoned the notion of a single authorship in favour of an architecture that is based on participation, not only by her team members but also by clients. The role assumed by the practice is that of professional service-givers who seek not to produce a work of art but to look after their clients' interests and well-being, as she explains this through the following statement:

> Our profession depends on the clients we have. If you do a good job, you will have more opportunities, but unfortunately it does not always work that way. For me, everything is still a challenge and it is the same to design a little house, or a room, or a 20,000 square metre building. This is what is wonderful about our profession. The interest it brings, regardless of its size. They (students) have to love the profession or if not, they should leave it. They should not expect to become rich either. I believe that it is a profession in which you have to be in for the long haul. Some of the young architects that have worked for us want to start designing immediately, but you have to start from the bottom, little by little.[83]

Alberto Kalach (1960–)

Kalach is often regarded as one of the most talented architects currently working in Mexico City (Figure 1.11). His designs share a formal concern that goes beyond functional restrictions to produce a sensual feel that has been described as 'the disarticulation of space, juxtaposition of planes, and sensually crafted details with the physicality of luscious materials'.[84] As a rebellious and provocative designer with an undoubtedly creative sensibility, Kalach's work at the beginning of his career was mainly concentrated on residential designs that received national and international acclaim and were highly publicized.

Kalach is another who is clearly a discursive author who imprints his authorship through his control over the architectural expression of each project, not least in his concern for architectural details. This can be seen in the Departamentos Rodin building, with its suspended façade, which he later took to a monumental level in the suspended floors of the Biblioteca Vasconcelos (Figure 1.12) in 2007. Kalach's buildings convey a perfectionist obsession in

Mexican Architecture as an Academic Discipline

Figure 1.12 Alberto Kalach: Biblioteca Vasconcelos, Mexico City, 2007.

Mexican Architecture as an Academic Discipline

their use of materials and their detailing. Still, he sees himself not as a hero or form-giver, but as an architect calmly concerned with the realities of each design experience:

> I do not believe that architecture is a way of saving the world. It is only a small job, even one we can do without, like many other jobs. It is a contribution. It is a job for which you get a fee to enjoy yourself, to have a house, a car. But in the end, it is just a job.[85]

Javier Sordo Madaleno (1956–)

As the son of Juan Sordo Madaleno, a distinguished Mexican Modern architect of the second generation, Javier Sordo Madaleno (Figure 1.11) carries his father's legacy in the firm bearing their name. In 1982, he took charge of this firm; after his father's death, he turned it into a highly successful company by undertaking large development projects, such as hotels and commercial business districts. Today, Javier Sordo Madaleno – now with the collaboration of his sons Javier, Fernando and José Juan – have turned this architectural firm into an even more ambitious enterprise that has branched out into real-estate development.

Besides being a great promoter, Javier Sordo Madaleno is also considered by many to be an excellent designer. His architecture falls into two phases: the first used local materials, colour, monumentality and a Mexican spirit influenced by his mentors, Francisco Serrano and Ricardo Legorreta; this was followed by another period full of technological advances and expressive iconic shapes that respond to contemporary trends. The Westin Regina Los Cabos Hotel is considered one of the best examples of his first phase for its use of intense colours, sensual textures and monumental scale.[86] His second phase, with its formal metaphors and bold geometries, can best be seen in the recently finished Plaza Artz Pedregal.

Madaleno's great care towards detailing helps to create a strong formal character of monumentality, theatrical effect and geometry that also greatly considers its context. He can thus be seen as a discursive author, keen to provide a professional service, with a particular interest as a developer who wishes to contribute to the city and to the financial interests of his clients. As he explains:

> I believe that what I have contributed a little is in giving it a more integral vision, on how to see architecture as a whole. That is, to see the whole not only the

Mexican Architecture as an Academic Discipline

aesthetic part but also all the rest that we have mentioned before. I am very concerned with budget control, and also to ensure that everything is finished on time. I like everything that surrounds this. I like to know that what I am proposing is in accordance with the wishes of users, technically and functionally. I enjoy this challenge. For example, in commercial buildings you must distribute the shops so that they work commercially. I even like to establish what type of shops should go in certain places. I get involved in things that go beyond design. This is the kind of vision that will become more important each day for an architect. [87]

In each of their ways, these 13 key Mexican architects, through their professional careers and their bodies of work, have contributed to the construction of Modernist architectural discourse. Their ideas and projects are featured in the most important books, and their own testimony, as gathered from published texts and personal interviews, demonstrates their collective contribution to the academic discipline in Mexico and their participation in the cultural issues that will be examined in the following chapters.

Firstly, 'the academic power structure' refers to that which presents architecture as a learned discipline and mode of practice. As such, it exerts its control through schools of architecture, professional publications and other similarly institutionalized formats. The main premise for looking at it here is to establish how this power structure contributed to the discourse and practice of Mexican Modernism by defining and controlling its classification systems, paradigms, archetypes, models, journals, monographs, etc.

To conclude, this chapter has shown that twentieth-century Mexican architectural discourse was essentially that of a normative academic discipline, rooted in Modernist Functionalism, and validated in terms of professional practice as established by architectural schools and guilds/associations to legitimate and justify its ethical and moral values, all of which follow Western standards and paradigms. Therefore, this academic power structure comprised all the mechanisms needed to produce architects for Mexican society via an educational process that served to reinforce belief in its own discourse; as such, the profession got to decide what is considered to be architecture and who could be considered to be an architect. This contribution to the making of Mexican Modernism was achieved through publications that presented both written-architecture and photographed-architecture within an organized classificatory system, sustained largely by functionalist theory and an anti-theoretical ethos, well-rooted in Western architectural paradigms. It also is important to point out that there were no architectural movements in Mexico during this period, theoretical or otherwise,

Mexican Architecture as an Academic Discipline

that questioned or challenged this power structure as there were, for instance, in Chile with the Valparaiso School during the 1950s-1970s or Paolo Soleri Cosanti Foundation that in a way followed Frank Lloyd Wright Taliesin School, which also functioned outside the academic radar; for it had no proper accreditation until 1989. Hence, this chapter's intention of pulling apart this academic power structure is to show how it operated, unveiling the underlying power mechanisms, and to challenge its dominance and legitimacy so that other alternatives might be produced. Along the same line, the following chapter will address the economic/political power structure that determined and controlled the production of Mexican twentieth-century architecture as part of Mexico's modernization and westernization process.

NOTES

1 The term 'discourse' here refers to the one adopted by Michel Foucault in Foucault, Michel. *The Archaeology of Knowledge and the Discourse on Language*. Translated by A. M. Sheridan Smith, New York, Pantheon Books, 1970.

2 These rituals create a bias, or subjectivity, to which people choose to conform and accept as a body of knowledge that exerts its power through expert groups and institutions, as explained in Hubert L. Dreyfus and Paul Rabinow, *Michel Foucault: Beyond Structuralism and Hermeneutics*. Chicago, The University of Chicago Press, 1982.

3 'Governmentality' is a term established by Michel Foucault that refers to conduct, or an activity meant to shape, guide or affect the conduct of people. Ibid.

4 Cuff, Dana, *Architecture: The Story of Practice*. Cambridge, MIT Press, 1991, p. 43.

5 Rittel, Horst. 'Evaluating Evaluators'. *Accreditation Evaluation Conference of the National Architectural Accrediting Board*. New Orleans, March 1976, pp. 77–91.

6 Larson, Magali Sarfatti. 'The Rise of Professionalism'. In *A Sociological Analysis*. Berkeley, University of California Press, p. 1977.

7 Cuff, Dana, *Architecture: The Story of Practice*. Cambridge, MIT Press, 1991.

8 Donald, P. 'The Relationship between College Grades and Achievement: A Review of Literature'. *American College Testing Research Reports*. No. 7. Iowa City, Research Development Division, 1965.

9 Ramírez Ugarte, Alejandro. *Conversación con Luis Barragán*. Guadalajara, Arquitónica, 2015.

10 Hernández, Agustin. Personal interview with the author. Mexico City, 17th March 2000.

11 Mijares, Carlos. Personal interview with the author. Mexico City, 30th May 2000.

12 Zevi, Bruno. *History of Modern Architecture*. London, Faber and Faber, 1950.

13 Mijares, Carlos. Personal interview with the author. Mexico City, 30th May 2000.

14 de Buen, Clara. Personal interview with the author. Mexico City, 16th October 2000.

15 Sordo Madaleno, Javier. Personal interview with the author. Mexico City, 27th May 2000.

16 Toca, Antonio. 'La Crisis de la Modernidad: Un nuevo fin de siglo'. In Fernando González Gortázar (ed.), *La arquitectura mexicana del siglo XX*. México, Consejo Nacional para la Cultura y las Artes, 1994.

17 Ibid.

18 Zabludovsky, Abraham. Personal interview with the author. Mexico City, 31st May 2000.

19 Legorreta, Ricardo. Personal interview with the author. Mexico City, 16th October 2000.

20 Zabludovsky, Abraham. Personal interview with the author. Mexico City, 31st May 2000.

21 Ibid.

22 This translation is possible using the premise of Roland Barthes in Barthes, Roland. *The Fashion System*. London, Jonathan Cape Ltd., Trinity Press, 1985.

23 Ibid., pp. 3–4.

24 Ramírez Ugarte, Alejandro. *Conversación con Luis Barragán*. Guadalajara, Arquitónica, 2015.

25 Ibid.

26 Legorreta, Ricardo. Personal interview with the author. Mexico City, 16th October 2000.

27 Mijares, Carlos. Personal interview with the author. Mexico City, 30th May 2000.

28 de Anda, Enrique X. *Historia de la Arquitectura Mexicana*. México, Gustavo Gili, 1995, p. 237.

29 de Buen, Clara. Personal interview with the author. Mexico City, 16th October 2000.

30 Sordo Madaleno, Javier. Personal interview with the author. Mexico City, 27th May 2000.

31 Kalach, Alberto. Personal interview with the author. Mexico City, 26th May 2000.

32 Choay, Françoise. *The Rule and the Model on the Theory of Architecture and Urbanism*. Edited by Denise Bratton, London, MIT Press, 1997, p. 8.

33 de Anda, Enrique X. *Historia de la arquitectura Mexicana*. México, Gustavo Gili, 1995.

34 Pérez Gómez, Alberto. 'Mexico, Modernity and Architecture: An Interview with Alberto Pérez Gómez'. In Edward R. Burian (ed.), *Modernity and the Architecture of Mexico*, Austin, University of Texas Press, 1997, p. 38.

35 Ibid.

36 Ibid., p. 34.

37 Diaz Infante, Juan Jose. Personal interview with the author. Mexico City, 17th March 2000.

38 Ibid.

39 Ortiz, Cecilia and María Rosenberg. *Las Pieles del Espacio: Space, Speed and Skin*. México, Díaz Infante Editorial, 1999.

40 Diaz Infante, Juan Jose. Personal interview with the author. Mexico City, 17th March 2000.

41 Ibid.

42 Ibid.

43 Ramírez Vázquez, Pedro. Personal interview with the author. Mexico City, 20th March 2000.

44 Treib, Marc. 'Foreword'. In Keith Eggener, *Luis Barragán's Gardens of El Pedregal*. New York, Princeton Architectural Press, 2001, p. xi.

45 Eggener, Keith. *Luis Barragán's Gardens of El Pedregal*. New York, Princeton Architectural Press, 2001, p. 89.

46 Ibid., p. 52.

47 This concept, developed by Foucault, explains this is a form of property claimed by the author as the expression of his or her ideas or body of work, also as a form of responsibility of the author's reliability and credibility, and finally as a form of creative power, standard of quality, conceptual coherence, stylistic uniformity and historical accuracy. See: Foucault, Michel. *The Order of Things: An Archaeology of the Human Sciences*. New York, Vintage Books, 1994, p. 143.

48 These two types of authors are further explained by Foucault in his book. Ibid., p. 148.

49 Benévolo, Leonardo. *Historia de la Arquitectura Moderna*. 5th Edición. Barcelona, Gustavo Gili, 1982.

50 Noelle, Louise. *Arquitectos contemporáneos de México*. México, Editorial Trillas, 1989.

51 Gómez, Lilia and Miguel Ángel Quevedo. 'Entrevista con el arquitecto José Villagrán García'. In *Testimonios Vivos 20 arquitectos*. México, Cuadernos de arquitectura. 15–16 INBA, Mayo-Agosto 1981.

52 de Anda, Enrique X. *Historia del arte mexicano: Arte contemporáneo*. Vol. 14. Edited by Juan Salvat and José Rosas et al. México, Editorial Salvat, 1986.

53 Noelle, L. and C. Tejeda. *Catálogo guía de arquitectura mexicana contemporánea, Ciudad de México*. México, Fomento Cultural Banamex AC., 1993.

54 Ambasz, Emilio. *The Architecture of Luis Barragán*. New York, Museum of Modern Art, 1976.

55 Browne, Enrique. *La Otra Arquitectura en Latinoamérica*. México, Gustavo Gili, 1988.

56 Hitchcock, Henry-Russell. *Latin American Architecture since 1945*. New York, Museum of Modern Art, 1955.

57 *Progressive Architecture*. Tokyo, Japan, No. 39, 1983, pp. 20–21.

58 Ramírez Ugarte, Alejandro. *Conversación con Luis Barragán*. Guadalajara, Arquitónica, 2015.

59 de Anda, Enrique X. *Historia de la arquitectura Mexicana*. México, Gustavo Gili, 1995.

60 Gómez, Lilia and Miguel Ángel Quevedo. 'Entrevista con el arquitecto Juan O'Gorman'. In *Testimonios Vivos 20 arquitectos*. México, Cuadernos de arquitectura 15–16 INBA, Mayo-Agosto 1981.

61 Cetto, Max. *Modern Architecture in Mexico*. New York, Praeger, 1961.

62 Browne, Enrique. *La Otra Arquitectura en Latinoamérica*. México, Gustavo Gili, 1988.

63 Trueblood, Beatriz. *Ramírez Vázquez en la arquitectura: Realización y diseño*. México, Editorial Diana, 1989.

64 Ramírez Vázquez, Pedro. Personal interview with the author. Mexico City, 20th March 2000.

65 Benévolo, Leonardo. *Historia de la Arquitectura Moderna*. 5th Edición. Barcelona, Gustavo Gili, 1982.

66 Noelle, Louise. *Arquitectos contemporáneos de Mexico*. México, Editorial Trillas, 1989.

67 Glusberg, Jorge. *Abraham Zabludovsky, arquitecto*. México, Noriega Editores: Consejo Nacional para la Cultura y las Artes, 1998.

68 Benévolo, Leonardo. *Historia de la Arquitectura Moderna*. 5th Edición. Barcelona, Gustavo Gili, 1982.

69 de Anda, Enrique X. *Historia de la arquitectura Mexicana*. México, Gustavo Gili, 1995.

70 Zabludovsky, Abraham Personal interview with the author. Mexico City, 31st May 2000.

71 García Bringas, Graciela. *Agustín Hernández, arquitecto*. México, Grupo Noriega Editores, 1998.

72 de Anda, Enrique X. *Historia de la arquitectura Mexicana*. México, Gustavo Gili, 1995.

73 Hernández, Agustín. Personal interview with the author. Mexico City, 17th March 2000.

74 Legorreta, Ricardo. Personal interview with the author. Mexico City, 16th October 2000.

75 Mijares, Carlos. Personal interview with the author. Mexico City, 30th May 2000.

76 Díaz Infante Nuñez, Juan José. *Del dolmen a la kalikosmia*. México, I. Maya Gómez, J. Torres Palacios, 1988.

77 Noelle, Louise. *Arquitectos contemporáneos de México*. México, Editorial Trillas, 1989.

78 Diaz Infante, Juan Jose. Personal interview with the author. Mexico City, 17th March 2000.

79 Ingersoll, Richard. *TEN Arquitectos Enrique Norten, Bernardo Gomez-Pimienta*. New York, Monacelli Press, 1998, p. 25.

80 Ibid., p. 26.

81 Ibid.

82 Norten, Enrique. Personal interview with the author. Mexico City, 30th May 2000.

83 de Buen, Clara. Personal interview with the author. Mexico City, 16th October 2000.

84 Betsky, Aaron. Introduction. *Kalach + Alvarez*. By Adriana León. México, Gustavo Gili, 1998.

85 Kalach, Alberto. Personal interview with the author. Mexico City, 26th May 2000.

86 Colle Corcuera, Marie-Pierre. *Sordo Madaleno: arquitectura en cuatro elementos*. México, Reverte Ed., 1998.

87 Sordo Madaleno, Javier. Personal interview with the author. Mexico City, 27th May 2000.

2
Mexican Architecture and Economic and Political Power

DOI: 10.4324/9781003318934-3

Mexican Architecture and Economic and Political Power

Architecture provides the built frames for everyday life, and as such it depends for its creation on internal and external political and economic power structures, thereby acting simultaneously as the container and the setting for our various social practices. These linked power structures undoubtedly contributed to the making of twentieth-century Mexican architecture, as implemented by dominant groups that lay within three spheres in Mexico: the public/governmental sector, the private business sector, and religious organizations. Members of these groups decided what should be built, where it should be built, and how it should be built. By studying some of the key architects and their buildings, the power relationships will become evident in the typology of each building, its location, infrastructure, construction technology, materials and style. What is revealed is how power groups influenced architectural and cultural patterns, showing the differing ways in which Mexico's entrenched power structures controlled the construction of Modernist architecture.

ARCHITECTURE AND POWER

Power in architecture can be used to empower its users through spatial and architectural elements, but also to control and manipulate them.[1] The power that operates through architecture is most clearly embedded in institutions such as hospitals, schools, corporations, factories and prisons, and it is this that Michel Foucault terms 'disciplinary power'. This power acts as a web of power, or 'micro-physics', that is developed between the built form, social events and individuals. Through these inter-relations, it is possible to locate or fix people in a precise place and to restrict them to certain gestures and habits.[2] Kim Dovey, in his book *Framing Places*, interprets these micro-physics of power in terms of what he calls forms of 'power over' people, as the types of control are produced as dominion or supremacy of one person or one group over another. These types of control can be identified in built form and are expressed through architectural elements such as space, scale and materials, as well as through the social behaviours and values that create and promote this control. Dovey defines these differences as the 'practice of force, coercion, manipulation, seduction and authority'.[3] Since the relationship between space and power is always dynamic, according to whichever social activities are taking place, the types of power are nonetheless always negotiated by built form. These negotiations are naturally complicated and multifaceted, and they tend to shift between various binary oppositions, such as Orientation-Disorientation, Publicity-Privacy, Segregation-Access, Nature-History, Stability-Change, Authentic-Farce, Identity-Difference, Dominant-Docile and Place-Ideology.[4]

Mexican Architecture and Economic and Political Power

To make visible the workings of power within built form, Dovey adopts Space Syntax methods devised by Bill Hillier and Julienne Hanson to identify the modes of control that are exerted through the micro-physics of spatial structure. Architectural plans are hence used to map spatial organizations to reveal the control that lies within them. A floor-plan analysis of a given building, using Space Syntax techniques, can be interpreted as a spatial diagram.[5] These diagrams show the depth or shallowness of any spatial segment in relation to the external point of entry into the building, as well as the overall depth of the spatial structure as a whole. According to Hillier, there are basically three main types of built diagrams: the 'loop'/'ring', the 'fan' and the 'linear' (Figure 2.1). The 'loop'/'ring' structure offers many possible paths for the occupants of a building, and consequently it becomes more difficult to use to exert control. The 'fan' disposition offers greater spatial control, even if it also offers alternative paths, since it only has one entry point through which all these paths must cross. The 'linear' diagram is, however, the spatial disposition that offers the highest degree of control both in terms of circulation routes and of chances of social interaction. Positions of power are thus usually located in the deepest cell of a 'fan' or 'linear' structure, and in such cases, an increase in depth indicates an increase in status. Yet, in some cases, the reverse can also be true; a building's deepest cells can be the places under greatest surveillance and control, as, for instance, in a prison cell.[6]

Built spatial structures thus allow us to interpret social relations of two kinds: those between inhabitants, such as kinship relations or organizational hierarchies; and those between inhabitants and visitors. In both, it is possible to recognise the use of space and built form as an instrument of control. To use these techniques

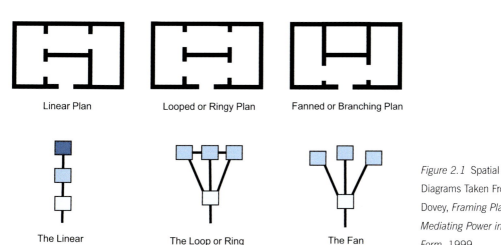

Figure 2.1 Spatial Diagrams Taken From Kim Dovey, *Framing Places Mediating Power in Built Form*, 1999.

75

Mexican Architecture and Economic and Political Power

to look at the power mechanisms within key Mexican twentieth-century buildings, it is necessary initially to identify the power groups that created this new architecture and that exerted power through it.

Main Power Groups in Mexico

Places are necessarily programmed and designed in accordance with the interests of certain power groups that are in pursuit of amenity, profit, status or political power, according to Dovey. As mentioned, in twentieth-century Mexico there were three main power groups who controlled the decision-making processes of the country: the public sector/governmental agencies, private enterprises/corporations and religious groups. Governmental groups in twentieth-century Mexico derived from the political organization of the United States of Mexico, which is made up of the 'classical' division of the three autonomous levels of government: legislative, judicial and executive. The business sector was comprised of private enterprises and corporations run by landowners, industrialists, businessmen, bankers and others in the commercial elite, and together they constituted Mexico's haut-bourgeoisie. Religious organizations make up the third power group in twentieth-century Mexico, with the Catholic Church serving as the main figure for Catholicism, by far the country's predominant religion. The first two groups continue to exert their power until this day; only the religious organizations have declined in status.

These three main power groups thus controlled the construction of Mexican Modernist architecture in the twentieth century. Their institutions and social practices followed those of Western countries in using architecture as the socio-spatial setting for their activities and as the formal representation of their belief systems. For instance, Mexico's political elite required public buildings for their official settings, and state-controlled institutions needed hospitals, schools and universities, as well as housing and transportation projects. All these structures and spaces demanded the appropriate image of dignity and authority. The private sector likewise needed its own spaces, structures and identity to house its social practices and investments, such as offices, banks, hotels and shops. Religious organizations also required special spaces to perform their ritualistic ceremonies with the appropriate character and formality. To understand how the power of these three groups participated in the making of Mexican Modernism, it is essential to establish the conditions that generated and sustained them. Perhaps the best way of doing so is by identifying the economic models that directed and controlled Mexico's power groups, particularly in terms of their architectural sponsorship and production.

TWENTIETH-CENTURY MEXICAN ECONOMIC MODELS

The history of twentieth-century Mexico is one of increasing capitalist development. Although at times the country took on slight socialist overtones, in general it remained part of the Western capitalist paradigm. Blended in with capitalist development, the other omnipresent element throughout the twentieth century was the 'project of modernity', which was interpreted as the level of economic and cultural development to which Mexico aspired in order to accomplish the dream of democratic progress, transforming its near-feudal agrarian economy into a capitalist, industrial one. Modernity was also portrayed as resulting in Mexico's economic, political and cultural independence. The ideal of modernity was, hence, at the core of the myth of the Mexican Revolution that took place in the years between 1910 and 1920. Through this myth, Mexico constructed a national project that constantly reinvented itself as a perpetual renewal of the nation and as a continuous attempt to reach democracy, equality, liberty and national sovereignty. Modernity in Mexico during the early-twentieth century lay mainly in the hands of the government, which, in this case, came from the single ruling party: the Partido Revolucionario Institucional (PRI), founded in 1929 and holding uninterrupted power for the next seven decades. The PRI was thus a constant element that determined not only economic and political life during the twentieth century, but also the architecture produced in Mexico. With the goals of modernity and progress in mind – and committed to a capitalist economy and the myth of the Mexican Revolution – the country pursues three sequential economic models: the 'Export-Led-Growth Economic Model', the 'Import-Substitution Economic Growth Strategy Model', and the 'Neoliberal Model'. All were to condition Mexico's power groups and the architecture that they commissioned.

The 'Export-Led-Growth Economic Model', which was implemented from 1880 through to 1940, is usually identified as the introductory phase for Mexican capitalism, with a heavy dependence on financial and technological investments from abroad. Its most important period was between 1926 and 1937, known as the 'reconstruction phase' following the Mexican Revolution and in which the government established the country's political constitution. As noted, this was also the time when the main political party, the PRI, was instituted. The period also coincided with the 1929 'Great Depression' stemming from the USA, which at first had serious negative effects but then led to an increase in Mexico's domestic production – leading thereby to the next economic model. The 'Import-Substitution Economic Growth Strategy Model', operating from 1940 until

Mexican Architecture and Economic and Political Power

1988, was characterized by a protectionist economy to encourage the growth of Mexican industries. It had four sub-stages. The first sub-stage (1940–54) saw the initiation of internal economic growth by introducing national products as substitutes for foreign imports, with the PRI government encouraging domestic investment and the nationalization of land, railroads and oilfields. The second sub-stage (1955–70) introduced the 'Stabilizing Development Model', considered to be a 'miracle' in curbing inflation and boosting economic development. This led to a period of relative social order, modernization and internationalization, as exemplified by the Mexican Olympic Games in 1968. During the third sub-stage (1970–76), the model was beginning to show signs of deterioration, leading to an economic crisis that escalated due to public spending and contradictory polices called 'Shared Development', whereby growing benefits of the private sector were shared through public investment. Ultimately, this unstable economic policy, along with rampant inflation, created an external debt crisis. Thus, the fourth sub-stage (1977–83) started with a phase of economic prosperity produced by newly discovered oil reserves, but this proved to be short-lived, as a worldwide fall in oil prices triggered an economic collapse in Mexico that was followed by a devaluation crisis and severe austerity measures.

Against this background, the 'Neoliberal Model' (1984 to present) became the new economic model, arguing that a much healthier economy could be created without the state's intervention, and in which free and unregulated supply/demand for goods and services would provide a 'natural' balance and harmony within the economy. It had two sub-stages. The first sub-stage (1984–94) saw the introduction of the model, with the highlight being the North America Free Trade Agreement (NAFTA) between the United States, Canada and Mexico, aimed at encouraging these three economies through privatization and deregulation. The second sub-stage (1995–2000) began with political turmoil and unpaid debts, generating a feeling of distrust that produced the flight of domestic and foreign capital, leading in turn to a financial crisis and the economic collapse of 1995. Due to this instability, Mexico's governmental leaders, and indeed the entire PRI political party, fell into disrepute. The PRI lost its first presidential elections in 2000; while it temporarily regained control from 2012–18, more recent accusations of state corruption and a crisis of mistrust in the existing political parties means that there are more than eight new political parties officially registered in Mexican elections, all of them attempting to gain control over the country's future.

These three economic models thus heavily contributed to fluctuations in architectural production, with buildings produced during the twentieth century

Mexican Architecture and Economic and Political Power

displaying the types of built form and spaces that Mexico's power groups required. It is impossible to dissociate social practices and social relations from the spatial distributions in which these take place, with each only being understood through the other.[7] Consequently, it is helpful to examine how Mexico's power groups commissioned architecture under the three different economic models, and what were the socio-spatial forms through which power was exerted.

Influence of Economic Models on Twentieth-Century Mexican Architecture

In order to establish the ways in which architecture is invested with power and its links to economic policies, a range of the buildings designed by the 13 selected architects can be studied. It is interesting to point out that, as Mexico has such a centralized governmental and economic system, most of these buildings are located in Mexico City. Using this list, it is possible to read the changes in architectural typologies and forms of patronage for each of the three economic models mentioned above. By analyzing these relationships, it is possible to reveal certain information about Mexico's power groups and their social practices and the way that they express power through architecture.

For instance, during the last sub-stage of the 'Export-Led-Growth Economic Model', from 1926 to 1938, some 73% of the key selected examples of Modernist architecture was sponsored by individuals, mainly for private houses (Graph 2.1). This period corresponded with the first years of professional practice of the first

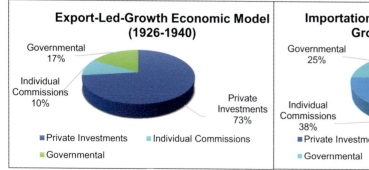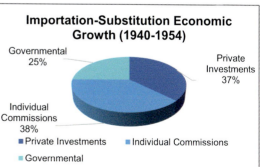

Graph 2.1

generation of Mexican Modernists, who were relying for commissions chiefly on the design of middle-class and upper-class dwellings. The governmental sector was responsible for 17% of the other examples, which included important social buildings, such as José Villagrán's hospitals and Juan O'Gorman's schools.

During the initial sub-stage of the 'Import-Substitution Economic Growth Strategy', between 1940 and 1954, things began to even out due to the increase in Mexican domestic production. Now, 25% of the selected buildings were sponsored by the state, 37% came from private business investment and 38 % were commissioned by wealthy individuals for houses and apartments (Graph 2.1). The latter, in particular, corresponded to Mexico City's rapid urban growth during that era. The state buildings were once again mostly hospitals and schools, yet the single most important governmental investment during this period was the campus of the Universidad Nacional Autónoma de México, generally known as CU, or Ciudad Universitaria. For this project, the buildings were designed by the most important Mexican architects, epitomized by Juan O'Gorman's celebrated library, or Biblioteca Central.

Architecture during the sub-stage known as the 'Stabilising Development Model', from 1955 to 1969, experienced an even greater diversification in typologies, suggesting a widening of social practices that resulted from Mexico's drive for modernization and internationalization (Graph 2.2). For instance, the state now sponsored 22% of the selected buildings, among them a group of museums that were all located in Mexico City's main central park, the Bosque de Chapultepec, of which perhaps the most famous is the Museo de Antropología. Although the state continued to build schools and hospitals, it also built the brand-new Mexican

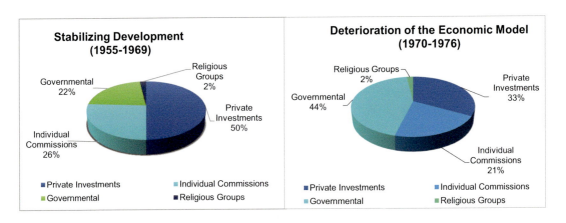

Graph 2.2

Secretariat of Foreign Affairs, known as the Torre de Tlatelolco, in the increasingly popular Modernist style. While individual commissions, at 26%, created new private houses and apartments, business investors diversified, too, increasing their now share to 50% of the key selected buildings. New hotels were built across the city, such as the Hotel Maria Isabel and the Hotel Camino Real, and many office blocks sprouted up. This era also validated the role and status of architects within Mexican society, since it was then that most of the country's most famous architects became wealthy enough to build their own houses and studios in Mexico City.

During the sub-stage of the 'Deterioration of the Economic Model', from 1970–76, architecture again underwent major transformations, including a period of intense state intervention in which 44% of the selected projects were governmental commissions (Graph 2.2). Thus, earlier housing experiments to provide workers' homes were transformed during this period into enormous housing projects like Las Torres de Mixcoac and La Patera. These were accompanied by other important state office buildings, such as the Delegación Cuauhtémoc building and the Instituto del Fomento Nacional de Vivienda, usually known as the INFONAVIT building. Meanwhile, business investment in office buildings remained strong, at 33%, while private individual commissions for houses and apartments formed 21% of the sample.

This situation did not last, however, due to the 'Devaluation Crisis' in Mexico between 1977 and 1983. Now, the types of building commissions changed even more dramatically. Architectural ventures sponsored by the state diminished to a mere 15%, including a bus station, a university campus and a legislative building. Individual commissions, stable at around 19%, were again mostly for new private homes (Graph 2.3). Most notably, business investment shot up to 66%,

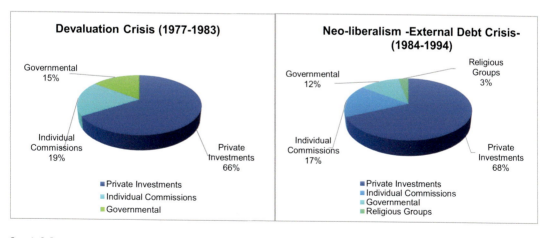

Graph 2.3

Mexican Architecture and Economic and Political Power

mainly in terms of offices and shops. For instance, Juan José Díaz Infante alone built ten bank office buildings during the early-1980s.

During the first sub-stage of the 'Neoliberal Model', from 1984 to 1994, religious buildings remained stable at their typically low level, being just 3% of the selected examples, while individual private homes were again at around 17% of the total (Graph 2.3). Governmental commissions were again low, at only 12%, with subways stations, auditoria and cultural centres as part of the state-sponsored restructuring of Mexico City. Corporate business investment remained consistent at 68%, with more banks, private schools, shopping centres and even car-park buildings by famous architects. Many were in the centre of Mexico City, as part of the restructuring project, whereas others tended to be concentrated in Santa Fe, a new development district set up by the PRI government.

The next sub-stage, the 'End of the Century Stage', from 1995 to 2000, although marked by financial crisis, saw business investment continue at around 66% by further diversifying its typologies with mixed-use company headquarters, a hotel, a television studio and even a Jaguar motorcar agency, thus dominating Mexican architectural production in the late-twentieth century (Graph 2.4). Now, government investment decreased to just 7%, while private housing stayed steady at 25% of the total.

As shown in the graphs, the different economic models played a critical role in the architecture created by Mexico's power groups, affecting also people's socio-spatial and cultural practices. It is important now to look in more detail at how power was exerted by analysing some key Mexican Modernist buildings to find the

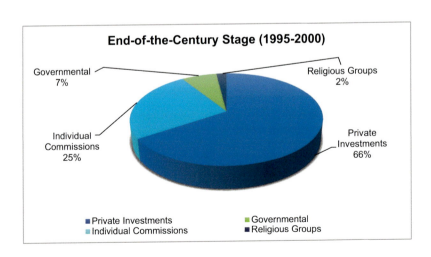

Graph 2.4

Mexican Architecture and Economic and Political Power

hidden elements of control within architectural elements, such as walls, rooms, doors and corridors. Such elements ensure the distribution of people in space, as well as surveillance and control. The sample buildings were analysed based on my personal visits, the testimonies of their author, and their spatial diagrams that I created from a study of their floor plans. To help frame the discussion, these buildings are organized according to their typologies.

POWER IN TWENTIETH-CENTURY ARCHITECTURAL MODERNISM IN MEXICO

As noted, the typology of buildings is largely determined by their patronage. Buildings by the Mexican state were generally in the form of hospitals, public buildings, museums, cultural centres, housing estates and transportation buildings, whereas business investment was usually concentrated in hotels, banks and shops. Office and school buildings could be financed either by private or public clients, while churches and chapels were primarily sponsored by religious organizations. Each of these typologies will be addressed in turn, and each one or two particular examples will be analysed in order to detect the workings of power in their architectural spaces and forms. These selected buildings are limited to those designed by the 13 key architects selected, and all of them were built in or around Mexico City.

Hospitals

During the twentieth century in Mexico, most hospitals were built during the period from the late-1920s to the late-1940s. This corresponded to a national programme that, along with schools and housing, was seen as part of national reconstruction after the Mexican Revolution. Two important examples are the Sanatorio para Tuberculosos de Huipulco (1929) and the Instituto Nacional de Cardiología (1937), both designed by José Villagrán García – a pioneer from the first generation of Mexican Modernists – and yet which show a clear change in his architectural approach. Both of these hospitals present a clear definition of what is intended as public and what is private, and they operate very strict control over access. Their circulation patterns thus tend to be well defined, giving a strong sense of internal orientation. The identity of each building is given not so much by the materials or the stylistic expression, but rather by the medical activities taking place within them.

The sense of dignity needed in a state building is thus given not by the Modernist style, but by the scale of the building. In the case of the Sanatorio

Mexican Architecture and Economic and Political Power

para Tuberculosos de Huipulco (Figure 2.2), there are still elements that are reminiscent of Neoclassical order, due to the building's symmetrical elevation and repeated rational rhythm of its bays. The floor plan is very simple, with controlled access at the centre and two wards placed on each side of the supervision area. The linear disposition gives those who run it the greatest amount of control over its patients through the power of constant surveillance (Figure 2.3).

Figure 2.2 José Villagrán García: Sanatorio para Tuberculosos de Huipulco, Mexico City, 1929.

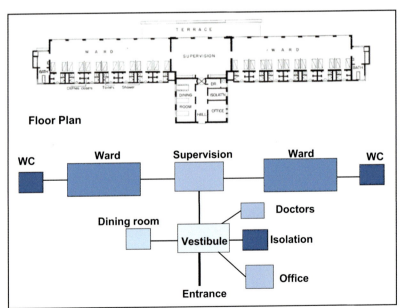

Figure 2.3 Sanatorio para Tuberculosos de Huipulco, Floor Plan and Spatial Diagram.

Figure 2.4 José Villagrán García: Instituto Nacional de Cardiología, Mexico City, 1937.

The Instituto Nacional de Cardiología (Figure 2.4) is completely different, however, due to its asymmetrical composition with lack of decoration, being a clear attempt to find expression through contemporary materials and constructional systems.[8] This building has since been remodelled, yet it nevertheless remains one of the best examples of Modernist architecture due to its horizontality, use of cubic lines and unadorned blank surfaces. This hospital also demonstrated the language of Modernism in its Corbusian-style access ramp and the carefully studied circulation route that links the two asymmetrical volumes of the composition. The division between these two main blocks was functionally motivated, given that one held the more restricted private wards, whereas the other contained the public areas of the hospital. The spatial diagram indicates a deep structure, with the wards being the last segment that requires the visitor to traverse various control points before arriving there (Figure 2.5).

These hospitals were sponsored by the state and were constructed with the ideal of public service in mind. The hospital as a typology exerts power over its patients by secluding them in the furthest place in the building, where they can be closely supervised and where their access and exit is heavily monitored. The doctors and nurses, on the other hand, are placed in areas with a privileged position that enable them to see and control the entrance and departure of both visitors and patients. Both of these example hospitals

Mexican Architecture and Economic and Political Power

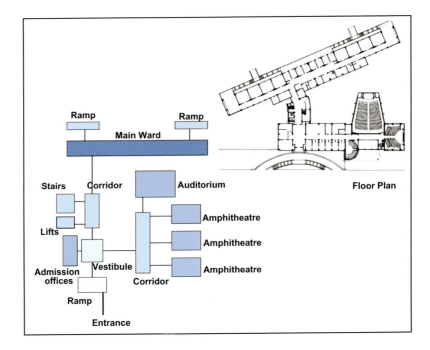

Figure 2.5 Instituto Nacional de Cardiología, Floor Plan and Spatial Diagram.

sought to be functional and efficient, emulating the patterns of contemporary European architecture.

Museums

Cultural centres and museums only began to be built by the Mexican state in the 1960s. Prior to then, old colonial buildings had usually been transformed for use as museums. During the 1960s, as part of Mexico's more stable and expansive political agenda, a designated group of museums were built in Mexico City that included the Museo de Arte Moderno, the Museo de Historia of México and the Museo Nacional de Antropología. All are located in a central wooded district known as the Bosque de Chapultepec, which is Mexico City's most popular park. Each of these museums were designed by Pedro Ramírez Vázquez, a leading figure from the second generation of Mexican Modernists, yet the most important of them was the Museo Nacional de Antropología, built in 1964.

As in most museums, the movement of visitors is vital, and in this sense, the Museo Nacional de Antropología is perhaps the best example of a controlled manipulation. Its circulation is organized counter-clockwise around a quadrangle, or central patio, although there is always the possibility of departing from the set course by taking a break in this central plaza. This plaza has the dimensions of a

Mexican Architecture and Economic and Political Power

quadrangle at Uxmal, a famous pre-Hispanic site, as will be seen in Chapter 5, but has a modern character with a large concrete umbrella structure that serves also as a fountain (Figure 2.6).

As the floor plan shows, there is no explicit force intended, just an underlining and seductive manipulation that is exerted over the visitor as he or she moves from one gallery to another (Figure 2.7). Before one reaches the main gallery – the

Figure 2.6 Pedro Ramírez Vázquez: The Museo Nacional de Antropología, Interior Courtyard, Mexico City, 1964.

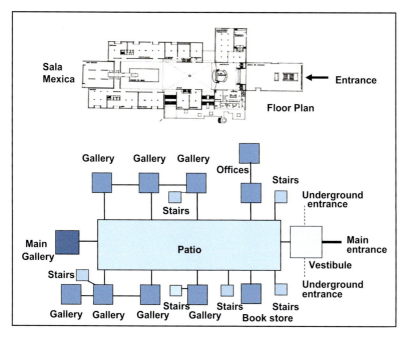

Figure 2.7 The Museo Nacional de Antropología, Floor Plan and Spatial Diagram.

Mexican Architecture and Economic and Political Power

Sala Mexica, where the Aztec Calendar (Figure 2.8), the museum's centrepiece, is located – you are enticed just as you leave the previous gallery by a small window that provides a glimpse of the Calendar even before you enter the main central hall. The spatial diagram suggests a loop-like disposition in which the patio occupies the main spatial position through which all paths must cross. By placing the main gallery as the furthest cell, this space becomes the most secluded and prominent.

What makes this and the other buildings designed by Ramírez Vázquez distinctive is the way that it deals with the need to handle a tremendous number of people. He is able to direct them through the different spaces without making them aware of this subtle system of control. Ramírez Vázquez also credits, for this particular museum, the collaborative intervention of an expert designer of theatre-sets:

> *I believe that in a museum, there are two main personalities or elements involved: the visitor and the object. Both must come into contact and come to an understanding. It is not a matter of placing things like a vase in a house. The visitor must not leave the museum without seeing the main piece. The visitor must be manipulated and made to behave in the way the scientific advisor decided, so that the visitor can understand the message of the exhibition.*[9]

Following these 1960s museums, there were other important examples built during the 1980s, such as the Museo del Templo Mayor (1987), also by Ramírez Vázquez, and the Museo Tamayo (1981), by Abraham Zabludovsky and Teodoro González de León. The Museo Tamayo is also located near the previous museums; while the Museo del Templo Mayor is located near the site where the archaeological

Figure 2.8 Sala Mexica With the Aztec Calendar, Mexico City.

remains of this pre-Hispanic ceremonial centre were found. The Museo Nacional de Antropología and the Museo del Templo Mayor both share similar façades which are based on large blank walls (Figure 2.9). Ramírez Vázquez, in his attempt to minimize its presence, resorts to two blank walls on an overwhelming scale with a central entrance as a backdrop to this archaeological site.

In the Museo del Templo Mayor, the circulation is the main concern, and the floor plan is split into different levels to make the visitor climb unnoticeably from one level to the next and across to the next gallery, until finally they reach the top (Figure 2.11). Through this clever way of spatial control, the visitor tours the whole exhibition, which revolves around a central atrium where the Tlaltecuhtli – the biggest piece of sculpture found to this day, made by the Mexicas – is located (Figure 2.10).

Figure 2.9 Pedro Ramírez Vázquez: The Museo del Templo Mayor Main Façade, Mexico City, 1987.

Figure 2.10 The Museo del Templo Mayor Interior With the Tlaltecuhtli as the Centrepiece of the Museum.

Mexican Architecture and Economic and Political Power

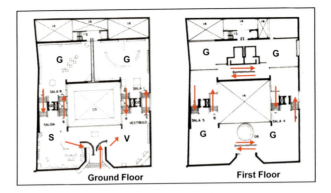

Figure 2.11 The Museo del Templo Mayor, Floor Plans Showing the Circulation Pattern in Red Arrows.

The Museo Tamayo, on the other hand, responds to their authors' Brutalist style with exposed concrete and textured walls as its main characteristics (Figure 2.12). Its pyramidal shape is reminiscent of pre-Hispanic architecture, although the architects insist that this indented shape is their response to the need for the building to be inconspicuous within the wooded park, as well as its internal illumination requirements (Figure 2.13).

Figure 2.12 Zabludovsky and González de León: Museo Tamayo Exterior, Mexico City, 1981.

Mexican Architecture and Economic and Political Power

The circulation route in the Museo Tamayo also revolves around a central covered patio, in which some sculptures are located. Through a predominant use of a linear spatial arrangement that loops around this inner patio, and the use of a diagonal entrance into the galleries and two central ramps, visitors can traverse the space and discover at every turn a different part of the exhibition before completing a circuit that ends with them arriving back at the main entrance (Figure 2.14).

These museums from different decades and by different architects express spatial power by the use of scale, location and materials, and by resorting to archetypical elements of 'Mexican' identity, such as the patio. They seek to control and conduct people through orientation or disorientation in their public and private spaces, aiming to produce docile domination as part of a process of continuous, serial stimulation for the visitor.

Figure 2.13 Zabludovsky and González de León: Museo Tamayo Interior, Mexico City, 1981.

Mexican Architecture and Economic and Political Power

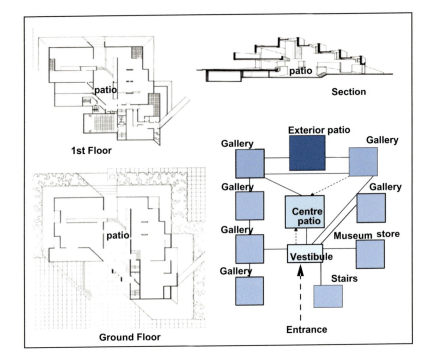

Figure 2.14 Museo Tamayo, Floor Plans, Section and Spatial Diagram.

Hotels

The construction boom for hotels in Mexico City happened in several stages. An early period was during the 1960s, when Mexico was modernizing and internationalizing its image. During this era, the Hotel María Isabel (Figure 2.15) was completed in 1963 by a team of architects/engineers that included José Villagrán García from the first generation and Ricardo Legorreta from the third generation, and it used the most sophisticated technical advances to guard against earthquakes. This hotel is located on one of the busiest and most beautiful avenues of Mexico City, Paseo de la Reforma, and to one side of the United States Embassy, thereby guaranteeing American visitors and diplomatic employees a sense of convenient proximity during the height of the 'Cold War' era. Although now part of the Sheraton Hotel Group, with its façade totally remodelled, its tall profile and prime location give it the authority and identity it demands. The internal distribution, as with traditional hotel layouts, allows for a totally controlled entrance, closely surveyed lifts and a linear arrangement of bedrooms. The upper stories are reserved for distinguished guests in the most secluded and private spaces in the building (Figure 2.16).

Mexican Architecture and Economic and Political Power

Figure 2.15 José Villagrán Garcia, Juan Sordo Madaleno, Ricardo Legorreta and José Adolfo Wiechers: The Hotel Maria Isabel, Mexico City, 1963.

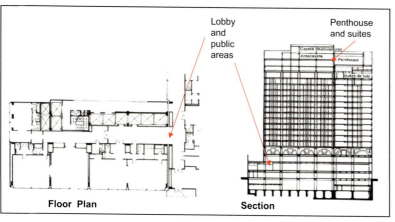

Figure 2.16 The Hotel Maria Isabel, Floor Plan and Section.

    The Hotel Camino Real also responded to the era of internationalization, being inaugurated for the 1968 Olympic Games. Here, its author, Ricardo Legorreta, opted for a horizontal building instead of a vertical tower to suit the more

93

Mexican Architecture and Economic and Political Power

Figure 2.17 Ricardo Legorreta: The Hotel Camino Real Front Patio and Fountain, Mexico City, 1969.

residential area in which the hotel is located. This design also responded to his intention of echoing the Mexican hacienda typology but in a modern fashion. It indeed offers a powerful retrieval of the hacienda's identity with its massive walls, colourful spaces and direct contact with the courtyards and gardens. The front patio (Figure 2.17), with its iconic fountain, is used to welcome the guest, while also keeping out strangers and protecting occupants from the hectic city. The back patio, or garden, is surrounded by the guest rooms, giving customers a sense of privacy. The generous spaces in its public areas, such as the main lobby, contrasts with the private corridors leading to the bedrooms.

The spatial diagram demonstrates how a fan-like disposition in the Hotel Camino Real gives more control whilst offering various alternative paths: one for the hotels guests to get to the rooms that loop around the garden; and another path for the outside visitors to access the ballroom, restaurants or bars (Figure 2.18). The service areas, on the other hand, are the most secluded spots, being located outside the main circulation and accessible only through the protected service entrance.

The Hotel Camino Real, by evoking the image of the Mexican hacienda, offers an image of cultural tradition and identity that appeals mainly to foreign visitors – in contrast to tower structures like the Hotel María Isabel, which convey the different image of an international hotel. Its skyscraper typology gives command and privacy to the top floors, along with astonishing views of the city, as part of its package. In

Mexican Architecture and Economic and Political Power

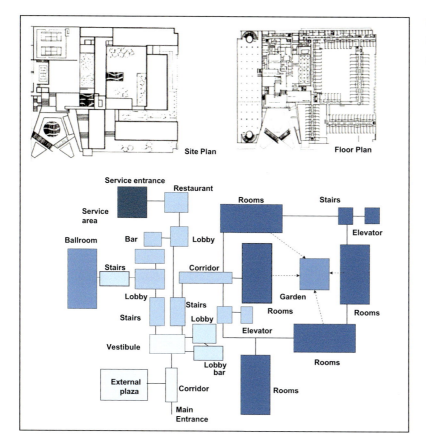

Figure 2.18 The Hotel Camino Real, Floor Plans and Spatial Diagram.

both of these hotels, a sense of seduction and desire is also created through the luxurious materials, textures and generous internal spaces.

Transportation Buildings

Most buildings of this type carry the implicit obligation of contributing an urban icon that is easily identifiable. This is certainly the case of the Terminal de Autobuses de Oriente bus station (1978), commonly known as TAPO and designed by Juan José Díaz Infante from the third generation of Mexican Modernists; however, this is not the case of the Estación del Metro de Pantitlán Linea A (Figure 2.19), as completed in 1991 by the firm of Nuño, Mac Gregor and de Buen, leading representatives of the fourth generation. The TAPO bus station (Figure 2.20) uses an identifiable domed shape, while the concrete structure of the Estación del

Mexican Architecture and Economic and Political Power

Figure 2.19 Nuño, Mac Gregor and de Buen: The Estación del Metro Pantitlán Linea A, Mexico City, 1991.

Figure 2.20 Juan José Díaz Infante: The Terminal de Autobuses de Oriente (TAPO), Mexico City, 1978.

Metro de Pantitlán Linea A is barely visible amongst the numerous vendors that surround it.

In both of these examples, the importance given to circulation is based on efficiency rather than hierarchy or power of one person over another. These spaces are thus more democratic and do not distinguish or privilege any of their users. In fact, at peak hours, due to the large amount of people, these spaces totally alienate the users by turning them into a huge mass in which the individual person becomes indistinguishable.

Mexican Architecture and Economic and Political Power

The TAPO bus station (Figure 2.21) is a truly an exceptional building. It was erected as part of a transportation renewal programme that aimed to decentralize Mexico City's main bus terminal. The design was based on Díaz Infante's 'Kalikosmia' theory of creating more built space by using less materials:

Figure 2.21 Juan José Díaz Infante: The Terminal de Autobuses de Oriente (TAPO), Mexico City, 1978.

> *The TAPO bus station is built in reinforced concrete, a dome-like structure, similar to the Pantheon where space corresponds to its form . . . We built TAPO in 14 months. There was money then, and it was also part of a transportation programme for Mexico City . . . TAPO was the answer to terribly important urban needs.*[10]

Díaz Infante used a circular floor plan with a central dome that allows a complete view from one side to the other, giving the traveller an immediate sense of orientation. The use of a loop or ring disposition for the internal spaces allows for numerous lateral connections, thereby offering more options or choices but, at the same time, less control. Control is nevertheless achieved by directing people along the periphery and by restricting both entry and exit to the central domed space by only providing two access tunnels. TAPO's recognizable shape and dimensions give it a sense of authority and legitimation within the urban setting. Its panopticon-like design allows everybody to see everybody else, which, in a way, helps also as a self-policing device, discouraging assaults or thefts (Figure 2.22).

Mexican Architecture and Economic and Political Power

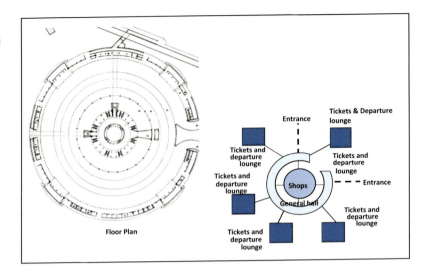

Figure 2.22 The TAPO Bus Station, Floor Plan and Spatial Diagram.

Efficiency, control and surveillance thus appear to be the main emphasis of these transportation designs, enabling them to conduct and orientate the travellers to effectively reach their destination. A strong presence in the city is expressed through elements like TAPO's dome and the steel canopy for the Estación del Metro de Pantitlán Linea A.

Banks

In Mexico, banks have almost always belonged to the private sector. They were only nationalized for a short time after the Mexican Revolution, from 1917 to 1920, and then again from 1982 to 1984, after which they were privatized again. During the 'Neoliberal Economy' phase, a series of important new banks were designed by Abraham Zabludovsky and Teodoro González de León, a team from the second generation, who created a completely new expression for this building type. Their contribution is particularly evident in a cluster of banks in Lomas de Chapultepec, an elite residential district in Mexico City. In these buildings, such as Multibanco Mercantil (now Actinver M. Lomas de Chapultepec) and Centro Financiero Banamex Lomas (now Citibanamex C.F. Lomas), completed in the late-1980s (Figure 2.23), they skilfully coped with the residential context and strict planning controls in producing a suitable, exalted image and dignity for a banking institution. Zabludovsky explains that they wanted to express great scale, but without great height:

> Banco Mercantil (now Actinver M) as well as Banco Nacional (now Citibanamex), both in Lomas de Chapultepec, had a 21 meters front and were allowed only 15

Mexican Architecture and Economic and Political Power

metres in height. This gave them a (volumetric) solution similar to a house. In order to give them an adequate image, we created a portico that, due to its height, is the main characteristic of the bank and contributes also as an urban icon.[11]

In analysing the spatial diagram of the Citibanamex C.F. Lomas (Figure 2.24), it is possible to see that the public areas are framed by a massive portico that gives glimpses into a large lobby on the ground floor and to open-plan offices on the first floor. The most private cells are the rooms on a semi-linear pattern in the perimeter, as in the case of the vault and security zones, or the private offices above.

In contrast with their previous use of impressive porticos, Abraham Zabludovsky and Teodoro González de León created in Mexico City's centre, as part of the area's urban renewal,[12] a new extension to the Baroque convent of Las Capuchinas as the new office spaces of Citibanamex Oficina Central. Their design mimics the scale and rhythm of the colonial façades, using exposed concrete, an element that was their brand image (Figure 2.25 and Figure 2.26). In this bank, a covered inside patio organizes the building's circulation, as the spatial diagram shows (Figure 2.27). The deeper cells or spaces at the back have more privacy and seclusion, while the patio is used to monitor everyone that enters.

In all of these designs, regardless of their style, there is a highly monitored entrance that leads to a vestibule and later into an open banking area in which people either queue in front of the tills or else are served by staff in office cubicles. The internal activities of the banks are kept isolated and invisible to customers, who in turn are kept under careful surveillance in the ample open areas. Within

Figure 2.23 Zabludovsky and González de León: Citibanamex C.F. Lomas, Mexico City, 1989.

99

Mexican Architecture and Economic and Political Power

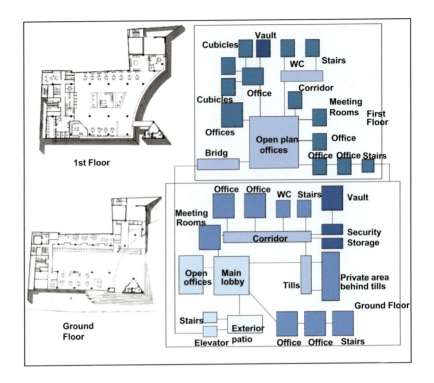

Figure 2.24 Citibank C.F. Lomas, Floor Plans and Spatial Diagram.

Figure 2.25 Zabludovsky and González de León: Citibanamex Oficina Central, Mexico City, 1987.

Mexican Architecture and Economic and Political Power

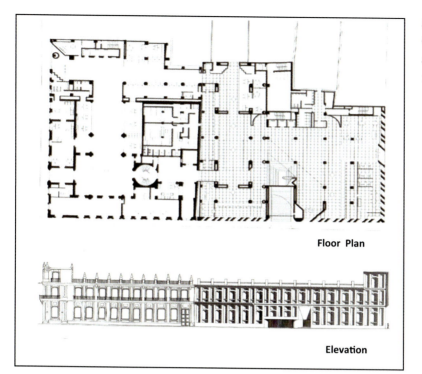

Floor Plan

Elevation

Figure 2.26 Citibanamex Oficina Central, Floor Plan and Elevation, Mexico City, 1987.

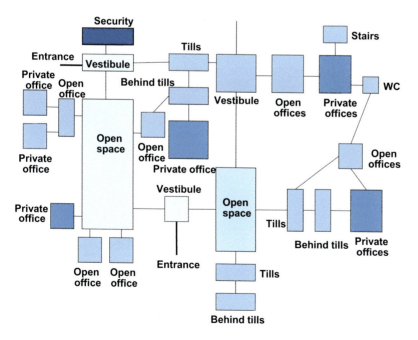

Figure 2.27 Citibanamex Oficina Central, Spatial Diagram.

Mexican Architecture and Economic and Political Power

the styles exhibited in these buildings, from Brutalism to urban integration, there remains an expression of control, stability and authority, creating an image that wants to speak of high status.

State Buildings

The most obvious locations where overt power resides are in state buildings. Although their typology often resembles that of office buildings, in providing the spaces for official public activities, they need to be designed for large numbers of people who conform to certain rituals and protocols. Three well-known Mexican architects are particularly noted for designing public buildings during the twentieth century. Perhaps the most famous is Pedro Ramírez Vázquez, one of the best second-generation Mexican Modernists. Besides his museum designs, he is renowned for the Palacio Legislativo de San Lázaro, Mexico's parliament (Figure 2.28), built in 1980. Ramírez Vázquez designed the Palacio Legislativo de San Lázaro in a rundown area of Mexico City, also during a time of economic crisis, which forced him to reduce both its size and its construction time. Again, he focussed on creating a symbolic image on a monumental scale, in this case by designing an enormous, flag-like façade that used blank walls in materials which resemble Mexico's national colours. He used bronze to produce the green colour, tezontle (a local stone) for the red and marble for the white. Ramírez Vázquez also inserted a large mural by Chávez Morado to graphically convey the building's

Figure 2.28 Pedro Ramírez Vázquez: Palacio Legislativo de San Lázaro, Mexico City, 1981.

importance to every Mexican person. Once again, he shaped the plan around a central patio of enormous proportions to organize the spaces and provide control through surveillance. In addition, there was an evocation of pre-Hispanic monumentality similar to his Museo de Antropología.[13] Ramírez Vázquez explained the need to resort to this type of design by stating:

> *Well, yes, because in our political organization of power (it didn't used to be but now it is changing), power is fundamentally found in the legislative branch. Here is where the direction of the country is set; it states what should be done. The executive branch enacts power, and the judicial branch keeps watch over it, but the legislative power is what determines the life of our nation. This is why the building had to show the same stature of the National Palace and the Supreme Court. Here the country's presence should be evident and forthright, as a fundamental power. A totally strong image!*[14]

Abraham Zabludovsky and Teodoro González de León, also from the second generation, have likewise been responsible for major public buildings in Mexico City. The most celebrated examples include the Delegación Cuauhtémoc (Figure 2.29),

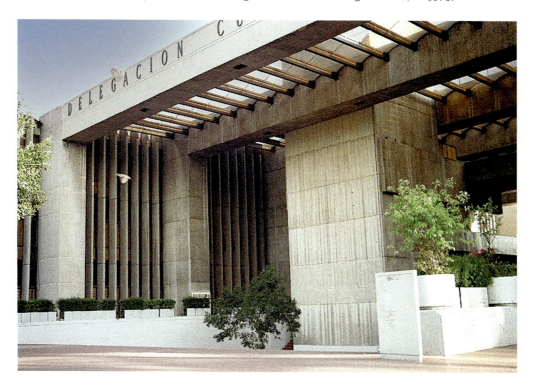

Figure 2.29 Zabludovsky and González de León: Delegación Cuauhtémoc Building, Mexico City, 1973.

Mexican Architecture and Economic and Political Power

the main offices of one of the city's administrative boroughs, completed in 1973. In this scheme, they expressed the municipality's authority through the texturing of the reinforced-concrete columns, beams and trellises. It formed part of their long experimentation with rough, exposed concrete that became their trademark, as Zabludovsky mentions:

> Well, yes . . . concrete should be used in all its force. This was the characteristic of our era . . . [and so] we applied at a very large scale this material. This became a sort of style that was used everywhere in the country. It was even used in different colours according to the place. In Chiapas, for example, they have yellow sand, and in other places they have white sand. Of course, we have used it in the other buildings we made afterwards, like Colegio de México, Museo Tamayo, Delegación Cuauhtémoc, and many others too.[15]

In the Delegación Cuauhtémoc building, there is an explicit intent to create a public plaza, or exterior atrium, that can engender a celebratory mood, as well as being a place for social interaction. This is most evident in the complex visual composition that exaggerates the scale of the columns and beams in order to frame this inner court. The result is what feels like a central stage in this plaza, whereby anyone who enters can be easily observed from the different upper levels. Zabludovsky notes:

> The city was divided into boroughs or delegations and each one needed an administration building and also a public building that would be a symbol and that would also be used to commemorate national celebrations such as the one of the 16th of September where a balcony is needed and a plaza for the ceremony of the 'Grito'. Consequently, in Delegación Cuauhtémoc we created an external space delimitated by trellises as part of the internal space of the offices that surrounded this plaza. We use exposed concrete as the main element for the structural and for the formal expression. This has become an icon in Mexican architecture.[16]

In public buildings such as these, there is a typical pattern used to filter the level of access through to the most private areas. The transition from the open outside atrium is followed by the entry into the building's lobby, after which the circulation route narrows down into corridors that lead to the private offices, which are usually located at the back of the ground-floor plan, out of plain view. Even more private are the offices in the upper floors, all of which is true of the Delegación Cuauhtémoc building (Figure 2.30). Most public buildings thus express their hierarchy through their overall size and their internal spatial hierarchy. The segregation

Mexican Architecture and Economic and Political Power

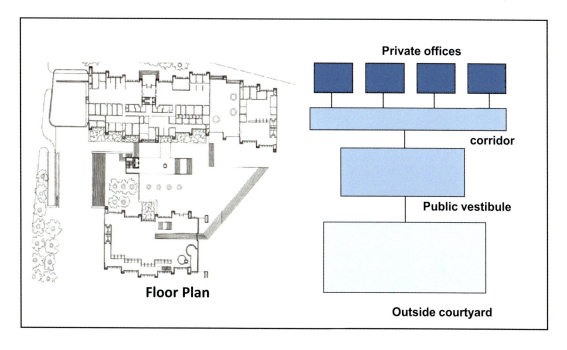

and manipulation of staff and visitors is experienced through circulation patterns that link open spaces to ample vestibules to narrow corridors to closed-off offices.

Figure 2.30 Delegación Cuauhtémoc Building, Floor Plan and Spatial Diagram.

Private and Public Office Buildings

The office typology sponsored both by the public and private sectors relies mainly on two alternative genotypes: the skyscraper and the elongated block. Several of the most important Modernist skyscrapers in Mexico City in the twentieth century are the work of Pedro Ramírez Vázquez, from the second generation, and Juan José Díaz Infante, from the third generation. These buildings adopt iconic shapes that are visually unmistakeable. The Torre de Tlatelolco (Figure 2.31), for instance, was completed in 1960 by Ramírez Vázquez for the Mexican Secretariat of Foreign Affairs during the administration of President Adolfo López Mateos. Ramírez Vázquez recalls how he was assigned the design of this building:

> *Originally this site was part of (architect) Mario Pani's master plan for that area. Pani had decided to build a hotel there . . . I pointed out to (President) López Mateos that it was not right to locate a hotel in Tlatelolco, a place with pre-Hispanic and colonial roots. The site would be like a showcase for the hotel, and this was not appropriate. On the other hand, the Foreign Affairs Office building should be*

Mexican Architecture and Economic and Political Power

seen like the living room of a house, a place where you could receive your visitors and you could display pictures of your grandparents. Tlatelolco was the place for the Foreign Office Building, and not a hotel. This argument convinced the Foreign Office Minister, Manuel Tello, and so they rejected Mario Pani's project for the hotel there and gave me the assignment for the Secretariat of Foreign Affairs building.[17]

Figure 2.31 Pedro Ramírez Vázquez: Torre de Tlatelolco, Mexico City, 1960.

Mexican Architecture and Economic and Political Power

Ramírez Vázquez also revealed that the formal appearance of this skyscraper was driven by the power and ideology that President López Mateos felt it should portray:

> I asked him (the President) what he wanted this building to express, and he answered: 'Simply the verticality and purity of Mexican international politics'. I answered, there you have the programme and the solution of the project. The building is a tower. Its verticality represents Mexican international politics and its purity, and so it is all in white.[18]

The design thus corresponded to the idea of the Modernist skyscraper, albeit with some elements of its façade being aimed at expressing the President's intentions as a crucial part of the programme. Its vertical form amid low surroundings gives it the desired sense of authority and legitimation. Common to all skyscrapers, the lower floors are the most public, whereas the top floors are restricted to a privileged few in the governmental hierarchy (Figure 2.32).

As another office skyscraper in Mexico City, the stock market building, known as La Bolsa Mexicana de Valores (Figure 2.34), which was completed by Díaz Infante in 1990, also provides a powerful urban icon. It is a very curious project, as it was transformed from a half-built hotel that lay in ruins after being abandoned due to the 1980's economic recession. Díaz Infante recounts the origin of the design:

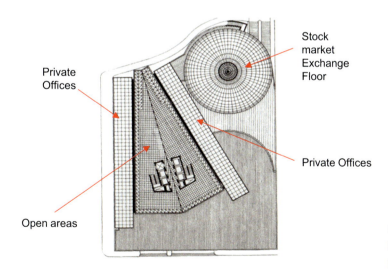

Figure 2.32 La Bolsa Mexicana de Valores, Site Plan.

Mexican Architecture and Economic and Political Power

Figure 2.33 Juan José Díaz Infante: La Bolsa Mexicana de Valores Exterior, Mexico City, 1990.

The columns determined its form. Everybody thinks that one day the muses appeared bringing the pointed shapes and all. But it was the pillars that defined the rooms, which were slanted in black, and the centre patio became the pointed element in white to compensate. The stock exchange floor is an adaptation of the Pantheon that used to be the hotel's ballroom.[19]

Because the existing structure greatly determined the building's form and internal layout, it does not contain open-plan offices and, consequently, the interior spaces feel rather constricted. The exchange floor is located under a domed area that offers a panopticon-like arrangement in which everyone can see all of the financial dealings (Figure 2.33). Again, the topmost floors are reserved for the elite, particularly the highest central peak that consists of a panoramic room for conferences and special events.

Mexican Architecture and Economic and Political Power

Figure 2.34 Juan José Díaz Infante: La Bolsa Mexicana de Valores Interior, Mexico City, 1990.

An elongated office block is an alternative model, as in the case of the Instituto del Fomento Nacional de Vivienda, usually known as INFONAVIT, an institution that runs national housing projects. Designed in the mid-1970s by Zabludovsky and González de León (Figure 2.35) of the second generation of Mexican Modernists, its long, low structure and horizontal circulation routes allow more efficient

Mexican Architecture and Economic and Political Power

communication between the different departments, instead of relying constantly on lifts as in the case of skyscrapers.[20]

This building can best be described as an asymmetric, monolithic volume of massive dimensions with an atrium framed by its monumental entrance. Once inside, the lobby leads into an open-plan office area that surrounds an inner patio, with the more private areas located around the perimeter of this open space, as the floor plan and spatial diagram indicate (Figure 2.36).

Figure 2.35 Zabludovsky and González de León: INFONAVIT Building Main Entrance, Mexico City, 1975.

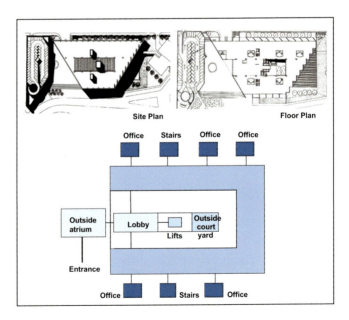

Figure 2.36 INFONAVIT Building, Floor Plans and Spatial Diagram.

Mexican Architecture and Economic and Political Power

More recently, and completed in 1997, the Corporativo IBM Santa Fe (Figure 2.37) is a scheme by Nuño, Mac Gregor and de Buen, from the fourth generation. It creates an identity for this global corporation by using exposed concrete on a massive scale. Horizontal circulation is optimized by placing the entrance in the centre, in a rather monumental fashion; as a consequence, the end offices on the ground floor and those on the upper floors become those with the most privileged locations (Figure 2.38).

By comparing the designs for the skyscraper tower or the low elongated building, we see that the towers lack a subtle manner to filter accessibility, having almost no transitional spaces. The horizontal building, on the other hand, allows a more careful transition between open public and private office spaces. Much has been written about open-plan office spaces, and while some regard them as more democratic spaces because they give an equal position to almost every occupant, it has also been pointed out that they offer minimum privacy and thereby homogenize and control their inhabitants in this way.

Figure 2.37 Nuño, Mac Gregor and de Buen: Corporativo IBM Santa Fe, Mexico City, 1997.

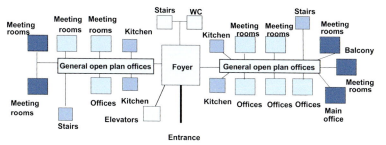

Figure 2.38 Corporativo IBM Santa Fe, Floor Plan and Spatial Diagram.

Mexican Architecture and Economic and Political Power

Public and Private Schools

School construction was especially encouraged after the Mexican Revolution, ranging from the modest rural school to the urban university, since education became a major governmental priority. One of the most avid designers to experiment with low-cost and efficient construction of school prototypes was Juan O'Gorman. In his design for Escuela Técnica Industrial (Figure 2.39), in the mid-1930s, there was a concerted search for simplicity. Rooms were designed for different functions, and classrooms and workshops were joined together by a covered outdoor corridor that provided the building's main axis. The auditorium is located at the centre of this corridor, facing the main entrance, giving it a prominent position, as well as optimum accessibility. The spatial diagram shows how the end rooms, although placed far away from the entry, enjoy a privileged position as the focal point at the end of the hallway (Figure 2.40). The outdoor corridor seems to be the main element for providing the required spatial hierarchy inside the school.

Figure 2.39 Juan O'Gorman: Escuela Técnica Industrial, Mexico City, 1934.

Mexican Architecture and Economic and Political Power

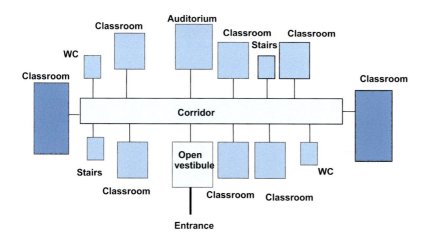

Figure 2.40 Escuela Técnica Industrial and Spatial Diagram.

Much later, two private schools from the 1990s also used outdoor spaces to organize their control of power. They were the Colegio Alexander Von Humboldt (Figure 2.41) and the Colegio Monte Sinai (Figure 2.42), as designed by Clara de Buen's firm and by Abraham Zabludovsky, two influential practices from the fourth and second generation of Mexican Modernists, respectively. The siting of these schools on uneven terrains resulted in the use of stairs that seems appropriate to symbolic commemorative entrances and courtyards. These stepped, open patios, however, allow a full view of the rooms around the central spaces, aiding the surveillance of their occupants.

Colegio Monte Sinai has recently been remodelled, yet it still conforms to its original design with a rather similar organization to O'Gorman's secondary school from the 1930s. There is, again, a spatial organization that is centred on a central corridor that unites classrooms and courtyards to give them the desired hierarchy (Figure 2.43). The corridor also provides a privileged position to the auditorium located at the end. These examples also appear to emulate the imposing monumental scale of higher education establishments, such as Universidad Pedagógica Nacional and El Colegio de México (Figure 2.44), both of which were designed in the mid-1970s by Abraham Zabludovsky and Teodoro Gonzalez de León.

El Colegio de México, a highly prestigious school of postgraduate studies, is set on an irregular, sloping topography and is organized around a main atrium, or plaza, that controls the internal circulation routes. As in most of these architects' projects, the plaza, or atrium, is the main organizing element, as shown in the floor plans (Figure 2.45). The plaza is located as the main entrance and arranges the circulation through a series of stairs that direct the visitor and the inhabitant in

113

Mexican Architecture and Economic and Political Power

Figure 2.41 Nuño Mac Gregor de Buen: Colegio Alexander Von Humboldt, Mexico City, 1990.

Figure 2.42 Abraham Zabludovsky: Colegio Monte Sinai Complex, Mexico City, 1994.

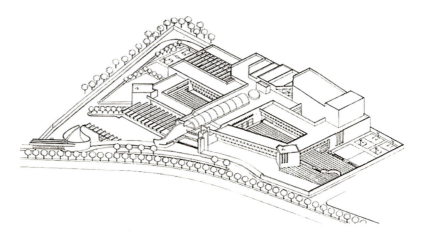

Figure 2.43 Colegio Monte Sinai, 1994.

Mexican Architecture and Economic and Political Power

Figure 2.44 Zabludovsky and González de León: El Colegio de México, Mexico City, 1975.

different directions. Hierarchy of spaces and activities is provided by their location either on the lower levels or on the higher levels. Control is made possible by watching everybody's movement across the plaza from corridors on the upper levels. As with the other designs by Zabludovsky, the use of exposed textured concrete and the large-scale structural components provide a dominant presence, as well as the sense of stability and authority (Figure 2.46).

Figure 2.45 Zabludovsky and González de León: El Colegio de México Patio, Mexico City, 1975.

Mexican Architecture and Economic and Political Power

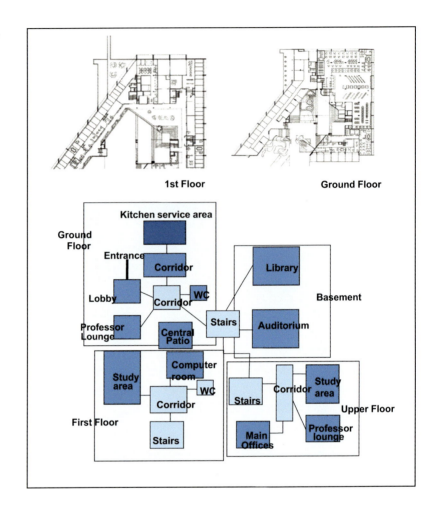

Figure 2.46 El Colegio de México, Floor Plans and Spatial Diagram.

Religious Architecture

Perhaps surprisingly for what is such a Catholic nation, religious architecture had the smallest role to play in twentieth-century Mexican Modernist architecture. There were a few exceptions, with, for example, important contributions being made by Félix Candela's concrete shell structure for La Iglesia de La Medalla Milagrosa, completed in Mexico City in 1955, and the entirely different mystical feel of El Convento de las Capuchinas by Luis Barragán, which opened in 1960. However, the two key examples of religious architecture to be studied here are both, again, in Mexico City. One is La Basílica de la Vírgen de Guadalupe (1976)

Mexican Architecture and Economic and Political Power

by Pedro Ramírez Vázquez, of the second generation of Mexican Modernist, and the other is Christ Church (1989) by Carlos Mijares, one of the leaders of the third generation.

Christ Church is an Anglican Church located in Lomas de Chapultepec – as noted, a prestigious residential area. The building consists of a single, centralized space that gives a sense of dignity and importance (Figure 2.47). The layout is a simple, square floor plan with a geometrically complex roof of symmetrical and structural brick-ribbed arches. All the activities and rituals are concentrated in this single, all-encompassing space, giving the church a real sense of unity. It also allows an easy visual control over everybody and everything inside it. Mijares designed the church using a diagonal axis that leads from the entrance to the altar as the focal point and higher part of the composition. Spirituality and contemplation were evoked by the careful manipulation of daylight filtering down through the elegant, ribbed arches (Figure 2.48).

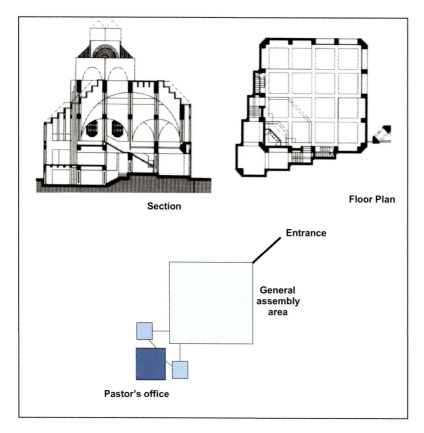

Figure 2.47 Christ Church, Floor Plan, Section and Spatial Diagram.

Mexican Architecture and Economic and Political Power

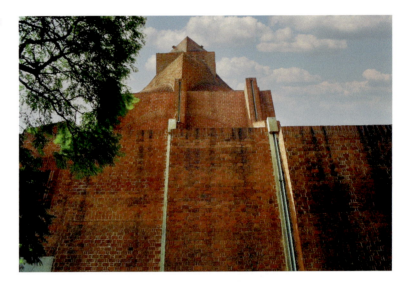

Figure 2.48 Carlos Mijares: Christ Church Exterior, Mexico City, 1989.

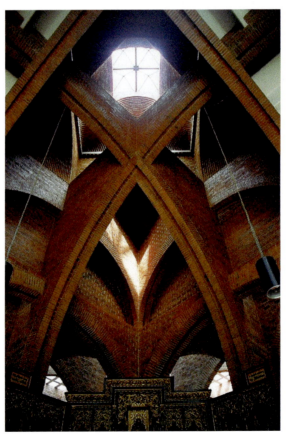

Figure 2.49 Carlos Mijares: Christ Church Interior, Mexico City, 1989.

Mexican Architecture and Economic and Political Power

La Nueva Basílica de la Virgin de Guadalupe, as designed by Pedro Ramírez Vázquez, is perhaps the most important religious building of this period. The Virgin of Guadalupe is, after all, the patron saint of all Mexicans, and so this building not only symbolizes the power of the Catholic Church but also the faith of Mexican people. The building is a concrete shell structure that functions like a gigantic tent with an off-centre mast that supports it (Figure 2.50), with the much-revered icon of the Virgin of Guadalupe on the wall underneath. Given that this painting constitutes the most important element in the basilica, everyone who enters from any point needs to be able to see it – even from the lateral chapels situated on the church's periphery. The basilica offers a Mass service every day from 6:00 am to 8:00 pm, continuously. This means that, when the pilgrims arrive, they have to be able to see the images of the Virgin of Guadalupe without interrupting the Mass.

The basilica's circular floor plan has a 100-metre diameter, and there are seven entrances/doors facing the altar and four lateral chapels on each side of the doors (Figure 2.52). Some have criticized the design as being an enormous tent that lacks religious and spiritual character. However, this does not seem to bother Ramírez Vásquez, who justified every design decision and detail in relation to the correct functional operation of the building. He claimed that the layout provides easy circulation for the vast number of people who visit daily as part of their pilgrimage to see the image of the Virgin of Guadalupe, while also offering the possibility of conducting smaller ceremonies simultaneously in the lateral chapels. As he explained:

> The basilica is the result of a type of devotion that is exclusive to Mexico and is not seen in any other part of the world, not even at the Vatican. For this reason, the requirements for the basilica were unique. The main requirement is the pilgrimage. The devoted pilgrim requires, according to our tradition, to be in front of the Virgin's image, and as close to it as possible. They want to see the image, and they want the image to see them. The number of people that visit the basilica is very large. It is not even comparable to any other church in Mexico. We needed to accommodate these thousands of pilgrims, without interrupting Mass.
>
> The lateral chapels are unique too, since there is no other church with this type of chapels. Chapels are usually located along the side of a church, each one has its own altar, and they are only used periodically. In the Basilica, these

Mexican Architecture and Economic and Political Power

chapels all face the same image, the image of the Virgin, and they are used all the time by people to celebrate a wedding anniversary or their first communion. So many people want to celebrate these events here, that there would not be enough time for so many masses. These chapels allow eight masses to take place simultaneously around the same image. This can only happen due to Mexico's devotion to the Virgin of Guadalupe, and so it demands a totally different architectural solution.[21]

The church clearly seeks to overwhelm visitors through its enormous, all-encompassing internal space (Figure 2.51). Its fan-like layout offers various alternative routes towards the altar, as well as secondary paths leading to the side chapels. Ramírez Vázquez cleverly designed a lower-level circulation route behind the altar so that pilgrims could enter, rather submissively, to view the painting of the Virgin of Guadalupe; that is, to stand in front of this image, pilgrims must obediently get onto a conveyer belt, or moving walkway, that strictly controls the time they can view the

Figure 2.50 Pedro Ramírez Vázquez: Basílica de la Virgen de Guadalupe Exterior, Mexico City, 1976.

Mexican Architecture and Economic and Political Power

Figure 2.51 Basílica de la Virgin de Guadalupe, Floor Plan, Section and Spatial Diagram.

painting, thereby creating a continuous flow for visitors' circulation. As in most of Ramírez Vázquez's buildings, this clever manipulation of movements and actions is used to provoke certain feelings – in this case, reverence and spirituality.

As we have seen in this chapter, Mexican Modernist architecture was determined by the dominant power groups and the prevailing economic model that they had adopted at that time. As Abraham Zabludovsky categorically declared, 'Architecture is an activity that is not exerted as a simple wish, it can only be created until it is assigned by a person or by an institution. Architecture is done by assignment'.[22] Consequently, the buildings produced in twentieth-century Mexico were the result of such assignments, created by the will of power groups and their associated institutions. Although it cannot be said that all architects consciously tried to use power to create subjectivities and manipulate the users, it must be acknowledged that forms of power were always being exerted – and thus it is vital that architects are aware of this and assume responsibility for this aspect. It should also be acknowledged that architects as the designers of built form are required to change to conform to changing social needs, situations and practices. This is particularly evident in the current condition of the 'Neoliberal Model' that

121

Mexican Architecture and Economic and Political Power

Figure 2.52 Pedro Ramírez Vázquez: Basílica de la Virgen de Guadalupe Interior, Mexico City, 1976.

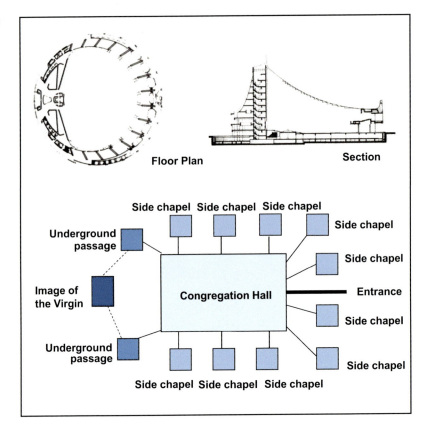

dictates the production of Mexico's contemporary buildings. Private enterprises and corporations, due to their need for competitiveness, rely upon information/communication media to publicize themselves and increase their control over the economic market. Promotion and control thus are part of the consumption system within twentieth-century Mexican architecture, as a system of signs and a system of meaning, as will be examined in the next chapter.

NOTES

1 Michel Foucault explains that architecture exerts power through its spatial organization and has thus been used at times to avoid revolts, epidemics, changes, or to reinstate control measures and express cultural identity. See: Foucault, Michel. *The Foucault Reader: An Introduction to Foucault's Thought*. Edited by Paul Rabinow. Harmondsworth, Penguin Books, 1986, p. 245.
2 'Disciplinary power' and 'micro-physics' of power are terms established in Foucault, Michel. *Discipline and Punish: The Birth of the Prison*. Translated by Alan Sheridan, New

Mexican Architecture and Economic and Political Power

York, Vintage, 1979. See also: Foucault, Michel. *On Power*. Edited by L. Kritzman, New York, Routledge, 1988.

3 Dovey, Kim. *Framing Places: Mediating Power in Built Form*. London, Routledge, 1999, p. 19.

4 Ibid., pp. 15–16.

5 Spatial syntax analysis discounts metric distances to prioritize measuring the topology; hence, the use of spatial diagrams. For more information see Kim Dovey states, Space Syntax Dovey, Kim, Elek Pafka and Mirjana Ristic. *Mapping Urbanities Morphologies, Flows, Possibilities*. New York, Routledge, 2017.

6 Dovey, Kim. *Framing Places: Mediating Power in Built Form*. London, Routledge, 1999, p. 24.

7 Foucault, Michel. *The Foucault Reader: An Introduction to Foucault's Thought*. Edited by Paul Rabinow. Harmondsworth, Penguin Books, 1986, p. 246.

8 Noelle, Louise. *Arquitectos contemporáneos de México*. México City, Editorial Trillas, 1989.

9 Ramírez Vázquez, Pedro. Personal interview with the author. Mexico City, 20th March 2000.

10 Diaz Infante, Juan Jose. Personal interview with the author. Mexico City, 17th March 2000.

11 de Garay, Graciela. *Historia Oral de la Ciudad de México Testimonios de sus arquitectos (1940 90) Abraham Zabludovsky Investigación y entrevista*. México City, Instituto Mora, 1995, p. 27.

12 Ingersoll, Richard quoted in Adria, Miguel. *México Arquitectura de los 90s*. México, Gustavo Gili, 1998, pp. 2–8.

13 Ibid.

14 Ramírez Vázquez, Pedro. Personal interview. Mexico City, March 20, 2000.

15 Zabludovsky, Abraham. Personal interview with the author. Mexico City, May 31, 2000.

16 de Garay, Graciela. *Historia Oral de la Ciudad de México Testimonios de sus arquitectos (1940 90) Abraham Zabludovsky Investigación y entrevista*. México, Instituto Mora, 1995, p. 79.

17 Ramírez Vázquez, Pedro. Personal interview with the author. Mexico City, 20th March 2000.

18 Ibid.

19 Diaz Infante, Juan José. Personal interview with the author. Mexico City, 17th March 2000.

20 de Garay, Graciela. *Historia Oral de la Ciudad de México Testimonios de sus arquitectos (1940 90) Abraham Zabludovsky Investigación y entrevista*. México, Instituto Mora, 1995, p. 83.

21 Ingersoll, Richard, as quoted in Adriá, Miquel. *México Arquitectura de los 90s*. México, Gustavo Gili, 1998.

22 de Garay, Graciela. *Historia Oral de la Ciudad de México Testimonios de sus arquitectos (1940 90) Abraham Zabludovsky Investigación y entrevista*. México, Instituto Mora, 1995, p. 27.

3

Mexican Architecture as Social Status in a System of Consumption

DOI: 10.4324/9781003318934-4

Mexican Architecture as Social Status in a System of Consumption

Mexican architecture is often considered to be an elitist realm reserved only for those select few who can afford it.[1] However, the impact of architecture is, of course, far more complex and widespread than this, as we saw in the last chapter when looking at the ways in which Mexican Modernist architecture was subject to the influence of successive economic models over the decades. This chapter will, likewise, examine the interdependence that Mexican twentieth-century architecture had with the patterns of social status which were formed in the country as part of a more generalized system of capitalist consumption. Architecture hence became a commodity that could be used by certain citizens as an interchangeable good or a financial investment within the local and global economy. Mexican architects, as we have seen, were also deeply immersed in this environment due to their upbringing, their training, and their practice – all of which ultimately determined their professional opportunities and even their probability of success and of thus becoming in effect a commodity themselves. By analysing the location, infrastructure and typology of key buildings, and the social connections required by key Mexican architects, it will become evident how this developing system of consumption contributed to the making of Mexican Modernist architecture.

MEXICAN ARCHITECTURE AND CONSUMPTION

Architecture in all countries cannot avoid engagement with the prevailing economic realm as a mode of production,[2] yet it is not its role in economic production, but instead economic consumption, that determines its value and forms the basis of social order.[3] Jean Baudrillard has argued that there are four different 'logics' involved in the creation of any consumer object.[4] The first logic consists of the functional logic of 'use-value' that is based upon its utility and functionality, with the object being, in effect, viewed as an instrument. This is followed by an economic logic of 'exchange-value', or 'price', whereby the value of a commodity or article of trade is determined by whatever people are prepared to pay for it in the market. Then there is the logic of 'symbolic-exchange' that, like a gift, symbolizes not a sense of use-value or exchange-value, but of the relationship to an event, time or place. And finally, the logic of 'sign-exchange' is when a consumer object becomes a sign for others to interpret in terms solely of its status value in that society, operating, therefore, in a pure process of symbolic exchange, whereby that sign is substitutable for other signs seen to be of a similar value.

Architecture has long been considered as a response to human needs and therefore its value could thus be claimed to be based on its utility and

Mexican Architecture as Social Status in a System of Consumption

functionality. Modernist architecture particularly tried to appeal to this logic of use-value, yet paradoxically, it was during the twentieth century that architecture came to be seen more and more as an interchangeable good subject to the logic of exchange-value. When architecture is transformed into a cash product, it requires there to be a healthy economy and the capability, indeed willingness, of customers to buy the finished product. Architecture's economic competitiveness thus depends on factors such as its typology, its urban construction, its materials, as well, of course, as its design. As Abraham Zabludovsky states:

> Just like architecture has structural elements, functional elements, formal elements and obviously spatial elements, we also need to know that architecture has a cost element and is an investment than you can recuperate.[5]

In Mexico, architecture was already becoming a market commodity, a tradeable good, by the beginning of the 1940s, when houses, apartments and other urban buildings flourished as a consequence of the growth of Mexico City, with their design now inspired by the new 'International Style' from the USA and Europe. By this time, developers had gained direct control over decisions about land, typology, materials and labour, as well as over the choice of architects. In order to be part of this process, architects needed to become promoters themselves. Luis Barragán was one of the first Mexican architects who decided to take control of this process by becoming a developer. That way, he felt more in control and not at the mercy of other people's decisions and whims. Barragán has said:

> In 1936, I went to Mexico City to work and I began to practice architecture. I got work designing houses and buildings, but nothing very big until 1940 when I realized that I could earn more by speculating with land (since I could help clients find property), than by practicing architecture . . . Back then, one would earn very little, so I quit the profession in 1940 to deal mainly in real estate. I began to construct to sell the land. This was between 1940 and 45.[6]

Perhaps one of the best examples of Barragán's work as a developer is the residential neighbourhood of Jardines del Pedregal, designed in the mid-1940s (Figure 3.1). This project is considered one of the best housing projects in Mexico City, both for its inherent beauty and also for its ability to transform the natural, exotic landscape, consisting of lava formations, into a suburban paradise. What is less known is that this project was actually a speculative commercial venture for Barragán, who had become disenchanted with his clients and wanted to take

Mexican Architecture as Social Status in a System of Consumption

control over his projects. He was, of course, fully aware of the complexity of undertaking this project, and the economic constraints:

> *El Pedregal needed to become a corporation with a financial investor; I invited José (Alberto) Bustamante. He accepted, obviously with a financial interest. So, this is how the neighbourhood of Jardines del Pedregal was born. I was in charge of the urban planning of the project. I also designed several houses, the gardens, and I was also getting involved in the financial and public relations, including the publicity.*[7]

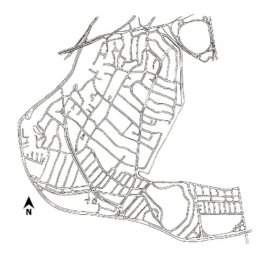

Figure 3.1 Jardines del Pedregal, Mexico City, Urban Layout, Mid-1940s.

Figure 3.2 Mathias Goeritz: Plaza 'El Animal del Pedregal' at Jardines del Pedregal.

128

Mexican Architecture as Social Status in a System of Consumption

Barragán's design followed the international model of the garden suburb, like other residential developments in Mexico City at that time, such as Lomas de Chapultepec (originally Chapultepec Heights), which followed Chicago's celebrated Riverside estate. Along with its suburban layout, El Pedregal also included several gardens and squares, like the Plaza de las Fuentes, with the famous sculpture of 'El Animal' by Mathias Goeritz located at its entrance (Figure 3.2). Or the Plaza del Cigarro and the Fuente de los Patos: 'These gardens were intended to entice prospective buyers and demonstrate Pedregal's potential as a site for a garden-home'.[8] The scheme also included two demonstration houses by Barragán and German-Mexican architect Max Cetto, which were designed to exemplify the 'correct' way of building in 'harmony' with the unique landscape of this place.[9] In spite of his involvement in this project, Cetto complained about El Pedregal's 'loud and propagandistic showiness . . . suited to the general taste of this country'.[10] All of its publicity was directed to ensuring the commercial success of the venture as envisioned by Barragán.

Luis Barragán, observes Keith Eggener, bought the land and immediately proceeded to work on the publicity promotion, which included a brief essay by Diego Rivera in which the basic aims of the project were described, calling, for instance, for the preservation of this natural site.[11] The endorsement by such an influential celebrity within Mexican society was echoed by a high-class brochure that has been described as 'having the character of an art book, showing the superiority of this space above other residential zones'.[12] It was also accompanied by a short colour film that was shown in the best movie theatres in Mexico City. El Pedregal was also repeatedly advertized in leading newspapers like *Novedades* by using slogans such as 'The Most Beautiful and Exclusive Subdivision in Mexico City', 'The Residential Zone with the Best Future in Mexico', and even 'The Most Admired Residential Zone in the World'.[13]

Barragán also reached out to an international market through an article written by Mary St. Albans in 1946 for the New York-based magazine, *Modern Mexico*, as published by the Mexican Chamber of Commerce of the United States. This was 'evidently a publicity piece, completed with the architect's cooperation',[14] and was geared towards American businessmen who, at that time, were investing in Mexico and who might even be interested in establishing a second residence in this new residential estate. In this way, El Pedregal's architectural design and urban layout readily became part of the capitalist consumption system by using a series of connotations and denotations that were made identifiable in Mexican society via a well-organized publicity campaign.

Mexican Architecture as Social Status in a System of Consumption

Much later, in the mid-1980s, Mexico's economy seemed to offer few opportunities for architects due to lack of economic stability in the market. This inspired Javier Sordo Madaleno to become a developer after his father, from whom he inherited his architecture practice, passed away. Relying on the firm's reputation and its social network, Madaleno transformed his father's office by encouraging new business opportunities and becoming, in effect, an entrepreneur. He explained why:

> I devoted myself to consolidate our work and also to look for work. I have become a developer since it is very hard for an architect to get a project. It is very hard because there are many architects, and so many clients and so many options that each time it is more difficult to get projects. So, I have devoted myself to look for projects and have tried to do everything. [15]

Thus, by the late-twentieth century, Mexican Modernist architecture had not only become widely commodified but had also begun to circulate as a sign, a status symbol, according to the fame reached by some of the most distinguished architects. Architects and buildings were adapting to their new roles as signs within Mexico's consumption system.

Mexican Architecture as a Sign Within the Consumption Cycle

In order to understand how architects and buildings become signs within the consumption system, it is essential to question the meaning of architecture itself; to ask if it ever corresponds to what people really want and need. It is therefore necessary to go beyond the purely economic sphere and take into account a semiotic reading that considers every object/commodity to be a sign whereby the signifier and the signified are correlated, not through financial relationships, but through human desire. [16] This realization removes any real claim that human need, in the case of architecture, is predicated on use-value as something fundamentally true and meaningful. In other words, any potential use-value of a building is overridden by an exchange-value system that then turns architecture into an object of symbolic-exchange and sign-exchange, circulating through its claim to carry social meaning and to present an image of reality. This observation, of course, diminishes or even destroys architecture's root meaning, and instead reveals its operations as an interchangeable sign within the consumption cycle.

Mexican Architecture as Social Status in a System of Consumption

Thus, when the 'Modern Movement' was being promoted in Mexico as a supposedly functionalist aesthetic, this was, in fact, simply an ideological proposition being introduced as a code whereby Modernist architecture, as a new signifier, was creating a new signified, conveniently under the term 'functionalism'. Functionalism became, in effect, the alibi used by early Mexican Modernists, such as Villagrán Garcia and Juan O'Gorman, to defend concepts of architectural purity and usefulness, and to attack 'false' ideals, such as decoration. In other words, terms like 'purity' and 'use' held no real meaning outside the consumption system that was enabling functionalist ideals to circulate. The same could be said of the contextual design approaches of Carlos Mijares, Clara de Buen and Javier Sordo, or of Juan José Díaz Infante's 'Kalikosmia' theory, or indeed Luis Barragán and Ricardo Legorreta's so-called 'emotional' architecture. All the architectural ideologies that Mexican architects were proclaiming, as listed in previous chapters, were promulgated in terms of explaining the underlying meaning of architecture, yet ultimately were just an alibi that allowed their buildings to circulate as signs within Mexico's capitalist system.

Although architecture bears no fundamental, 'real' meaning, this does not make it irrelevant. It is still capable of exerting a great deal of control as part of the consumption system, even if only as a sign that circulates within the general manipulation of signs. Here, architecture is not consumed so much as a sign, but in relation to other objects. Consequently, objects become categories of objects that denote and connote social status. Social differentiation thus becomes organized by the system of objects, in which the relational differences in quality and cultural value of an object are used to classify consumers. Architecture is, hence, used as a status object which categorizes the people who consume it.

Architects, just like their buildings, can become commodities and signs. Their signatures are a unique gesture that proclaims 'originality'; when this happens, it is not about architecture anymore, but about the architects themselves. As a result, some Mexican Modernist architects became abstracted from social reality to become a signature and a sign of their own work. This can be witnessed in the work of several successful figures, such as Luis Barragán, Ricardo Legorreta, Abraham Zabludovsky, Pedro Ramírez Vázquez and Enrique Norten. All these architects have also capitalized on their status by producing signature objects. Barragán, for instance, commissioned furniture inspired by Mexican tradition, like the Silla Miguelito (Figure 3.3), which was at first attributed as his design. This was later rectified by recognizing Clara Porset as its author, appointed by Barragán. She was frequently commissioned by him to produce furniture to suit his houses. Legorreta followed closely Barragán's influence by creating his own

Mexican Architecture as Social Status in a System of Consumption

Figure 3.3 Clara Porset, Comissioned by Luis Barragán: Silla Miguelito.

Figure 3.4 Ricardo Legorreta: Silla Vallarta, 1973.

designs for both modern and traditional chairs (Figure 3.4). Similarly, Pedro Ramírez Vázquez conceived new designs based on Mexican furniture, like the *equipal*, a traditional handcrafted chair, to produce a modern *equipal* (Figure 3.5) in an attempt to dignify Mexican crafts. Abraham Zabludovsky, Agustín Hernández and Enrique Norten have also created interesting chairs, often using steel and glass to create these signature objects, like Hernández's Silla Gala (Figure 3.6).

Buildings also cash into this consumption cycle by promoting architectural styles or trends that can be endlessly consumed and collected. This is usually related to architects with a particular style or form of expression, as in the case of Barragán, Legorreta (Figure 3.7) and Sordo Madaleno's (Figure 3.8) trademark use of colour

Mexican Architecture as Social Status in a System of Consumption

Figure 3.5 Pedro Ramírez Vázquez: Equipal Moderno.

Figure 3.6 Agustín Hernández: Silla Gala Chair, 1997.

and massive walls, or of Zabludovsky's use of rough, exposed concrete. As Clara de Buen notes, this has given those figures an upper hand in relation to the rest:

Only some architects are the ones who have an image. I am not going to mention names, but there are some architects who have managed to achieve an image and a place in society as very predominant figures; this no one will argue. But these are very few, so few that you can count them on one hand. The rest of us do not have this image.[17]

Mexican Architecture as Social Status in a System of Consumption

Figure 3.7 Ricardo Legorreta: Museo MARCO, Monterrey, Mexico, 1991.

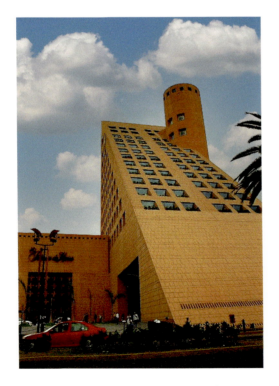

Figure 3.8 Javier Sordo Madaleno: Plaza Moliere; Now Palacio de Hierro Plaza Moliere, Mexico City, 1997.

Mexican Architecture as Social Status in a System of Consumption

Carlos Mijares explains how the consumption cycle triggered a need in Mexico to produce designs that could give an architect an edge within a highly competitive profession:

> There is a general obsession with the idea of the architect and his or her architecture as having a leading role. The moment this obsession exists, trendy expressions are just one step away. This means that architecture, seen as a fashion, requires an image, does it not? It becomes an ever-changing image, an image that changes into different manifestations. Therefore, they (architects) become stereotypes. What is more, people demand brands. When this need for a strong central character develops in architecture, it has the tendency of becoming an endless consequence of fashion. Therefore, most architects end up thinking this way too. Or the circumstance makes them think this way. Or perhaps they also lack a critical spirit that will not allow them to get out of this situation.[18]

Mijares thus openly condemns the use of a trademark style, whereas others like Javier Sordo argue that a clear architectural approach, such as one that alludes to ancient Mexican architecture, can provide an advantage:

> A trademark is what you develop along with your personality . . . I believe that architects should or must keep to their roots . . . [and so] if you are a Mexican architect, you have certain roots that you need to express. I believe that this is the only element that will give the Mexican architect an edge, or the possibility to defend his work and his position in the architectural world. Often, we do not have within our hands the technology or the budget or many of the elements that are present in countries that are more industrialized than ours. So, how is a Mexican architect going to compete if he forgets his creativity and his roots? He has nothing to compete with. What is important is to have roots.[19]

Alberto Kalach agrees that there are architects who resort to preconceived styles or stereotypes, but he rightly claims that this stance is not exclusive to Mexico:

> Yes, but it is not only Mexican architects. This is also the concern of Daniel Libeskind. He has a form (shape) and has used it for 15 years. Every time they give him the chance of a building, he will explore this form. Or Richard Meier, he has a language that he, when given the opportunity, will use whether in Barcelona or in Hong Kong.[20]

Mexican Architecture as Social Status in a System of Consumption

Yet, even this observation by Kalach confirms the participation of certain Mexican Modernists in creating a trademark architecture as an object of consumption within what is now a globalized system. By joining in with the process of turning architecture into a commodity and a sign, they thereby helped to transform Mexican architecture during the twentieth century.

THE IMAGE OF MEXICAN ARCHITECTS

Many architects have enjoyed celebrity since the Renaissance, with figures like Palladio or Michelangelo, mainly due to the significance of the buildings they designed and their close relationships to the elite. Architectural fame was further fuelled during the twentieth century, as seen by the enormous appeal of the bestseller, *The Fountainhead*, in the late-1940s, and by the work of historians and theorists such as Lewis Mumford, Siegfried Giedion and Nikolaus Pevsner, and of fame-making institutions like New York's Museum of Modern Art.[21] Despite contrary feelings generated by worldwide critiques of Modernist architects in the 1960s, the process continued. For example, Walter Gropius complained that he had become a person covered in labels. He also remembered how much his mother disapproved of his fame when his name started to appear in newspapers.[22] Fame has nevertheless become a requirement for architects and, living within an increasing culture of celebrity architecture, realizing that they, even more the younger ones, need publicity. In fact, twentieth-century architects were required to publish, exhibit and network if they wanted to build. Architects learned to promote themselves and their buildings, regardless of the quality of their work. Hence, as the architectural critic David Dunster observed: 'branding, marketing and even being famous require only the appearance of originality and robust abilities to brand and rebrand, in order to keep that spotlight where it belongs'.[23]

Despite this all-too-apparent phenomenon, many architects continue to deny their participation in the fame-game, and some emphatically assert that their careers are solely built on their design merits and sheer hard work. Although theoreticians like Roxanne Kuter Williamson are sad to admit it, the reality of the fame-game within the contemporary architectural discipline means that any student learns that they manipulate their career somehow to become a famous architect.[24] Therefore, architects must achieve the status of what the French sociologist and philosopher, Pierre Bourdieu, called the 'consecrated avant-garde'.[25] This means that their work must have 'architectural qualities that are acknowledged as being worthy, valorised by people in position of influence. Such a position is

Mexican Architecture as Social Status in a System of Consumption

distinguished from the majority of architects who are run-of-the-mill building designers with comparatively little cultural status'.[26] Once architects are aware that this 'consecrated avant-garde' is a limited field, they now begin to design their own image by resorting to the mechanisms of social media. According to Julia Chance, we live in a culture with a short-term memory and a habit of consuming vast quantities of highly sophisticated visual images, and thus architects use their own image as a recurring portrait to create a constant visual reference or a subtle kind of label to be identifiable despite the diversity of their projects.[27]

Mexican architects have equally become aware of the importance of creating a marketable image, and they resort to publicity in their quest for fame and commissions. Written-architecture as well as photographed-architecture are both pivotal for this purpose. This is evident in the number of monographs published during the twentieth century – and which are still being published today – as a means to promote and disseminate certain architects. Likewise, it is notable that the leading Mexican Modernists began ever more to use their own faces to portray their design ideals. By examining the pictures of these architects, we can see how, through use of their portraits and other elements within the photographs, they could cast a hidden (or at times overt) message. What thus follows are some of the most-often-published photos of these celebrated figures and a brief interpretation of what is being said by each.

To cite a classic example, Luis Barragán was usually photographed impeccably dressed, depicted as an aloof and private character, often with folded arms, caught in a reflective pose. He was also typically seen in his own surroundings, as here in his own house in Tacubaya (Figure 3.9).

Although there are few photographs of José Villagrán García available, this photograph of him as a relatively young man shows him as an affable and confident architect, looking securely into the camera (Figure 3.10).

Juan O'Gorman, in this early photograph by Esther Born, appears as a young architect with a clean-cut and professional look, very much in tune with his functionalist ideals at that time (Figure 3.11).

Pedro Ramírez Vázquez is usually photographed in one of his many buildings, but here he is working behind his desk in his office, sitting amongst his possessions. He is portrayed as a serious professional and a religious man, with a cross on the wall, and highly patriotic, with the Mexican flag behind (Figure 3.12).

Agustín Hernández is likewise frequently photographed in his own office. Through this picture, he both reveals the unusual design of his studio and presents himself at work as a highly creative architect who is rather removed from the ordinary cityscape beyond (Figure 3.13).

Mexican Architecture as Social Status in a System of Consumption

Figure 3.9 Luis Barragán in His House/Studio.

Abraham Zabludovsky is captured here in one of his buildings, where you can observe its harsh texture. Like Alfred Hitchcock in his movies, he frequently appears in his buildings participating in the space and environment he created. As he explained jokingly, he always likes to return to the scene of the crime (Figure 3.14).

There are only a small number of photographs of Carlos Mijares that ever appeared in publications, but in all of them, he appears as having a friendly and relaxed disposition and a suitably thoughtful and knowledgeable expression (Figure 3.15).

Mexican Architecture as Social Status in a System of Consumption

Figure 3.10 José Villagrán García.

Figure 3.11 Juan O'Gorman.

Mexican Architecture as Social Status in a System of Consumption

Figure 3.12 Pedro Ramírez Vázquez in His Office.

Figure 3.13 Agustín Hernández in His Studio.

Mexican Architecture as Social Status in a System of Consumption

Figure 3.14 Abraham Zabludovsky in One of His Buildings.

Figure 3.15 Carlos Mijares in His Office.

Mexican Architecture as Social Status in a System of Consumption

Ricardo Legorreta usually appears in all his photos in a deliberately casual and informal attitude, much like his architecture. Here we find him in a lecturing mood, raising his hand and pointing with his finger to emphasize his enthusiasm for the subject (Figure 3.16).

Juan José Díaz Infante's image is hardly ever shown in publications, yet in this image, he is captured sitting inside his office, surrounded by the paraphernalia of his collected items that are intended to convey his playful, boyish and less conventional character (Figure 3.17).

Enrique Norten, reclining against a wall inside one of his buildings, is portrayed as an intense professional, framed within an acute photographic perspective. He is dressed all in black, as per the international architects' code, and yet is surrounded by highly tectonic elements, all very stylish and avant-garde (Figure 3.18).

Alberto Kalach refrained from promoting his own image during the early part of his career, and therefore there are few pictures of him. This one is a close-up taken from a photo that will appear in the following chapter where he is standing with all the member of his studio (Figure 3.19).

Figure 3.16 Ricardo Legorreta in His Office.

Mexican Architecture as Social Status in a System of Consumption

Figure 3.17 Juan José Díaz Infante in His Office.

Figure 3.18 Enrique Norten.

Mexican Architecture as Social Status in a System of Consumption

Figure 3.19 Alberto Kalach.

Figure 3.20 Clara de Buen in the Earlier Part of Her Career.

Clara de Buen and her partners rarely appear in photographs. Here, she is standing between her team members, Mac Gregor and Nuño, stressing the collaborative nature of her work, and unpretentiously looking away from the camera as if she is, in fact, uninterested in the notion of fame (Figure 3.20).

Mexican Architecture as Social Status in a System of Consumption

Figure 3.21 Javier Sordo Madaleno in the Late 1990s.

In this photo, Javier Sordo Madaleno, on the far left, is represented at work amongst five of his team members. Here he is portrayed as a determined, hardworking professional – as the leader in charge (Figure 3.21).

Each of these photographs, although, of course, always staged in some way for publication, manage to reflect quite accurately the personality of each architect. They also demonstrate the various facets and roles of the architect within the profession. Self-branding was rare at the beginning of Mexican twentieth-century architecture, but by the latter part of the century, such photos started to appear more frequently in printed publications or on the internet – the latter being that which is favoured by many of the younger generation of Mexican architects.

Mexican Architects and Their Social Status

A factor that motivates an architect, consciously or unconsciously, within his or her professional career is that of obtaining recognition from their peers and critics. Yet it is ultimately more important for them to gain the acceptance and patronage of the elite social group, first at a local or national level, and later, perhaps, at the international level. This essentially is how they can guarantee more assignments, more future commissions, and thus financial security. This process of acceptance and recognition requires a series of shrewd decisions, as well as fortuitous events, all of which conform to the social and cultural trajectory of any professional career. Any

Mexican Architecture as Social Status in a System of Consumption

Map 3.1 Key Architects' Houses, Studios and House/Studios in Mexico City.

series of decisions and events can be mapped into a variety of social connections that are derived from where the architect studied, under whom they studied, with whom they worked, who were their relatives, who are their friends and acquaintances and so on. Also very important is where they live and where they work. Map 3.1 thus indicates the location in Mexico City of the homes and studios of the selected architects, showing how these are concentrated in the most prominent

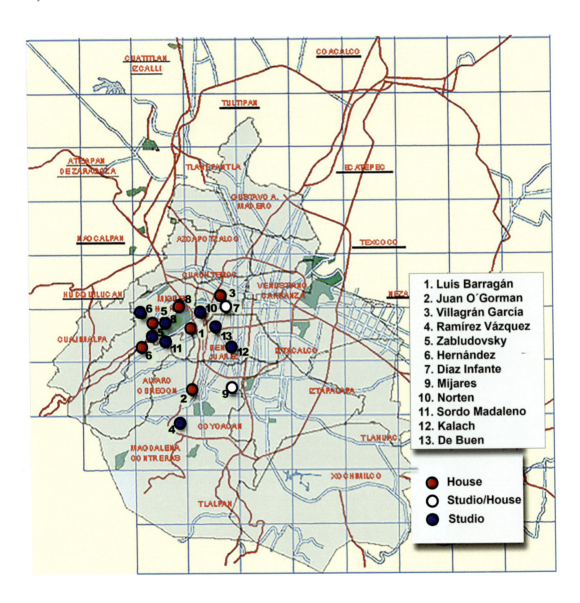

Mexican Architecture as Social Status in a System of Consumption

neighbourhoods in western and southwestern parts of the city, such as Lomas de Reforma, Lomas de Chapultepec, La Condesa and Coyoacán.

The social connections of Mexican Modernist architects can be interpreted by analysing the list of buildings they have had the privilege to design. One of the most important aspects of any architect's career is determined by their very first commissions. These may vary widely, although most of these architects had modest beginnings to their careers. Their first projects were mainly houses commissioned by friends and relatives. For instance, Hernández stated that his first job assignments came from 'people that I knew like my parents and friends, or the friends of my parents; something like that . . . mostly houses'.[28] Mijares similarly noted that his 'first projects were houses, always houses, relatives' houses, friends' houses'.[29] Likewise, Enrique Norten's and Alberto Kalach's first projects were also commissions for private houses. Kalach explained, 'It has to do with the fact that people are not going to ask a youngster to design a big building. They ask him to remodel a bathroom or maybe, if they want to be adventurous, to design a house'.[30]

These early assignments will hopefully translate into greater local recognition, more design offers, and ultimately social promotion and class mobility. Architecture is a profession that can provide such opportunities, as has been shown by figures such as Abraham Zabludovsky and Pedro Ramírez Vázquez. Both came from very humble upbringings. Zabludovsky, for instance, arrived in Mexico at a very young age, as the son of Polish immigrants. He recalled, 'Our family income came from a small store near La Merced, a traditional public market in Mexico City, managed by my parents. So maybe the financial aspect and the need of having an income, and also to be able to work and to study at the same time, influenced my decision [to study architecture]'.[31] Ramírez Vázquez also remembered how his family's modest business consisted of selling used books in one of the plazas in Mexico City,[32] and how he was first discouraged from studying architecture due to the profession's elitist reputation:

> My elder brothers, 14 and 16 years older than me, were studying law and starting their practice back then. The older one was a judge, and when I told them I wanted to study architecture, he said: 'Architecture? That is a profession for rich people, and we do not know anybody rich.'[33]

Despite their modest backgrounds, both these famous Mexican architects, through work and dedication, as well as their professional and social connections, were

147

Mexican Architecture as Social Status in a System of Consumption

able to forge distinguished careers. For instance, Ramírez Vázquez, although he had been working for the administrative committee for the federal programme for school construction (Comité Administrador del Programa Federal de Construcción de Escuelas, or CAPCE) and was involved in other important governmental projects, got his big opportunity by building the house of Adolfo López Mateos, later to become the Mexican President in 1958. This relationship thus helped launch his career as Mexico's official architect during several presidential administrations. As even he admitted of his friendship with López Mateos:

> I was introduced to him socially. He was a good friend of Diego Rivera, and I was a good friend of Rivera's daughters, Ruth and Lupe [Rivera]. Adolfo López Mateos, who was very interested in the arts, would invite us for lunch every Saturday, or we would go to Federico Canesi's home for lunch. We all got together then, and that is how I met him.[34]

Similarly, Abraham Zabludovsky recounted the way that he and Teodoro Gonzalez de León both got the opportunity to move beyond private houses and apartment blocks and take on larger public projects, simply as a result of their friendship at school with Guillermo Rossell de la Lama, a Mexican politician who was the Secretary for Tourism:

> One of our classmates became a high-rated public servant in one of the State Secretariats. The three of us got together regularly, and one day he said: 'Why don't you do something for us?' I believe that it was the general plan of the city of Poza Rica. He was Guillermo Rossell, the first official of state heritage at that time.[35]

Eventually, this enabled Zabludovsky and González de León to design a series of public housing projects and the headquarters building for the new public institution known as INFONAVIT:

> It is interesting how people consider that this INFONAVIT building was given to us by 'dedazo' [being assigned without the usual formalities]. But the real story is different. We had just finished, two years before, Las Torres de Mixcoac housing project, considered the best one made by this housing institution. So, when Jesus Silva-Herzog Flores, who was the director, decided that his institution needed its own building, he said: 'Let those who built the best housing project, build the main INFOVAVIT building too.'[36]

Mexican Architecture as Social Status in a System of Consumption

Juan O'Gorman also confirmed that it was through a social connection – in his case, his friendship with Narciso Bassols, a lawyer and socialist politician – that he was awarded the opportunity to transform Mexico's public schools:

> When Narciso Bassols became the Minister of Education, he asked me to design the project for the school buildings. The central department gave one million pesos annually to start the programme of primary schools in the poorest neighbourhoods in Mexico City.[37]

Social connections were thus very relevant in Mexican Modernist architecture, as they are in any country, but it also helps, of course, if the architect also comes from a wealthy family or one already related to a high-level architecture practice. Luis Barragán, for example, came from a wealthy rural family from Jalisco; likewise, Ricardo Legorreta belonged to a prominent family of bankers. Javier Sordo Madaleno, as the son of Juan Sordo Madaleno, a renowned Mexican architect from the first generation of Modernist architects, has continued the family tradition. He inherited his father's office and transformed it into a major business, as mentioned above. Clara de Buen also has close relations to the construction industry, being the daughter of Oscar de Buen, a prominent civil engineer and member of the firm Colinas de Buen, and thus part of one of the top civil engineering companies in Mexico City. So, through social connections and the right kind of networking, architects were able to achieve social recognition and social status. These connections often produce their big break that serves to make their career. In a few cases, these are also prompted by academic connections, as noted in the previous chapter, but in the majority of cases in Mexico, such breaks come through social and family connections.

Clara de Buen remembers the way in which she and her firm got their first important large commission for the Estación del Metro de Pantitlán Linea A:

> In 1984, my father's office, which has always been a structural office, was invited to participate in the metro project. The metro project had traditionally been done by the construction company ICA (Ingenieros Civiles Asociados). This meant that ICA had been participating in these projects for over 20 years, and it was during the government of President Miguel de la Madrid that they decided to open this project to other participants . . . even though ICA still had the main part of the project. It was a very important project in Mexico City. They invited the office of Colinas de Buen and other offices for the civil engineering part, as well as the metro stations that consisted of the architecture and the engineering part of all of

> the stations. They asked us to be part of the architectural project. Afterwards, we
> designed the complete project for the Linea 'A'.[38]

Javier Sordo Madaleno considers that the Centro Cultural Arte Contemporáneo was the project that gave him his start, or *'alternativa'*, a term that refers to a bullfighter's brutal process of initiation. He notes:

> This building was designed when my father was very ill. He died of cancer, and at
> that time he was in his final stages. When the opportunity to design the Centro
> Cultural came along, Emilio Azcárraga Milmo [an entertainment tycoon], asked
> me to make a presentation and my father doubted very much whether they were
> going to award it to me, if he was not there. So, it was a great satisfaction for me
> when we won the project.[39]

As pointed out before, one of Ricardo Legorreta's most beloved buildings is the Hotel Camino Real, completed in 1968. This project allowed him to achieve international recognition and also gave him the opportunity, in 1985, to design the house of Ricardo Montalbán, then a well-known, Mexican-born Hollywood actor. Montalbán had been very impressed with the hotel's design, as Legorreta did not fail to mention:

> Montalbán is a marvellous person. He wanted to establish [with his house] in the
> United States the awareness that Mexico had good architecture, and that it was
> not just a country, as he described it, with tiled roofs, burros and siesta. So, he
> gave me that job after staying in the Hotel Camino Real.[40]

It was thus through a combination of social and family connections, but also of hard work and successful designs, that the key Mexican Modernists earned their reputation – which then transformed them into a commodity, ensuring their participation in further architectural projects and thus guaranteeing their success. Consequently, these architects became sought out by many clients and developers, showing that they had become an economic asset in their own right.

Mexican Architects and Their Social Image

Although all the architects analysed in this book have achieved social acceptance in Mexico, and even a certain prominence that has made them part of the consumption

Mexican Architecture as Social Status in a System of Consumption

system, they have also expressed concern about the difficulty of asserting and promoting their image within a Mexican society which does not seem to understand the architectural profession. Apparently, this problem was far more acute earlier in the twentieth century, when Mexican architects were generally considered to be second-rate engineers. José Villagrán Garcia has explained how, at the beginning of his professional practice, he struggled to establish and maintain the distinction between an architect and an engineer, as will also be seen in the next chapter:

> I had to emphasize the fact that architects should be called architects . . . [There were] those who believed that engineering and architecture were the same thing, and that there was no reason to differentiate them. At that time, it did not worry anyone that architects were not called architects but were instead called engineers. 'Señor Ingeniero', because to utter the word 'architect' sounded strange.[41]

Abraham Zabludovsky echoed this view and attributed the substantial changes in the social perception of the architectural profession to the efforts of pioneering figures from the previous generation, such as Villagrán:

> There was a time when an architect who studied in the school of San Carlos was considered a dilettante of the Beaux Arts. Some studied architecture in the way that young girls would study piano, in order to entertain in family parties. Many considered architecture to be something like that. In spite of this, there were several architects in our time who gave it an extraordinary support and encouragement, changing that concept. We must acknowledge people like Villagrán, who introduced modern architecture to Mexico. And we cannot forget the special contribution of Mario Pani and his large-scale projects and architectural concepts.[42]

Zabludovsky was thus one who tried to work hard to alter this stereotype. He considered himself first and foremost a constructor and an administrator – and credited this notion not only to his success as a commodity but also as a modifier of the social understanding of his profession. Given his modest beginnings as a contractor, he always conveyed a sense of someone engaged in commercial professionalism instead of artistic whim:

> I developed a very important rule or guideline that has helped me very much, especially in housing projects; that is to give your clients a fixed price. Architects have been called many bad names because we do not know how to give fixed prices. I believe that it is very important . . . and in our economy, this has become essential.[43]

Mexican Architecture as Social Status in a System of Consumption

According to Ricardo Legorreta, the tainted image of the artist-architect still persisted in Mexico late into the twentieth century. When asked if there is a stereotype with which an architect is associated in Mexican culture, he replied:

> Sometimes an architect is associated with an artist who deals in the field of whims and caprices, and this is something that we have to correct. We architects must rectify this in order not only to have a job, but also to benefit our profession. [44]

Clara de Buen likewise believes that the image that Mexican people gained of the architectural profession during the course of the twentieth century still needs to be tackled and changed:

> In general, architects are considered unimportant; we lack prestige. I think that people consider architects as unnecessary, as someone who makes buildings more expensive, and their role is not very clear because people think they can be architects themselves. It is not very clear what we do, or if we really do anything. I believe that this has been in part due to bad public relations from our associations and schools of architecture, because, for example, engineers and other professions do possess a certain prestige. [45]

Within the sphere of practicing architects in any country, there will always be hierarchies that separate the elite designers from those seen as less important. One such hierarchy is that determined by specialists like critics, historians and other architects, often located within the academic sphere either nationally or internationally. Furthermore, there is a hierarchy shaped within the social and cultural sphere by power groups, such as clients and developers. Both kinds of hierarchy classify architects in an ascending order rising from the unknown architect to the averagely-known figure to the up-and-coming architect who is worth watching out for, and finally up to the elite architect who is favoured by academic circles, as well as by wealthy patrons.

Clara de Buen acknowledges the existence of this hierarchy within Mexican architecture, particularly in terms of the presence of a select group of architects of which she believes she still is not a part:

> There are some architects who have managed to achieve an image and a place in society as very predominant figures . . . [we] do not have this image. We have

Mexican Architecture as Social Status in a System of Consumption

had to work very hard to get and to keep our clients. We have more work because we keep our same clients. They like our buildings, but more than anything, I think, they like the service we can give them.[46]

In Mexico, it is clear the type of client not only determines the relationship between the architect and society, but also a building's typology. Architects that manage to

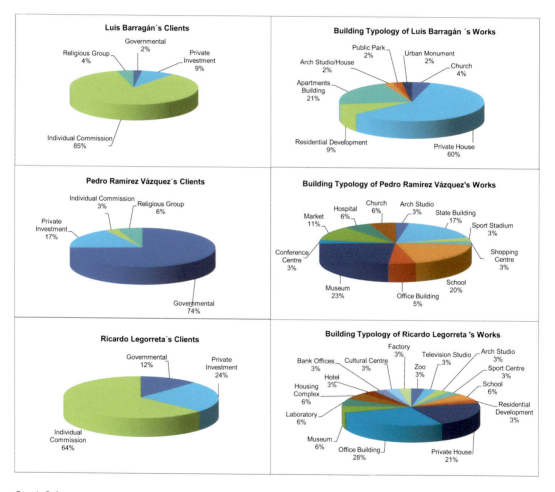

Graph 3.1

get away from individual domestic commissions are those that then build for the government or for businesses, gaining more diversity in their oeuvre. This is shown in the graphs, which were created by mapping the list of key buildings by three of the selected architects to the typologies that were being erected during the twentieth century. From this, it is easy to see that Luis Barragán was engaged primarily on individual houses and thus had little diversity in his work. In contrast, Pedro Ramírez Vázquez did more work for the government and Ricardo Legorreta, for private companies, and hence their oeuvres were more diverse.

What enables architects to reach an elite position and to achieve diversity in their projects, as well as cementing their commodity status, is determined by these factors: their ability in networking, the enduring quality of their designs and their ability to remain on top in the local and international hierarchies of status. Aside from such considerations, they are also required to conform to the complex codes established by social and cultural patterns, so as to remain loyal to the patronage of the elite group for which they work, and which they represent in built form. Their architecture needs not only to attract those with power, but also to demonstrate economic wealth. At an academic level, successful Mexican Modernist architects needed to conform to the cultural images created by Western architecture, as mentioned in the previous chapter. Ultimately, only those architects who are part of the decision-making control of the elite group, and who could keep up with architectural changes in western countries, were able to secure the most valued, state-of-the-art commissions.

SPATIAL AND SOCIAL MARGINALIZATION IN MEXICO CITY

The architectural form and urban structure of Mexican cities together shaped and depicted social relationships in the twentieth century, mainly by privileging a select few and marginalizing the underprivileged.[47] Urban form also contributed to the construction of social and cultural patterns and to the construction of individuals and their social stratification.[48] The urban structure of Mexico City thus allows us to read social status, as is evident in Luis Barragán's residential neighbourhood of El Pedregal. Here, the design follows the model of a North American type of automobile suburbia, denoting its high status.[49] If we compare it with the nearby, lower-class and similarly-named El Pedregal de Santo Domingo (Map 3.2) – located on the other side of the UNAM, or CU, campus – then there is an enormous difference in terms of the width of the streets and the size of the housing plots, as well as in the quality of the infrastructure.

Mexican Architecture as Social Status in a System of Consumption

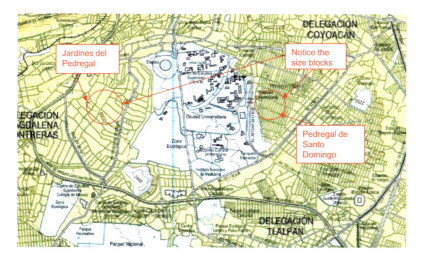

Map 3.2 Map of Mexico City With Jardines del Pedregal (left) and Pedregal de Santo Domingo (right).

Social stratification is thus evident in the cases of El Pedregal and El Pedregal de Santo Domingo, but it is important to point out that the whole urban structure of Mexico City marginalizes its inhabitants. The lowest classes are relegated to the driest and dusty parts of the city, located on the north-eastern and eastern areas. In contrast, the wealthier classes are located on the north-western, western, south-western and southern parts of the city, which also correspond to the greener and higher areas. This spatial difference between social classes can also be shown by drawing a map of Mexico City (Map 3.3) to show the location of the main buildings designed by the selected members of the four generations of Mexican Modernist architects.

From this map, it is clear that the most famous buildings are concentrated in the western districts that make up the wealthiest and most prominent areas of Mexico City. Boroughs in which these buildings are located have larger plot sizes, better infrastructure and higher-level incomes (indeed the highest anywhere in the nation). These districts thus correspond to the new developments that appeared in Mexico City from the mid- to the late-twentieth century. By looking at the list of the buildings by these selected architects, we can also deduce their size and cost, as well as their social importance. Although most of the buildings that are considered to be the most important in this book are theoretically accessible to everyone, in fact it is only the older parts of Mexico City that are pedestrian-friendly and possess the requisite level of public transport; instead, the city's western districts, such as Bosques de las Lomas, due to their scale and design, are able to restrict pedestrians' access in order to favour people with automobiles – hence privileging the high-class elite.

Mexican Architecture as Social Status in a System of Consumption

Map 3.3 Key Buildings by the Four Generations of Modernist Architects in Mexico City.

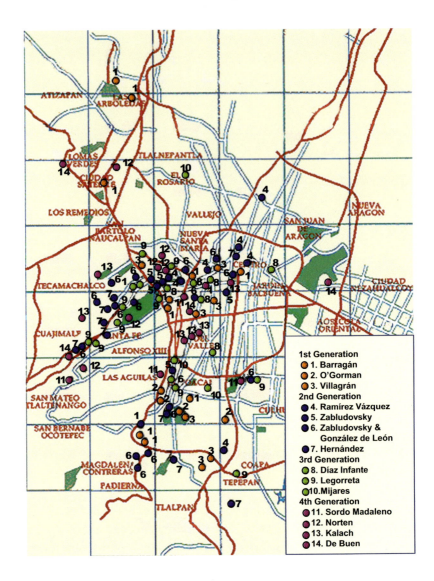

The social and cultural construction of classes is expressed and maintained through architecture and urban space.[50] Therefore, it is also important to note the ways in which Mexican Modernist architecture has helped to construct a class hierarchy that is linked to the social construction of ethnic divisions and of gendered identities, as will be discussed in the following chapters. Additionally, it is also evident that the spatial order and arrangement in Modernist architecture and urban design plays its role in supporting and strengthening class divisions. By analysing the selected buildings of famous Mexican Modernist architects as valuable examples, the power structures involved in creating different social classes can be revealed.

Mexican Architecture as Social Status in a System of Consumption

It is thus notable that these celebrated Mexican Modernist buildings often display certain distinguishable signs of status in terms of their location, monumental scale, luxurious materials, and need for many staff for their upkeep. Typical examples tend to be fashionable restaurants, hotels, commercial centres, department stores, as well as private clubs, private schools and private universities. These may be accessible to lower classes, perhaps, via back doors and entrances, or during night hours when lower social groups are allowed to enter these buildings, usually as cleaners. Or there might be spaces and places that are inherently more socially neutral and that are open for use by anyone, such as museums or churches. Then, the only problem tends to be their location in less accessible elite areas, which may prevent or at least discourage visitors from poorer social classes.

Social class distinction is always expressed through power, as a form of domination and authority.[51] Architecture uses entrances, rooms, corridors and service areas to clearly define in a spatial way those areas that are designated for the privileged and those for the underprivileged. In this sense, it is possible to interpret the workings of power by examining the floor plans and spatial diagrams of key examples of Mexican Modernist architecture. No other typology expresses social hierarchy more clearly through built form than the domestic house, primarily in regard to spatialized services and social privileges. The house or apartment block as a cultural object sustains class hierarchies through their manipulation of space and their relative distribution.

In a household environment, social structure is so naturally embedded into the framework of everyday life that it appears to be less questionable, and thus successful. This is inferred in the explanation given by Abraham Zabludovsky about the relevance of domestic servants or hired help when one is designing houses and apartments:

> In Mexico, domestic help is affordable to most almost every income, and why not admit that most of us love the way that it takes away lots of problems, like washing dishes, running errands, serving food. Well, this 'institution' demands a different type of space. In an apartment block, that we have built in Tecamalchalco [a neighbourhood of Mexico City], La Templanza and in other areas, one of the first things that we take into consideration is the service areas. There are places that have two rooms for the hired help and one for washing and ironing with a patio. Here, too, it is important to take into account the fact that the elevator must be near to the service areas so that when the mother arrives from the supermarket, the servant will be waiting to take the groceries without entering the living room or dining room. This is not something that you see in other parts of the world.[52]

Mexican Architecture as Social Status in a System of Consumption

If we then analyse some of the apartment buildings by Zabludovsky, it is easy to see the importance that he gives to these areas for domestic servants, whether that is in the government-sponsored housing complexes like Las Torres de Mixcoac, which will be discussed in the next chapter, or in privately built middle-class apartment towers, such as La Templanza (Figure 3.22). The latter has more generous bedrooms and social areas than Las Torres de Mixcoac, or indeed most private residences in Mexico City, but the servants' areas in La Templanza remain more or less the same design as anywhere else in terms of scale and disposition (Figure 3.23). Looking closely at the spatial diagrams, we can see that the maids' quarters are the last cell in a linear disposition that requires one to cross through the kitchen and the service patio to get there. The maids' bathroom only includes a shower and a toilet, which means that the servants must wash their hand and brush their teeth in the laundry sink in the patio.

In both cases, Zabludovsky has paid special attention to the necessary proximity of the entrance to the servants' area. La Templanza has two separate entrances, one opening into the family's social area and the other into the kitchen; whereas Las Mixcoac Towers provides only one entrance that is located cleverly between the kitchen and the living room. The location of these areas for servants appears to denote functional efficiency and a suitable provision of services, yet it also connotes the social hierarchy of its inhabitants, in that the hired help is kept isolated, away from view, and is confined to the smallest areas of the apartment.

Architects' own homes in Mexico City also provide clear evidence of an embodied class structure in relation to architectural space. Zabludovsky, Legorreta and Barragán all placed their maids' quarters on the rooftop of their respective

Figure 3.22 Abraham Zabludovsky: La Templaza, Avenida Las Fuentes #34. Mexico City, 1971.

Mexican Architecture as Social Status in a System of Consumption

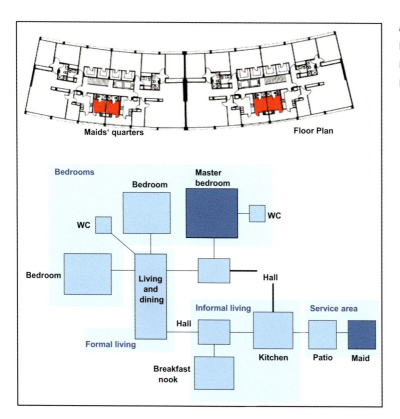

Figure 3.23 La Templanza, Floor Plan (Maids' Quarters in Red) and Spatial Diagram.

Figure 3.24 Abraham Zabludovsky: Casa Zabludovsky; Now Museo de la Intervención Arquitectónica, Palacio Versalles 235, Colonia Lomas de Reforma, Mexico City, 1969.

dwellings, thus placing these lower-status workers in secluded areas, away from everybody else's view. Zabludovsky's house (Figure 3.24) is located within an inclined terrain, so it makes sense to locate the service areas, such as the garage, laundry facilities and servants quarters, on the top floor; whereas the family's social areas and bedrooms could then be located on the lower levels to provide a better view and greater privacy. The master-bedroom is also located at the end of a linear spatial segment but on the main floor (Figure 3.25).

In Legorreta's house in Monte Tauro (Figure 3.26), the maids' quarters are located on the top floor, at the same level as the main bedroom, but placed at the rear and accessible only through a small circular service staircase. This room can be reached only via the kitchen and laundry facilities and, as shown in the spatial diagram (Figure 3.27), its location is in the deepest position within a linear structure. The master-bedroom is also positioned on the top floor but in a better spot, overlooking the garden.

Luis Barragán's famous own house/studio in Tacubaya included three different spatial sequences that are all interconnected, plus a separate entrance

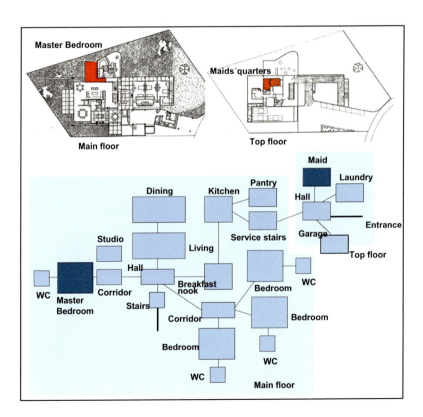

Figure 3.25 Zabludovsky House, Floor Plans (Maids' Quarters and Master-Bedroom in Red) and Spatial Diagram.

Mexican Architecture as Social Status in a System of Consumption

Figure 3.26 Ricardo Legorreta: Casa Monte Tauro in Monte Tauro #270, Lomas de Chapultepec, Mexico City, 1995.

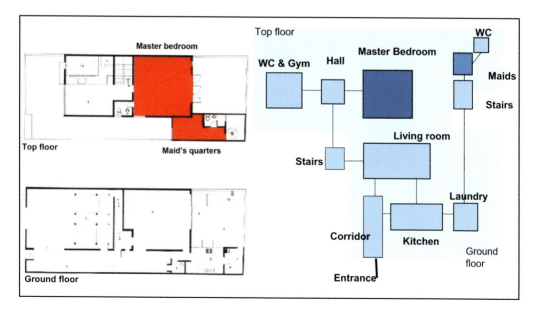

Figure 3.27 Legorreta's House, Floor Plans (Maids' Quarters and Master-Bedroom in Red) and Spatial Diagram.

Mexican Architecture as Social Status in a System of Consumption

sequence belonging to his studio. This was part of Barragán's clear need for privacy. The spatial diagram shows these sequences in various colours, with the servants' areas in green, the family's social areas in aqua, the studio in grey and the private family areas in blue (Figure 3.28). All these sequences use a hall or corridor in a fan disposition that provide control over the various alternative paths on offer. At the end of each sequence is the master-bedroom for his own use, plus the maids' quarters for the servants' area. It is important to point out that the

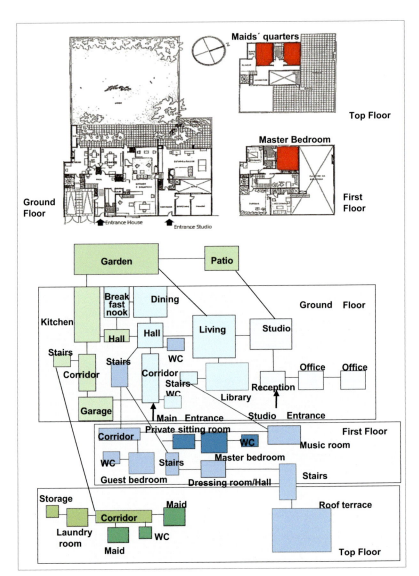

Figure 3.28 Luis Barragán: Casa Estudio Tacubaya, Floor Plan (Maids' Quarters and Master-Bedroom in Red) and Spatial Diagram.

Mexican Architecture as Social Status in a System of Consumption

servants' area is the most secluded, with its own entrance through the garage and its own service stairs. This guaranteed that the paths between the owners and their hired help would never cross.

The design for Casa GGG (Figure 3.30) by Alberto Kalach is an example of a truly elite residence, with a separation between the servants' area and the family area, as in the previous houses. Here, the servants' area is located on the lowest level and the maids' quarters are the last cells in this spatial sequence (Figure 3.29). In Mexico, most houses or apartments that include servants' areas usually allocate very small spaces for the maids' quarters and use for them very cheap

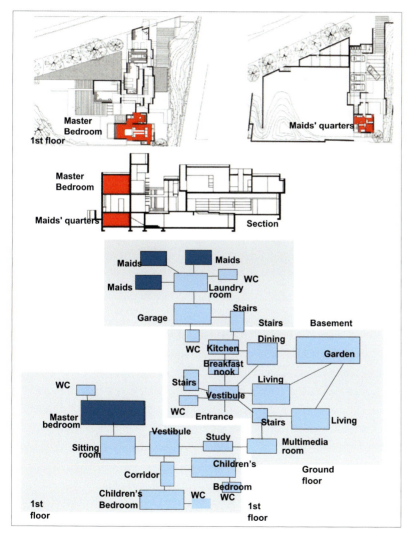

Figure 3.29 Casa GGG, Floor Plans (Maids' Quarters in Red), Section and Spatial Diagram.

Mexican Architecture as Social Status in a System of Consumption

Figure 3.30. Alberto Kalach: Casa GGG, Side view, Mexico City, 2000.

materials in comparison to that of the rest of the house. The same is true in Casa GGG, and the servants' area also has an underprivileged situation in terms of ventilation and views, as can be seen in the plans and sections.

To conclude this chapter, it is, of course, not only domestic architecture that reveals class distinctions in Mexico. Public buildings, such as the Torre Citibank Reforma by Juan José Diaz Infante, or the Hotel Camino Real in Mexico City by Ricardo Legorreta, also reveal how architecture is used to define social classes by isolating, marginalizing and controlling the spaces given to service workers and other lower-status groups (Figure 3.31).

The Torre Citibank Reforma is a typically modern, open-plan office block, and although all of the office space is theoretically accessible to the cleaning staff, that

Mexican Architecture as Social Status in a System of Consumption

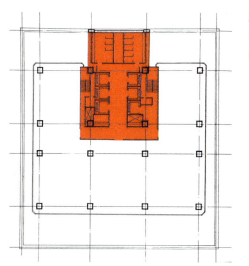

Figure 3.31 Torre Citibank Reforma, Floor Plan (Service Areas in Red).

Figure 3.32 Juan José Díaz Infante: Torre Citibank Reforma, Mexico City, 1989.

is only ever allowed to happen in the evening, after office hours. The spaces that are reserved as service areas are tiny and are either located at the rear near to the bathrooms and stairway or else in the basement floors next to the car parking area (Figure 3.32).

The Hotel Camino Real by Ricardo Legorreta likewise delineates social classes by giving the predominant and more capacious spaces to higher-class groups – in this case the hotel guests – and by relegating and scaling down the locations for service workers. This is evident in its grandiose public spaces, like its lobby (Figure 3.34). There is also a separate rear entrance to the service areas at the back, and in this way, while the hotel staff are always available, they are never seen (Figure 3.33).

Each of these examples established new architectural trends, as well as helping to construction a new social order through spatial techniques and built forms, revealing Mexico's hierarchical society. As a result, Mexican Modernist architecture was turned into interchangeable goods that were part of an economic consumption system wherein a network of signs served to express and sustain social differences. Mexican twentieth-century architecture, like in most parts of the world, was changed from a discipline predicated on ideas of usefulness and functionality, to one that was increasingly the object of the consumption cycle and a sign that symbolized not a sense of 'real' value, but status as part of a process of symbolic-exchange and sign-exchange. Mexican architects were also

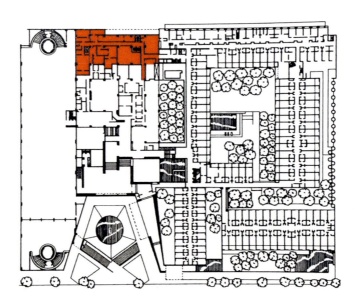

Figure 3.33 The Hotel Camino Real, Floor Plan (Service Areas in Red).

Mexican Architecture as Social Status in a System of Consumption

Figure 3.34 Ricardo Legorreta: The Hotel Camino Real Lobby Showing the Entrance to the Ballroom to the Right and the Front Desk to the Left, Mexico City, 1968.

commodified in the process and were increasingly required to establish social connections to promote their careers. They thus became part of the 'fame-game', designing and manipulating their own images as economic signs and status symbols within the system of consumption.

NOTES

1 Toca, Antonio. 'La Crisis de la Modernidad: Un nuevo fin de siglo'. In Fernando González Gortázar (ed.), *La arquitectura mexicana del siglo XX*. México, Consejo Nacional para la Cultura y las Artes, 1994.
2 The classic Marxist theory of historical materialism establishes a mode of production in every given period as a specific combination of the following factors: productive forces and the social and technical relations of production.
3 This is stated by Jean Baudrillard in Baudrillard, Jean. *The Consumer Society: Myths and structures*. London, Sage Publications, 1998.
4 'Four Logics of The Object' organizes objects in a system of consumption, as explained in Baudrillard, Jean. *For a Critique of the Political Economy of the Sign*. Translated by Charles Levin, London, Verso, 2019, p. 47.
5 Zabludovsky, Abraham. Personal interview with the author. Mexico City, 31st May 2000.
6 Ramírez Ugarte. Alejandro. *Conversación con Luis Barragán*. Guadalajara, Arquitónica, 2015.

Mexican Architecture as Social Status in a System of Consumption

7 Ibid.

8 Eggener, Keith. *Luis Barragán's Gardens of El Pedregal*. New York, Princeton Architectural Press, 2001, p. 25.

9 Ibid., p. 35.

10 Ibid., p. 46.

11 Ibid., pp. 21–22.

12 Ibid., p. 22.

13 Ibid.

14 Ibid., p. 23.

15 Sordo Madaleno, Javier. Personal interview with the author. Mexico City, 27th May 2000.

16 This semiotic reading is offered in Jean Baudrillard's many writings. See: Baudrillard, Jean. *Jean Baudrillard: Selected Writings*. Edited by Mark Poster, London, Polity Press, 1988.

17 de Buen, Clara. Personal interview with the author. Mexico City, 16th October 2000.

18 Mijares, Carlos. Personal interview with the author. Mexico City, 30th May 2000.

19 Sordo Madaleno, Javier. Personal interview with the author. Mexico City, 27th May 2000.

20 Kalach, Alberto. Personal interview with the author. Mexico City, 26th May 2000.

21 Williamson, Roxanne Kuter. *American Architects and the Mechanics of Fame*. Austin, University of Texas Press, 1991.

22 Gropius, Walter. *Scope of Total Architecture*. New York, Collier Books, 1962.

23 Dunster, David. 'Some Thoughts on Fame and the Institution of Architecture'. In Julia Chance and Torsten Schmiedeknecht (eds.), *Fame +Architecture (Architectural Design)*. London, Wiley-Academy. Vol. 71. No. 6, November 2001, p. 11.

24 Williamson, Roxanne Kuter. *American Architects and the Mechanics of Fame*. Austin, University of Texas Press, 1991, p. 230.

25 Stevens, Garry. *The Favoured Circle: The Social Foundations of Architectural Distinction*. London, MIT Press, 1998, p. 100.

26 Dunster, David. 'Some Thoughts on Fame and the Institution of Architecture'. In Julia Chance and Torsten Schmiedeknecht (eds.), *Fame +Architecture (Architectural Design)*. London, Wiley-Academy. Vol. 71. No. 6, November 2001, p. 34.

27 Chance, Julia. 'The Face of Jacques Herzog'. In Julia Chance and Torsten Schmiedeknecht (eds.), *Fame +Architecture (Architectural Design)*. London, Wiley-Academy. Vol. 71. No. 6, November 2001, p. 50.

28 Hernández, Agustín. Personal interview with the author. Mexico City, 17th March 2000.

29 Mijares, Carlos. Personal interview with the author. Mexico City, 30th May 2000.

30 Kalach, Alberto. Personal interview with the author. Mexico City, 26th May 2000.

31 de Garay, Graciela. *Historia Oral de la Ciudad de México, Testimonios de sus arquitectos (1940–90): Abraham Zabludovsky Investigación y entrevista*. México, Instituto Mora 1995.

32 Trueblood, Beatriz. *Ramírez Vázquez en la arquitectura: Realización y diseño*. México, Editorial Diana, 1989.

33 Zabludovsky, Abraham. Personal interview with the author. Mexico City, 31st May 2000.

34 Ramírez Vázquez, Pedro. Personal interview with the author. Mexico City, 29th March 2000.

35 Zabludovsky, Abraham. Personal interview with the author. Mexico City, 31st May 2000.

36 Ibid.

37 Gómez, Lilia and Miguel Ángel Quevedo. 'Entrevista con el arquitecto Juan O'Gorman'. In *Testimonios Vivos 20 arquitectos*. México, Cuadernos de arquitectura 15–16 INBA, Mayo-Agosto 1981.

38 de Buen, Clara. Personal interview with the author. Mexico City, 16th October 2000.

39 Sordo Madaleno, Javier. Personal interview with the author. Mexico City, 27th May 2000.

40 Legorreta, Ricardo. Personal interview with the author. Mexico City, 16th October 2000.

41 Gómez, Lilia and Miguel Ángel Quevedo. 'Entrevista con el arquitecto José Villagrán García'. In *Testimonios Vivos 20 arquitectos*. México, Cuadernos de arquitectura 15–16 INBA, Mayo-Agosto 1981.

42 Zabludovsky, Abraham. Personal interview with the author. Mexico City, 31st May 2000.

43 Ibid.

44 Legorreta, Ricardo. Personal interview with the author. Mexico City, 16th October 2000.

45 de Buen, Clara. Personal interview with the author. Mexico City, 16th October 2000.

46 Ibid.

47 McDowell, Linda. *Gender, Identity and Place*. Cambridge, Polity Press, 1999.

48 Carsten, Janet and Stephen Hugh-Jones. Quoted in Linda McDowell, *Gender, Identity and Place*. Cambridge, Polity Press, 1999.

49 Eggener, Keith. *Luis Barragán's Gardens of El Pedregal*. New York, Princeton Architectural Press, 2001, p. 127.

50 This has been argued by figures such as Henri Lefebvre.

51 Dovey, Kim. *Framing Places: Mediating Power in Built Form*. London, Routledge, 1999.

52 de Garay Arellano, Graciela. *Historia Oral de la Ciudad de México*, Testimonios de sus arquitectos (1940 90) Abraham Zabludovsky Investigación y entrevista. México City, Instituto Mora, 1995, p. 57.

4

Mexican Architecture and Gender

DOI: 10.4324/9781003318934-5

Mexican Architecture and Gender

In numerous countries around the world during the twentieth century, women began to participate in what had previously been an almost exclusively male-dominated architectural discipline. Not surprisingly, therefore, an important part of the making of Mexican Modernist architecture was shaped by gender issues. It was also during the twentieth century that gender configurations and their social system of meanings that encode sexual difference underwent profound changes worldwide, and again Mexico was no exception. To begin an analysis of Mexican Modernist architecture in terms of gender, it is necessary to acknowledge that, although the architecture discipline was traditionally immune to gender or sexual issues by relying on geometry and technological elements,[1] gender played indeed a very active role. Gender can be found at every level of architectural discourse, in, for example, its rituals of legitimation, in its hiring practices or in its professional ethics, to name a few.[2] It is also important to acknowledge that architecture, as an object, is never experienced by a neutral body.[3] The body, just as much as the building, forms part of the system of meaning and representation whereby architecture actively participates in maintaining gendering patterns.[4] With these thoughts in mind, this chapter will identify some of the gender issues present within the social and cultural mechanisms of Mexican twentieth-century architecture by revealing it as a gendered discipline, as a gendered profession, as well as a gendering artefact that played a very important role in shaping and defining male and female roles within Mexican culture.

Gender issues deal with the struggle in power relations within society related to women and men, and to the ways in which they interrelate their differences, particularly in terms of the spatial marginalization that it produces for females.[5] However, it is also important to recognize that gender relations are at the base of all relations of power, hierarchy and inequality, and cannot be understood simply as a dichotomy of dual male/female categories, since there are obviously still other variables, such as social class, race and religion. All these intersectional issues are especially relevant today in twenty-first century Mexico due to an increasingly strong female participation that is making claims for greater social justice and for a new urban order that would be more inclusive.

MEXICAN ARCHITECTURE AS A GENDERED DISCIPLINE

Architecture as a practice and an object has never been gender neutral. It was frequently portrayed in Greek Classicism as a beautiful woman. Architecture

Mexican Architecture and Gender

as a discipline was, hence, also gendered by classical academic theory, which proposed that a house was itself feminine and that the architect, by using the principles derived by his mind, could control the excesses in its use of matter and prescribe appropriate places for domestic activities. The feminine materiality of buildings was, hence, seen as being given a masculine order: the body of the building was constructed naked and then clothed by placing on it a thin layer of ornament. In essence, it meant that the task of the Classical architect and of architectural theory was to control ornament by restricting its mobility and domesticating it by defining its proper place.[6]

Ornament, as part of architectural aesthetics, has long been tied to effeminacy and decadence. This tradition continued through to become part of the ideology of Neoclassical architecture, which, into the twentieth century, associated ornament with characteristics deemed as feminine.[7] In Mexico in the early-twentieth century, we can see that ornament and aesthetics were clearly associated with effeminacy, as part of the architect's occupation, and was inferior as such. For this reason, in Mexico, an engineer's job was generally considered manly and superior to that of an architect. Modernism, since it was so heavily based on the rejection of ornament, wished to change this stereotype. José Villagrán García expressed this position clearly when he recalled, 'When I started practicing architecture, I made those that called me engineer, call me architect instead'.[8] For Villagrán, as a functionalist and a member of the first generation of Mexican Modernists, it was extremely important to reinstate the architect's good name by disassociating the architectural profession from the activities of decoration and ornamentation. Villagrán's preoccupation is not present in Mexican Modernists architects of the third and fourth generation, given that gender, social and cultural patterns had by then begun to change.

However, although Neoclassical architectural theory in Mexico was superseded by Modernism, the gendered nature of the profession itself was only slowly addressed, not least because it also remained so male-orientated worldwide. Gradually, therefore, Mexican women found themselves able to enter the architectural profession during the latter part of the twentieth century. From 1939, the year in which María Luisa Dehesa Gomez Farias graduated as Mexico's first female architect, the number of women studying architecture rose steadily.[9] In the 1970s, females began to study architecture in significant numbers, changing Mexican architectural schools by their enrolment. By the late-1980s, the number of women entering architectural courses was expanding significantly internationally,[10] and this situation was replicated, too, in Mexico (Chart 4.1). For instance, in 1977, around 26% of the students studying for bachelor's degrees in Mexican

Mexican Architecture and Gender

architectural schools were female, and by 1999 this percentage had increased one-third, to 33.6% of the cohort. Carlos Mijares affirmed this when he said, 'The situation was different in the 1930s, where there was probably only one girl in architecture in my generation. [When] I entered the school of architecture [at the end of the 1940s] there were only 10 girls and now there are 100 or more'.[11] Nonetheless, the percentage of females on Mexican architectural courses remains lower than on other university courses, where the gender split is 50/50, suggesting therefore that a structural bias still persists in architectural education, as shown in Chart 4.1.

Furthermore, there is a serious structural problem when one looks at what happens to female architects after graduating. Again, this situation is not limited to Mexico, since, once out of school, female architects worldwide have struggled and faced extensive prejudice both on- and off-site. International statistics show that, during the twentieth century, 'the number of women entering schools of architecture is inversely related to the number of women who actually went on to practice architecture. This was mainly due to having fewer work opportunities, lower salaries, more pressure to raise children and far less professional recognition than men with similar experience.'[12] Unfortunately, the same is true in Mexico. Mexican women who study architecture usually abandon their profession or never even practice it, especially after they get married. Agustin Hernandez, who taught architecture at Universidad Anahuac, said that 'The bad thing about women architects is that they get married! They are great students and suddenly I find they got married, and they don't want to know anything about architecture anymore'.[13] Javier Sordo Madaleno also offers a similar explanation: 'I have known from among my female classmates those that were good, but I have lost contact with them. I do not believe this is a problem of talent, but a cultural problem. Women who have a lot of talent, but after they get married, they stop working'.[14]

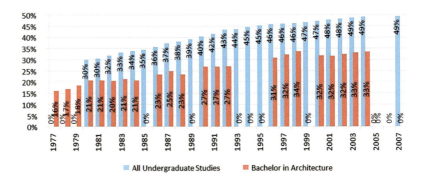

Chart 4.1 Mexican Women's Participation in Undergraduate Studies.

Mexican Architecture and Gender

As noted by Sordo Madaleno, this is an entrenched cultural condition, given that gender roles in Mexico determine to a great degree the extent and manner of participation of men and women in different aspects of Mexican society. Mexico is well known for its tradition of macho men and submissive women. Mexican culture views the man as the breadwinner and the woman as the homemaker. These roles are well-rooted in Mexican society throughout all social classes. Carlos Mijares believes that Mexico's male-dominated society teaches men a manner or behaviour that is very different from that which is taught to, or indeed imposed upon, women.[15] Mijares argues this is not a cultural but a historical condition:

> I would not be so sure that it is due necessarily to machismo. I believe that these were historical circumstances where women not only did not intervene in architecture, but also in many other activities. So, independently of the fact that there are people that are 'machistas', and this is detestable, I do not believe that was the reason women did not participate. These were more complex historical motives and cultural habits, because in countries that are not considered 'machistas', there were no women architects either. It was that way for centuries and not only here.[16]

Perhaps what he said was true, as the situation in Mexico only really began to change towards the end of the twentieth century, due mainly to economic and political transformations in Mexican society that included a real need for a larger number of educated women to become part of the active labour force. During the last two decades of the twentieth century, the rate of women's economic participation slowly increased, as is shown in Chart 4.2 – although it is still low compared to men, and the types of jobs available for women remain heavily limited by cultural prejudices and patterns of discrimination.

As Mexican women started to enter architecture schools and architecture practice in the twentieth century, this prompted the question as to how women might contribute to the architecture profession. In the typical architectural practice of the time, male architects were usually seen as assuming a commanding role, while women architects were expected to be pliable team members within the design and construction process. Hence, these fundamental differences were seen as residing in the way that both sexes approach design, as well as other aspects of the profession. Yet such differences could be recognized in a positive fashion, with women recognizing their own value and using this consciously in their attempts to make a sound contribution to architecture.[17]

Mexican Architecture and Gender

WOMEN AND MEN'S PARTICIPATION IN MEXICAN ECONOMY BY AGE GROUPS IN 1970 AND 1997.												
1970	**12–14**	**15–19**	**20–24**	**25–29**	**30–35**	**35–39**	**40–44**	**45–49**	**50–54**	**55–59**	**60–64**	**65 +**
Women %	7	24	25	18	18	18	17	16	16	15	14	12
Men %	12	50	78	88	87	90	89	89	87	85	77	53
1997	**12–14**	**15–19**	**20–24**	**25–29**	**30–35**	**35–39**	**40–44**	**45–49**	**50–54**	**55–59**	**27.9**	**65 +**
Women %	10.2	31.6	41.9	47.6	47.4	50.8	45.9	44.8	36.4	32.2	27.9	14.8
Men %	24.6	59.6	86	96.8	98.3	98.3	97.9	95.6	92.7	87.5	79.2	52.3

Chart 4.2

Some of the Mexican architects selected in this book did claim to be aware of key 'differences' between female and male architects. Juan O'Gorman, for one, proposed the contribution women can have when stating that:

> Among women there is a lot of intuition, more than amongst men. We hope that someday the world will be handled by them [women], because I believe that it would be better conducted by feminine intuition than by men's rationality. [18]

Javier Sordo Madaleno also declares that 'women definitely have a great sensibility'.[19] However, no one supported more clearly the female contribution to architecture than Ricardo Legorreta:

> I admire their [female] attitude and what they are accomplishing. They, for example, are breaking away from the idea that men have of trying to be superstars. Women are more humble, they accept perfectly to be part of a team with no intentions of being the leader, while men always want to be the team captain. This is a serious problem in Mexico and for the future of so many students that want to become 'star architects'. You must understand that architecture is at this moment the product of teamwork. For me at this moment, both men and women must find out what is their best position within the team, where they play better, and then concentrate on this. [20]

Despite this apparent recognition by Legorreta, during the twentieth century, female architects in Mexico, like in other countries, were usually marginalized into the areas of interior design or small-scale, mainly domestic, architecture. In fact, women have been marginalized even to the point where the key role of women in designing important buildings has often not been acknowledged.[21] For instance, many women architects do not always get equal recognition, particularly those who are partners in firms in which the

Mexican Architecture and Gender

other partners are male. Since many female architects have taken the route of a male-female architectural partnership, which on the surface gives females easier access in a prevailing male profession, this then creates problems in the important issue of authorship.[22] Similarly, publications and other media do not seem to acknowledge women's work on the same level as that of their male partners.

For instance, Clara de Buen, who is a partner in the firm Nuño Mac Gregor de Buen, despite the fact that this joint firm was founded in 1984, declared in her interview that initially she was not even credited for the projects like the Estación del Metro Linea 'A', completed in 1990. Indeed, many of the early designs of the firm were usually credited only to Aurelio Nuño (her husband) as the main 'star architect'. A similar case is that of Alberto Kalach's former wife, Adriana León. During the interview with Alberto Kalach, one of the first things that he did was to acknowledge her as having been one of his female classmates, but he didn't formally recognize her as being part of his firm. When asked if he felt that she might have been discriminated against professionally, he answered, 'No, I don't think so; that you would have to ask her'. Regrettably, I never did get the chance to ask her – but I did later find her picture (Figure 4.1) in a book that she had written, titled *Kalach+Alvarez*, which mentions her as part of the firm's support team, Taller de Arquitectura X, or TAX, but only as a collaborator in some buildings. Still today, her name appears after that of Kalach as part of TAX team.

Perhaps such problems will diminish and evaporate in time. In Mexico, as in many parts of the world during most of the twentieth century, women had a very hard time entering the professional workforce. It was difficult for women to leave their homes and their family duties and break away from the cultural patterns that defined their role in society as housemakers. This required a change in cultural paradigms, as Javier Sordo Madaleno pointed out:

Figure 4.1 Kalach + Álvarez Studio Staff in the 1990s: Daniel Alvarez on the Far Right, Alberto Kalach in the Centre and Adriana León Standing on His Right Side.

Mexican Architecture and Gender

> In Mexico, women study for their degree and many are very talented and could be marvellous architects. But psychologically, I don't know, in Mexico maybe they feel that men will not love them that much or that men would not like to be married to someone famous or to a famous architect. I think that all of this will have to change one day. And sure enough, not everyone will like it, but some will.[23]

Clara de Buen concurs with him, and she explains her experience as a mother, wife to Aurelio Nuño and a partner in their architectural firm:

> It is as if the two things, marriage and architecture, do not go together. I love architecture and I believe that you can combine the two things, the family responsibilities and the professional ones. I believe that this is the same thing that happens to women in any other profession. But it can be done, and I wish that there were more women doing it. I believe it is different for women than for men. I think that there are very modern families that share all the roles, but not in my case, even though Aurelio has always supported me . . . I know that there are men who would not let their wives work or to work with them. Well, I do not know what would bother them more. This is difficult, but I also think that this is something we women must earn . . . I am aware that I am in a privileged situation and that I have been very lucky in having my husband's support.[24]

Still, she feels that working with her husband is also tainted by cultural overtones:

> As for working with my husband, well there are many clients that know we are married, but in a professional relationship this is kept in private. The reason that it bothers me is . . . the minute that they know, suddenly I become the wife, 'La Señora' . . . it is a cultural phenomenon. Their attitude changes: well, not everyone's, but many feel they have to treat me with a certain respect as 'La Señora Nuño'. That is why we try to keep this, at least in the beginning, private.[25]

Clara de Buen exemplifies the way that, in Mexico, being married is considered a dignified state for a woman, since this gives her social credibility and an 'appropriate' and controlled surname. Although she has indeed contributed to this desire for emancipation, de Buen has had to maintain her family duties through the difficult task of juggling both the mother and the professional roles. As she notes:

> I believe women should not give up. If you like what you do, why do you have to abandon it? I have three children between eleven and fifteen, and I am freer now that they

Mexican Architecture and Gender

*do not need me as much as when they were little. That was a period of parenthood
that passes, and in the case of a woman, if she abandons architecture for this period
of 10 or 15 years, then it will be practically impossible to return. You must stay. I had
to divide my day in morning and afternoon. I would work in the office in the morning
trying to stretch time as much as possible, and the afternoons were for my children.
Now that they are older, I have more time to be in the office than before.*[26]

Importantly, Clara de Buen is also aware that gender patterns can be changed.
For instance, before, parents did not allow women to study, but this situation
has changed. She feels that women's role in society can also change, allowing
women to become professional persons: 'I suppose that this will change in time,
because males will study with their female classmates and accept them as their
equal and may marry them and somehow this will change'.[27] Ricardo Legorreta
also believed in promoting this change, when stating:

*Men's domineering passion, and the fact that traditionally men are considered
the only ones that accomplish things, has definitely been negative for women.
This is a disadvantage for women. But in today's environment this will change. I
can tell you that in many architecture studios, and particularly in mine, there is
no prejudice about gender, male or female.*[28]

Despite this statement, Legorreta – father to both a son and a daughter who became architects – replied, when asked why their professional development had
been so different:

*I think that my son is able to dedicate all of his time to architecture, while my
daughter is also a wife and a mother. In other words, she has another line of work
too. She studied photography, and she has taken photographs of all of our work.
She is also an extraordinary critic of architecture and helps us continuously with
her opinions in the interior and sensitive aspects of architecture. This gives her
the time that she needs for her family life and other things. This is the enormous
advantage that I see in the architectural discipline.*[29]

Here is another example of how it is acceptable for women to participate in the
professional arena, but only so long as this does not interfere with their duties
and obligations as wives and mothers, particularly since men were not involved
in child-rearing activities or in household chores during the twentieth century.
Hence, the envelope of professional architectural practice was being pushed to

accommodate the partial participation of women, as long as the traditional gender roles of male and female within family structure still prevailed.

These testimonies illustrate important issues about the situation of Mexican women working in the field of architecture in the twentieth century. Firstly, there is the notion of women as not being as suitable for professional life as their male counterparts. Secondly, there was only partial awareness that males had of the difficulties and discrimination that women encountered in the architectural field as a result of gender-based structures. Therefore, there grew a need, towards the end of the twentieth century, to challenge the notion of architectural practice as a male occupation and as a social construct that embodies male characteristics, as a means to encourage women to decide to participate in the profession and then to reduce the number of female architects who abandon the profession.

ARCHITECTURE AS AN ARTEFACT OF GENDER DIFFERENTIATION

Turning now to the analysis of buildings, it is clear that the idea that built form both affects and reflects social relationships is now widely accepted – as is the concept that space and place are gendered and sexed, and that therefore gender relationships and sexuality are spatially configured.[30] Architectural writers also usually concur that the social construction of gender combines both the material and social relations of symbolic representations that distinguish the masculine from the feminine. In a similar way, 'architectural space is not the container of identities, but a constitutive element in them'.[31] According to Mark Wigley, the US-based architectural historian and theorist, gender is always underpinned by the spatial logic that is masked within architecture. It is precisely here that patriarchal order is constructed, and the place where this is most evident is the house. The house is the stereotypical feminine space, particularly the sexualized, emotionalized, personalized, privatized, erratic sphere of the home and the bedchamber, as opposed to the structured, impersonal public realm.[32] For instance, houses are often thought of as bodies that share common features and fates, which affect our gender and our sense of self. Wigley writes, 'If people construct houses and make them in their own image, so also do they use these houses and houses-image to construct themselves as individuals and as groups'.[33]

Public buildings are also designed assuming a spatial distribution of the sexes which allocated spaces for men's use and for women's use, frequently distinguishable by evident signs of status. A good example is the differentiation in spaces given within the office environment to the manager, who is usually a man, and to his secretary, who is usually a female. This is also true for the segregated areas allocated to men and women in sports arenas and other public facilities. Buildings such as monasteries and convents are the most obvious examples, but so are schools and clubs that are strictly intended for one gender only. Such buildings, because of their association with one sex, exclude the other sex, such as pool halls or certain bars for women; and, for many men, perhaps the child health clinic and the maternity ward.[34] The social and cultural construction of gender relations is also linked with class and ethnic divisions that also form part of the social construction of particular versions of gendered identities in different places. Since it is now widely accepted that 'space and place are gendered and sexed, and that gender relations and sexuality are indeed spaced',[35] it is also important to acknowledge that, as cultures change, so does the gendering of spaces and places. Therefore, it is helpful to present examples from Mexican Modernism that show the role of architecture and the architect in producing gendered identities and to look at their consequent effects on building design and on gendered cultural patterns.

Women's Place in Mexican Architecture

A cultural- and gender-specific version of a space for a woman is the house, given that females are so often used to personify the concept of 'home' – the latter sharing the same characteristics as those assigned to a woman/mother/lover.[36] Typically, the specific places conceived for women within the house are the bedroom and the kitchen. In Mexico, as in many other countries, the bedroom is considered a private and intimate space, and as such is usually located as far away from the outside world as possible. The traditional Mexican house plan revolved around a patio, with the living areas in the front and the bedrooms in the middle, with little privacy. The bedrooms were sometimes even part of a spatial sequence that needed to be crossed to get to the kitchen. In other cases, the bedrooms were placed at the rear of a dwelling, on an upper floor, to give them more privacy, surveillance and control. High-status single-family houses clearly offered more variety in the disposition of the bedrooms, but generally corresponded to the same cultural pattern. Indeed, the analysis of the different housing solutions designed by all four generations of Mexican Modernist architects shows that they consistently relied on these received methods, either placing the bedrooms around a patio if adopting a more traditional layout or else locating them at the rear of the dwelling and on the top floors if it was a more contemporary arrangement.

The other space in the house that is usually allocated to women in homes around the world is the kitchen. Kitchens were long considered as part of the area

Mexican Architecture and Gender

for servants within Mexican dwellings, so were customarily placed at the rear of the ground floor. This typical distribution placed the kitchens and the women who worked there in the deepest cell within the house's spatial diagram. This can be compared to the 'reverse buildings' such as hospitals or prisons that locate their inhabitants in their deepest segment to increase the level of supervision and restraint. The different housing designs by the selected Mexican Modernist architects indeed reveal that the traditional tendency of placing kitchens at the rear gradually changed into their becoming part of the social area of the house, sometimes regardless of social status. Luis Barragán's adaptation of his existing family's holiday home in Chapala in 1931 (Figure 4.2), demonstrates the traditional model. Here, the bedrooms are placed on the top floor for privacy, with the typical balcony placed for surveillance of the street. The kitchen also obeyed Mexican tradition and is located in the floor plan at the rear, behind the patio, as part of the servants' area.

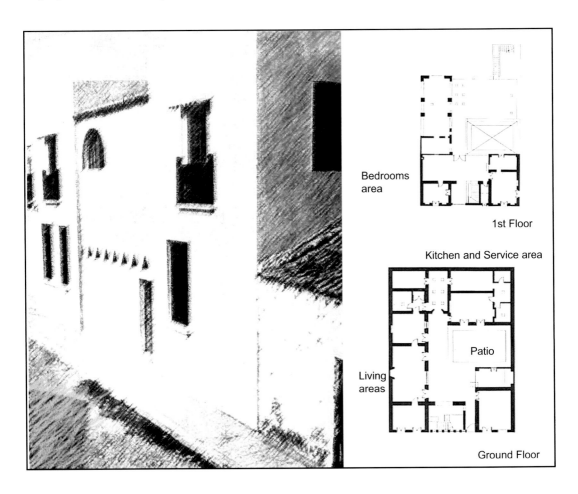

Figure 4.2 Luis Barragán: Family Holiday House, Chapala, Altered in 1931.

Mexican Architecture and Gender

Casa Efraín González Luna (Figure 4.4), also designed by Barragán, is widely considered to be his most important work from the period before the Second World War. Here, the central corridor acts as the visual axis that connects the front vestibule all the way to the rear patio and its loggia, while at the same time separating the living and dining areas to the right from the bedrooms to the left. Barragán used a central axis to separate the different spatial sections with a central route as the main distributor through which all paths must cross. As shown by the spatial diagram for this dwelling (Figure 4.3), the bedrooms, although interconnected, are separated from the main axis and do not surround the patio. The kitchen also appears to be slightly more segregated than in traditional layouts, with its only access being via the dining room and pantry or from the outside rear through the patio. This indicates the high status of this family that wished to keep the hired help well out of sight, while prominent spaces with the utmost privacy and hierarchy are the family chapel and library located on the upper floor, over the living room.

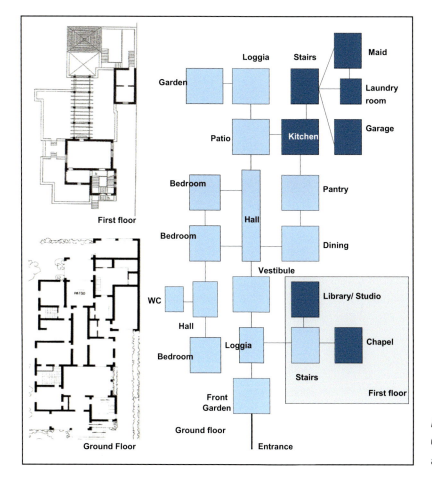

Figure 4.3 Casa Efraín González Luna, Floor Plan and Spatial Diagram.

Mexican Architecture and Gender

Figure 4.4 Luis Barragán: Casa Efraín González Luna, Guadalajara, 1928.

Two much later designs by Luis Barragán also reveal his preference for domestic privacy and seclusion. In the Casa Gilardi, completed in 1976, he again used a central axis, this time to separate off the servants' area, including the kitchen and maid's room, but this time primarily to create a more dramatic entrance into the dining room right at the back (Figure 4.5), with its internal pool and dramatic red wall as the main focus (Figure 4.6). The living room is located on the floor above, along with one of the bedrooms, while the other two bedrooms are given still more privacy by being up on the topmost floor (Figure 4.7).

Mexican Architecture and Gender

Figure 4.5 Luis Barragán: Gilardi House, Mexico City, 1976.

Mexican Architecture and Gender

Figure 4.6 Luis Barragán: Gilardi House, Swimming Pool, Mexico City, 1976.

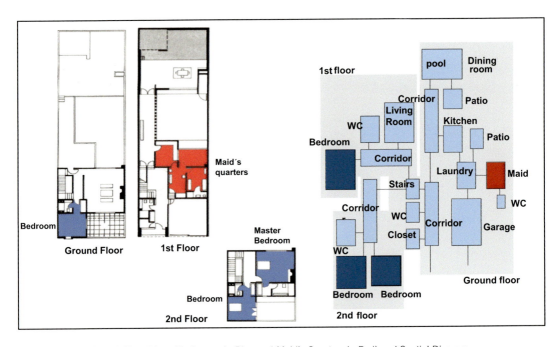

Figure 4.7 Casa Gilardi, Floor Plans (Bedrooms in Blue and Maid's Quarters in Red) and Spatial Diagram.

Mexican Architecture and Gender

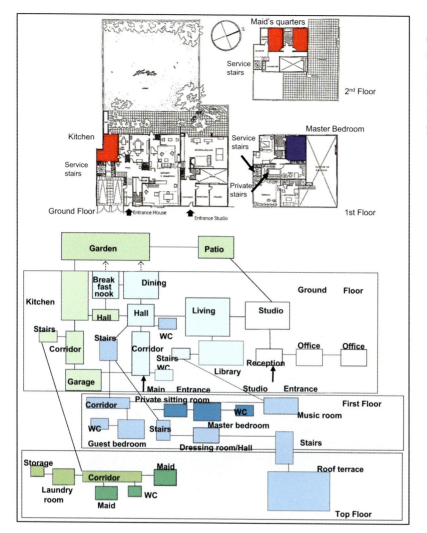

Figure 4.8 Barragán's Casa Estudio Tacubaya, Floor Plans (Master-Bedroom in Blue and the Kitchen and Maid's Quarters in Red) and Spatial Diagram.

But perhaps none more than Barragán's own house/studio in Tacubaya exemplifies his need of privacy and seclusion for the female areas within the dwellings, echoing the points made about the house in the previous chapter. By creating different spatial sequences, Barragán maintains the autonomy of each (Figure 4.8). For instance, only the hired help is allowed to go through servants' rooms like the kitchen, or up to the maids' quarters and laundry rooms; whereas the route that leads into the master-bedroom is kept private through its own staircase (Figure 4.9). In this design, the kitchen is located in the most inconspicuous corner, which can only be entered through the garage or via a private breakfast nook.

Mexican Architecture and Gender

Figure 4.9 Luis Barragán: Casa Estudio Tacubaya, Mexico City, 1947.

More recent examples, such as Enrique Norten's Casa LE, which were designed for younger families, defy the tradition layout and adopt a much more modern lifestyle. For instance, in Casa LE, the location of the kitchen between the living room and dining room keeps the woman (or perhaps the man) who is using this space in close contact with those adjacent spaces (Figure 4.11). Privacy and hierarchy are still given to the bedrooms, particularly the location of the master-bedroom at the end of the spatial sequence, as shown in the spatial diagram, with a balcony again overlooking the street (Figure 4.10).

Mexican Architecture and Gender

Figure 4.10 Enrique Norten: Casa LE, Mexico City, 1996.

Figure 4.11 Casa LE, Floor Plans (Bedrooms in Blue and Kitchen in Red) of the Spatial Diagram.

Mexican Architecture and Gender

Alongside these examples of the single-family house, the design of Mexican Modernist apartment blocks also offered gendering spaces. Although multi-family dwellings first appeared in Mexico City in the form of *'vecindarios'* in the late-nineteenth century, when old colonial monasteries and convents were transformed into multiple housing units, the apartment block as a typology in Mexico was very much a twentieth-century development. Indeed, the erection of apartment blocks truly emerged as a private business investment in the 1940s, in response to Mexico City's rapid growth and at a point when Modernism was starting to dominate. From the 1950s onwards, apartment blocks became part of public urban projects inspired largely by Le Corbusier's ideas for the modern city. From the architects interviewed for this book, Abraham Zabludovsky and Alberto Kalach are perhaps those with the most successful apartment designs, whether as private developments or as public housing projects, and so they can be used as the focus of study.

Zabludovsky, along with Teodoro González de León, completed their famous public project for Torres de Mixcoac in the early-1970s as a complex of 16 towers with three types of arrangement (Figure 4.12). The tallest towers each have four dwellings per floor, with the apartments comprising a combined living/dining area, three bedrooms, a kitchen, patio and maid's quarters. On entering each apartment, there are two possible routes: one for the inhabitants and their visitors

Figure 4.12 Abraham Zabludovsky: Torres de Mixcoac, Mexico City, 1971.

that leads into the living/dining room and beyond, and the other for the family's servant who enters the kitchen and only from there can they get to their quarters. Once again, the bedrooms (and especially the master-bedroom) are kept well away from the servants' area for maximum privacy and seclusion, as is shown in the spatial diagram (Figure 4.14).

Figure 4.13 Abraham Zabludovsky: Torres de Mixcoac, Mexico City, 1971.

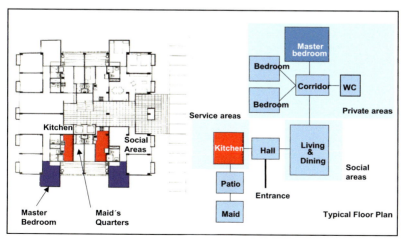

Figure 4.14 Torres de Mixcoac, Floor Plan (Master-Bedroom in Blue and Kitchen in Red) and Spatial Diagram.

Mexican Architecture and Gender

In contrast, the apartments in the Edificio Rodin by Alberto Kalach (Figure 4.15), dating from 1993, offer a far more open spatial arrangement, similar to Norten's Casa LE. Here, the kitchen is placed in a privileged position, near the entrance and overlooking the living room beneath. Consequently, this traditional place for females is given a key vantage point that monitors all type of activities within the dwelling (Figure 4.17).

Thus, for the Edificio Rodin, as in previous examples, the women's role within the house is at least partly determined by their social status. High-status homes with full-time servants usually have closed, isolated kitchens in order to keep the hired help out of sight. However, in more contemporary designs like those by Norten or Kalach, kitchen activities are integrated into the living areas of the house, suggesting perhaps even the participation of men in the kitchen while entertaining their guests.

Looking now at women's place outside the home, it is evident that this poses a threat to the gender patterns that society and culture has assigned them because 'a woman on the outside is implicitly sexually mobile and her sexuality is no longer controlled by the house'.[37] It is common to hear arguments that discourage women from venturing out to public spaces, with the latter being portrayed as dangerous either to security or integrity, with her turning perhaps into a *'mujer de la calle'*

Figure 4.15 Alberto Kalach: Edificio Rodin, Mexico City, 1993.

Mexican Architecture and Gender

Figure 4.16 Edificio Rodin, Detail.

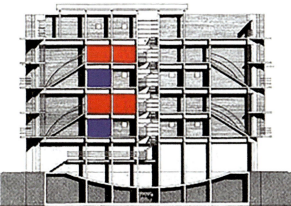

Figure 4.17 Edificio Rodin, Section (Bedroom in Blue and Kitchen/Dining in Red).

('woman from the street'). Carlos Monsiváis, a Mexican writer, has, for instance, written that it is in urban settings that women experience greater repression and violence.[38] Such views only contributed to the notion that woman should remain at home and not be out in the city, thereby reinforcing notions of women as static and men as dynamic. These concepts were certainly prevalent in Mexico in the twentieth century and corresponded to popular narratives in which females generally stayed at home, while males were drawn into heroic exploits and journeys.[39] Of the Modernist architects interviewed, Diaz Infante was one who tried to use ancient history to explain why women had been cast into a static life role:

> *It was women who planted and weaved and looked after the children. In her own body, she has milk and the way of caring for her children. Women made men sedentary because they were formerly like crazy goats. They still wanted to hunt mammoths, as was their duty. But it was women that made cities and pottery and the first water container.*[40]

By the late-twentieth century, there were a growing number of writers challenging this fixed, conventional notion about female social stasis. The British cultural theorist, Elizabeth Wilson, for one, pointed out that, although cities are portrayed as dangerous for women, it is in fact in cities where women have more freedom.[41] This was also true for Mexican women in the twentieth century, since statistics showed that it was at home where women experienced the most frequent and severe violence. Therefore, the home is both a place of conflict as well as rest, and paradoxically, many women had to leave home to forge their own identities.[42] Indeed, in Mexican twentieth-century cultural patterns, this mobility of women seemed to pose a threat to a settled patriarchal order – whether it be by going out to work or simply by becoming hard to find or constrain within the city. Diaz Infante observed this phenomenon in his remarks:

> *Women now have absolute liberty; firstly, they let her go into restaurants in their pyjamas or leotards. Secondly, they let her use pantyhose and she is able to cross her legs. This is a perfect use of her liberty. Women have evolved more than men. Now she is able to have children without a Señor or a man. Forget it, her liberty is scary. If you go to a discotheque, the boys there are scared, while the girls are jumping because women have realized that they can. And this is the way it should be.*[43]

Once outside the home, Mexican women began to occupy spaces that were traditionally exclusively male (albeit some architectural spaces, such as universities or shops, where women were free to enter, carried less explicit gender differences). Within the urban scene in Mexico, the twentieth-century space that was most typically female is that which was assigned to the office secretary or receptionist, who tended almost exclusively to be a woman. Office design in Mexican Modernist architecture followed the prevailing international patterns, which were increasingly for open-plan layouts with only a few senior figures in cellular rooms. Although the open-plan office space might appear to be more egalitarian, this was only on the surface. For, in these office spaces, it was women who typically occupied the 'open-floor' spaces and men more likely to occupy the 'closed-door' spaces.[44] Once the female office worker was placed into this quasi-public space,

Mexican Architecture and Gender

she was no longer protected or secluded, but instead was subjected to the male gaze and objectified by it.[45] Since the secretary's desk was usually placed in the front, close to the lobby or entrance, she was sitting in full view and with no privacy (Figure 4.18). In this way, she was not only controlled and monitored by her superiors, but also acted as a filter for her boss and other office workers higher up the social hierarchy. This may be one of the reasons why it became a common practice in prominent corporations in twentieth-century Mexico, as elsewhere, to hire secretaries according to their physical attractiveness.

Figure 4.18 Ricardo Legorreta: Plaza Reforma Offices, Mexico City, 1993. This Axial Entrance Places the Secretary as the Focal Point.

A clear example of this type of gendered office spaces was Juan José Diaz Infante's Bufete Industrial, completed in 1979 (Figure 4.20). In this building the office managers are located in the rear spaces with their own private bathrooms, whereas the secretary is far more exposed and placed in an open space beside the corridor, near to the open balcony, where – as the section shows – she was subjected even to the view of those working on the floors above (Figure 4.19).

195

Mexican Architecture and Gender

Figure 4.19 Bufete Industrial, Floor Plan and Section (Private Areas in Blue and Public Areas in Red).

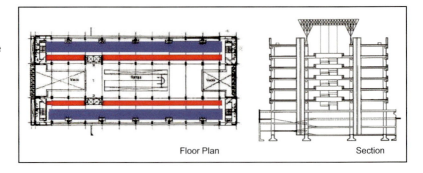

Floor Plan   Section

Figure 4.20 Juan José Díaz Infante: Bufete Industrial, Mexico City, 1979.

These kinds of examples all present spatial evidence of the gendering of space in houses, apartments and offices in twentieth-century Mexico, and of the ways in which women's place was definitely changing, as old patterns were altered and new, internationalized and westernized layouts were reproduced. The gendering of females by the use of space was, of course, also changing because certain spaces previously restricted exclusively to women, like the kitchen, were now also becoming available

Mexican Architecture and Gender

to men – although it must be recognized that this was altering the lives of relatively few Mexican women, who could acquire more mobility as they were part of the middle-class or highest-class urban population.

Men's Place in Mexican Architecture

At this point, it must also be recognized that gendering via space in twentieth-century Mexico pertained to both male and female identities. In other words, places for men were also being developed to create and perpetuate gender patterns and hierarchies. Male and female identities are always relational, since each constructs its identity in relation to the other. For instance, it has been observed that 'women and men grow up with personalities affected by different boundary experiences, different construction of inner and outer worlds and the preoccupation with different relational issues. Female sense of self is one connected to the world while male sense of self is separate, distinct and even disconnected'.[46] According to Octavio Paz, the Mexican poet and diplomat, the classic Mexican male, or macho, is a closed man who shuts himself off to protect himself. This macho is the ideal of manliness that never opens ('*no se raja*') to reveal his real inner self, which would be considered a sign of weakness. This restraint and imperviousness reveals distrust and suspicion of the world and is considered manly and stoic, as opposed to women, who are born open and vulnerable.[47] This seeming need of men to establish boundaries and maintain a closed and protected position within certain spaces can undoubtedly be found in Mexican Modernist architecture.

For instance, Luis Barragán has a distinct preference for domestic privacy and seclusion achieved on many occasions through the use of visual surveillance. His houses express what architecture professor Dörte Kuhlmann states: 'that visual surveillance is inseparably connected to the concept of privateness and privileges',[48] and in his case, also to his own personality. Barragán's own house/studio in Tacubaya offers a perfect, secluded sense of home and of a 'man's castle'. This house, as well as the Casa Gilardi, was designed for a single male owner. Every room in Barragán's home is carefully designed to provide this sense of security. Thus, the master-bedroom is the most protected room; you reach it only after entering the sitting room. Barragán designed special features to provide even more privacy: entrances to each room are guarded, the ceiling height is lowered or a screen is used to obstruct the view. For example, a screen protects access and views into the living room, while a low wall blocks the entrance to his library (Figure 4.21).

Mexican Architecture and Gender

Figure 4.21 A Low Wall Is Used To Divide and Provide Privacy. Luis Barragán: Casa Estudio Tacubaya, Mexico City, 1947.

Staircases also offer vantage points of surveillance. Barragán's most famous staircase leads up to his private music room, where the door does not actually reach the ceiling. It was designed to allow Barragán – he was himself 6 feet 3 inches in height, very tall for a Mexican man – to see down into the room below (Figure 4.22). Most of the staircases in Barragán's own house/studio were similarly left open for observational purposes.

Mexican Architecture and Gender

Figure 4.22 A Low Wall and Door Allow Surveillance From the Top Floor. Luis Barragán: Casa Estudio Tacubaya, Mexico City, 1948.

In the Casa Gilardi, the staircase is, in fact, used to provide seclusion and privacy for the bedrooms on the top floors (Figure 4.23). It allowed the owner to hear the footsteps of anyone approaching and to see him or her before they were allowed inside the most private areas. Once again, in this domestic interior, Luis Barragán – as for Adolf Loos before him – was treating it as a system of defence from the exterior, protecting itself by devising a hierarchy of internal gazes related to the internal circulation route.[49]

Mexican Architecture and Gender

Figure 4.23 An Open Staircase with No Banister Provides Easy Surveillance from Top Floors. Luis Barragán: Casa Gilardi, Mexico City, 1976.

A later, fascinating example of seclusion, but this time with a twist of grandiosity, was Agustin Hernández's own house in Mexico City, dating from 1989. This project was based on what he termed a 'bolt-and-nut' design, with the main body of the house being the bolt that is projected out over a sloping terrain (Figure 4.24). The design wishes to speak with the efficiency of an airplane, boat or even a spacecraft, with its different areas being separated on different levels or decks. The kitchen and servants' area are located down below, the entrance point

Mexican Architecture and Gender

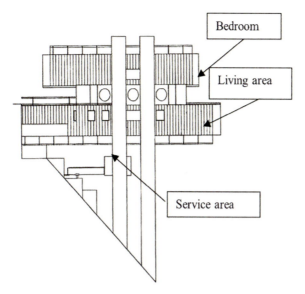

Figure 4.24 Agustín Hernández House, Side Elevation.

and living area is sandwiched in the middle and the private areas like the bedrooms are located on top to emphasize privacy. Hernández thus achieves a desired degree of male protection and hierarchy by defying traditional forms and seeking instead an avant-garde house that mimics a spacecraft in presenting an experience of social order, technological aesthetics and boys' own masculinity (Figure 4.25).

Figure 4.25 Agustín Hernández: His House, Mexico City, 1989.

Mexican Architecture and Gender

Figure 4.26 The Chimney is Used to Block the Direct View of the Studio. Luis Barragán's Studio.

In exploring the gendered mentality of the Mexican Modernist architects selected for this book, their own architectural offices also serve as excellent examples of the male need for seclusion and protection, as well as for a sense of hierarchy and dominance. Barragán's own studio was again a clear example of a secluded and protected place, being located just behind his living room, with its entrance screened by a low wall containing the fireplace (Figure 4.26).

Mexican Architecture and Gender

Figure 4.27 Luis Barragán: Casa Estudio Tacubaya, Exterior Studio Entrance, Mexico City, 1948.

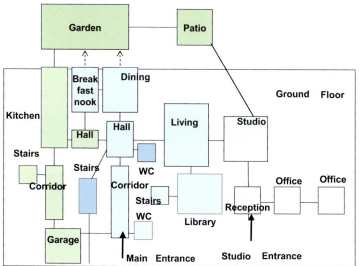

Figure 4.28 Luis Barragán's Studio, Spatial Diagram of Ground Floor Showing the Entrance to the House on the Left and the Entrance to the Studio on the Right.

There was also an entrance to the studio from the street, which meant a reception area needed to be crossed before reaching it (Figure 4.27). The spatial diagram of his combined house/studio (Figure 4.28) reveals the use of a linear syntactic structure in which the studio is placed at the end of the domestic sequence, and his own personal office was placed at the end of the studio sequence, thus indicating his status, power and control as a world-famous architect.

Mexican Architecture and Gender

Figure 4.29 Entrance to Ricardo Legorreta's Office. Ricardo Legorreta: His Studio, Mexico City, 1997.

In the case of Ricardo Legorreta's, the evident need in his own office for protection and seclusion was likely inspired by the precedent of Barragán's house/studio. Legorreta had an independent building for his architectural office, situated on a slope and with its entrance down several flights of stairs, emphasizing a sense of shelter (Figure 4.29).

Mexican Architecture and Gender

Figure 4.30 Reception Area of Ricardo Legorreta's Studio. To the Left and on a Lower Level, His Private Secretary and Office. To the Right, the Stairs that Lead to the Studio.

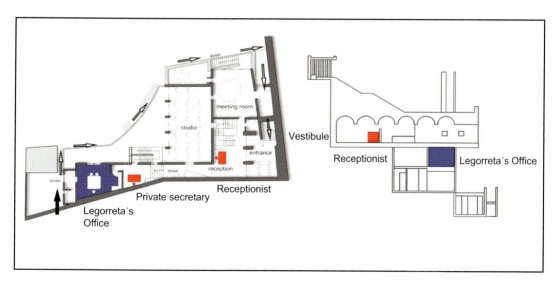

Figure 4.31 Ricardo Legorreta's Studio, Floor Plan (Reception in Red and Legorreta's Office in Blue) and Section (Reception Area in Red and Legorreta's Office in Blue).

205

Mexican Architecture and Gender

Figure 4.32 Abraham Zabludovsky: His Studio, Mexico City, 1992.

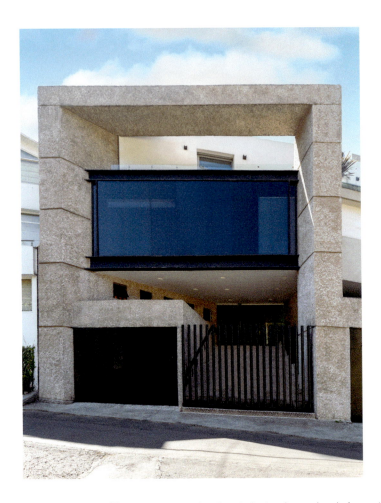

His private office space was also located at a lower level, in a strategic position far away from the entrance, screened by a receptionist and guarded by his personal secretary, who was kept out of view by an inclined wall and positioned at a lower level. The floor plan and photo (Figure 4.30 and Figure 4.31) reveal that Legorreta's own office room was located at the end of a sequence of careful spatial segments that provided both status and privacy, helping to establish a male sense of place and identity. Hierarchy and surveillance were also made evident by locating the atelier or studio on a lower level, where Legorreta could supervise his assistants from the main floor, allowing him visual control.

Abraham Zabludovsky's own office room (Figure 4.32) was suspended above the entrance of his Brutalist office building, as built in the early-1990s, allowing him unimpeded surveillance over any visitors as well as the surrounding landscape. This arrangement, however, did not then offer him visual control over his employees, since the main studio, located on the opposite side, followed the

Mexican Architecture and Gender

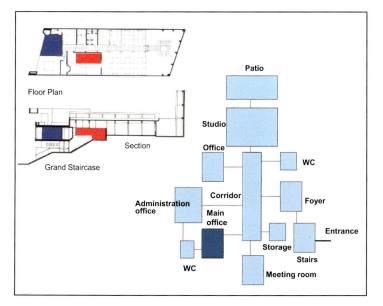

Figure 4.33 Abraham Zabludovsky's Studio, Floor Plan, Section (Reception Area in Red and Zabludovsky's Office in Blue) and Spatial Diagram.

building's central axis. But a sense of real drama and anticipation is created by the building's grandiose entrance (Figure 4.33), with its wide staircase leading to a reception/waiting area that is screened by the female receptionist.

An even more astonishing design is that for Juan José Diaz Infante's own house/office that was built after the earthquake of 1985 to be an anti-seismic building stabilized by three-dimensional trusses. Regrettably, this building was dismantled after Diaz Infante's death in 2012. His own private office – called 'La Geoda', short for geodesic dome, as popularized by Buckminster Fuller – was positioned within the open space of a three-storey structure (Figure 4.35). La Geoda

Figure 4.34 Juan José Díaz Infante: His Studio, Inside the Geodesic Sphere, Mexico City, 1990.

Mexican Architecture and Gender

Figure 4.35 Juan José Díaz Infante: His House and Studio, Mexico City, 1990.

gave him a very male sense of protection and hierarchy. Using a spiral-staircase, one had to venture across a suspended bridge to get to his spherical office – creating a sense of surprise as well as adventure. However, once inside his office, you did not feel at all threatened by its height because the space was closed off and did not allow you to see any of its surroundings (Figure 4.34).

A similar sense of adventure was required if one wanted to enter Agustin Hernández's office. Surveillance is an obvious element that guarantees protection and defence, and thus the gaze becomes an important element in the

Mexican Architecture and Gender

Figure 4.36 Agustín Hernández: His Studio, Mexico City, 1976.

construction of male identity. Hernandez's own studio operated mainly by control and domination through vision, with the tree-like structure of this building dictating the hierarchy of its interior spaces and uses (Figures 4.36). The difficulty of even entering the office was like an initiation process in which one must literally walk the plank (there are no protective handrails) to reach the front door (Figure 4.37). Once inside, a central spiral staircase offers the only access up to the main floor where the studio is located, and then to the even-more-private top floors.

Again, the spatial diagram reveals how Hernandez's own office room was given seclusion by being located on a higher level, while at the same time allowing him visual control over his employees (Figure 4.38). By looking at the building's spatial distribution as a linear syntactic structure, we can see how his private

Mexican Architecture and Gender

Figure 4.37 The Daring Entrance to Agustín Hernández Studio.

spaces were placed on the uppermost level where he could step out onto an open terrace with no railings or sense of restraint. Here, one is both secluded and given a sense of status and control, a feeling of being on the top of the world. The use of the gaze inside Hernandez's office thus worked as a closed and controlling mechanism, whereas on the outside, the gaze becomes an omnipresent sensation that,

Mexican Architecture and Gender

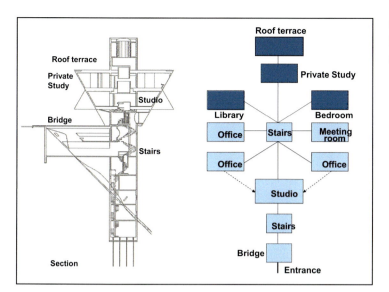

Figure 4.38 Agustín Hernández Office, Section and Spatial Diagram.

far from objectivising others, created an almost daredevil experience of freeing up the body – not at all suitable for those suffering from agoraphobia or vertigo.

In each of the examples presented here, we can see how this Modernist architecture played an important gendering role through its use of space and the hierarchy constructed through vision and position and levels of protection. In some cases, the location of spaces generated a sense of seclusion and safety, reinforcing the male need for privacy; whilst in others, techniques of visual surveillance provided hierarchy and a feeling of domination. Notably, however, not all the male architects interviewed seemed to feel this same need for protection, seclusion, control or domination, and so it must partly be due to individual psychology, as well. An interesting counter-example of an office space that holds no sense of hierarchy is the workplace of Nuño, Mac Gregor and De Buen's, where, perhaps due to the fact that all three architects hold an equal partnership and the fact that one of them is female, means that the spatial hierarchy based on that of a traditional late-nineteenth Mexican patio house, as shown in Figure 4.39, was transformed into an office that acts as a site of teamwork and collaboration.

Here, the spatial diagram reveals how the linear syntactic diagram typical of an older Mexican house was transformed into a fan-like spatial structure that, in effect, reuses the patio as its foyer. The office rooms are thus distributed around this patio: all of them have the same importance, giving no partner a higher status in relation to their role or gender. The three partners, indeed, share the spaces with specific functions as the main office, meeting room, reception area and – in what was customarily the servants' area at the rear – a kitchenette and storage

Mexican Architecture and Gender

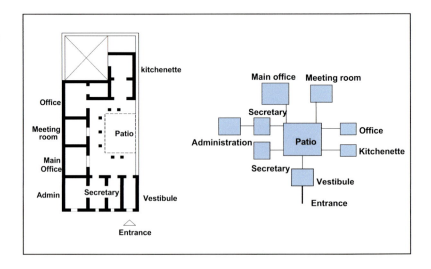

Figure 4.39 Nuño, Mac Gregor and de Buen's studio, Mexico City, Floor Plan and Spatial Diagram.

space. This example demonstrates how Modernist architecture can also develop new cultural patterns that do not perpetuate existing gender archetypes, helping to break the banally simple gender codes that have been reinforced for too long by architects.

To conclude, this chapter has shown that gender issues made an important contribution to Mexican Modernist architecture. As Mexican society changed during the twentieth century, so did its architecture, and new conditions evolved regarding gender roles and buildings. Examinations of this topic are still deeply relevant, as we all live in man-made environments in which it is not understood just how much women have been excluded.[50] Since our built environment affects our identity and our sense of gender, it is important to break this cycle by encouraging wider and more active female participation in its design. Thankfully, there is some evidence of changes in building designs and spatial dispositions that break with the traditional gendering of spaces, as, for instance, at an ordinary level through open kitchens that give women a new perspective and encourage men to participate in household chores. Nuño, Mac Gregor and De Buen's office is a further example of how Mexican gender patterns may be altered by built form; in that case, an office in which partnership at last goes beyond gender, however imperfectly.

Twentieth-century transformation in culture and in gendered configurations created the need to address gender issues within the Mexican architectural profession for three main reasons. Firstly, there was an increased participation from new generations of women studying and practicing architecture, especially towards the end of the century. Secondly, this exposed the unequal treatment and

Mexican Architecture and Gender

discrimination that female architects suffered in their careers. Thirdly were the critiques of established gender patterns and paradigms that were so prevalent within the profession, given that Mexican architecture continued to be gendered and exercised mainly by men. This provoked a persistent and growing dissatisfaction among women and the desire to motivate change in people who were intolerant, irrational or unwilling to reject old paradigms to construct newer ones. Therefore, it became imperative for women to be heard and noticed for them to become role models for future generations, as well as to debunk the unfortunate ideology that existed within Mexico's architectural profession. Conditions for female architects in Mexico have continued to improve marginally in the first decades of the twenty-first century, but it remains an unfinished project. For, unless women's viewpoint is heard more loudly in Mexican architecture and their participation is felt more clearly, there is little hope for change and for further intervention of female architects in the design of a better-built environment.[51]

NOTES

1 Ingraham, Catherine. 'Losing It in Architecture in Hughes'. In *The Architect Reconstructing Her Practice*. Cambridge, MIT Press, 1996.
2 Wigley, Mark. 'Untitled: The Housing of Gender'. In Beatriz Colomina (ed.), *Sexuality and Space*. New York, Princeton Architectural Press, 1992, p. 329.
3 Colomina, Beatriz (ed.). *Sexuality and Space*. New York, Princeton Architectural Press, 1992.
4 The body is closely related to architecture and built form, as are our gestures, clothes and the freedom with which we are able to move in space. See Grosz, Elizabeth. *Volatile Bodies: Towards a Corporeal Feminism, eBook*. London, Routledge, 2020.
5 There have been two principal ways that summed up the relationship between men and women, the first one as women having a subordinate status and the second one as women being 'different' or the 'Other'. See Porter, E. *Women and Moral Identity*. Sydney, Allen & Unwin, 1991 and Beauvoir, Simone. *The Second Sex*. Translated by Constance Borde and Sheila Malvonay-Chevallier, New York, Vintage Books, Random House, 2011.
6 Wigley, Mark. 'Untitled: The Housing of Gender'. In Beatriz Colomina (ed.), *Sexuality and Space*. New York, Princeton Architectural Press, 1992.
7 Schor, Nahomi. *Reading in Detail: Aesthetics and the Feminine*. London/New York, Routledge, 2007, p. 49.
8 Gómez, Lilia and Miguel Ángel Quevedo. 'Entrevista con el arquitecto José Villagrán García'. In *Testimonios Vivos 20 arquitectos*. México, Cuadernos de arquitectura 15–16 INBA, Mayo–Agosto 1981.
9 Hurtado Azpeitia, María Eugenia. 'Mujeres en la Arquitectura'. In *Enlace*. México, Colegio de Arquitectos de la Cd. de México A.C., 2013, p. 126.

Mexican Architecture and Gender

10 Lorenz, Clare. *Women in Architecture: A Contemporary Perspective*. New York, Rizzoli, 1990.

11 Mijares, Carlos. Personal interview with the author. Mexico City, 30th May 2000.

12 Doubilet, Susan. 'P/A Reader Poll: Women in Architecture'. *Progressive Architecture*. Vol. 70. No. 10, 1989, pp. 15–17.

13 de Buen, Clara. Personal interview with the author. Mexico City, 16th October 2000.

14 Sordo Madaleno, Javier. Personal interview with the author. Mexico City, 27th May 2000.

15 Monsiváis, Carlos. 'Lo Sagrado y lo Profano: México, Identidad y Cultura'. In *Identidad Nacional*. México, Universidad Autónoma Metropolitano, 1994.

16 Mijares, Carlos. Personal interview with the author. Mexico City, 30th May 2000.

17 These ideas were expressed by Margrit Kennedy, a German architect who has studied feminine and masculine values in architecture and has stressed their mutual importance in terms of an all-inclusive design process that could combine these values. See Lorenz, Clare. *Women in Architecture: A Contemporary Perspective*. New York, Rizzoli, 1990, p. 25.

18 Gómez, Lilia and Miguel Ángel Quevedo. 'Entrevista con el arquitecto Juan O'Gorman'. In *Testimonios Vivos 20 arquitectos*. México, Cuadernos de arquitectura 15–16 INBA, Mayo–Agosto 1981.

19 Sordo Madaleno, Javier. Personal interview with the author. Mexico City, 27th May 2000.

20 Legorreta, Ricardo. Personal interview with the author. Mexico City, 16th October 2000.

21 'Women, Architecture and Identity' – Personal Details, Stuart Hall with others, interview with Denise Scott Brown, BBC Open University, 1992.

22 Rendell, Jane. 'Introduction'. In Jane Rendell, Barbara Penner, and Iain Borden (eds.), *Gender, Space, Architecture*. London, Routledge, 2000, p. 228.

23 Sordo Madaleno, Javier. Personal interview with the author. Mexico City, 27th May 2000.

24 de Buen, Clara. Personal interview with the author. Mexico City, 16th October 2000.

25 Norten, Enrique. Personal interview with the author. Mexico City, 30th May 2000.

26 de Buen, Clara. Personal interview with the author. Mexico City, 16th October 2000.

27 Ibid.

28 Norten, Enrique. Personal interview with the author. Mexico City, 30th May 2000.

29 Legorreta, Ricardo. Personal interview with the author. Mexico City, 16th October 2000.

30 MacDowell, Linda. *Gender, Identity and Place*. Cambridge, Polity Press, 1999, p. 135.

31 Durning, Louise and Richard Wrigley. *Gender and Architecture*. Chichester, John Wiley and Sons, 2000, p. 1.

32 Wigley, Mark. 'Untitled: The Housing of Gender'. In Beatriz Colomina (ed.), *Sexuality and Space*. New York, Princeton Architectural Press, 1992.

33 Carsten, Janet and Stephen Hugh-Jones. Quoted in McDowell, Linda. *Gender, Identity and Place*. Cambridge, Polity Press, 1999, p. 93.

34 McDowell, Linda. *Gender, Identity and Place*. Cambridge, Polity Press, 1999.

Mexican Architecture and Gender

35 Probyn, Elspeth. 'The Body Which Is Not One: Speaking an Embodied Self'. *Hypatia*. Vol. 6. No. 3, Fall 1991.

36 Massey, Doreen. *Space, Place and Gender*. Cambridge, Polity Press, 1994, p. 10.

37 Wigley, Mark. 'Untitled: The Housing of Gender'. In Beatriz Colomina (ed.), *Sexuality and Space*. New York, Princeton Architectural Press, 1992.

38 Monsiváis, Carlos. 'Lo Sagrado y lo Profano: México Identidad y Cultura'. In *Identidad Nacional*. México, Universidad Autónoma Metropolitano, 1994.

39 Mulvey, Laura. 'Pandora, Topographies of the Mask and Curiosity'. In Beatriz Colomina (ed.), *Sexuality and Space*. New York, Princeton Architectural Press, 1992.

40 Diaz Infante. Juan Jose. Personal interview with the author. Mexico City, 17th March 2000.

41 Wilson, Elizabeth. *The Sphinx in the City: Urban Life, the Control of Disorder and Women*. London, Virago, 1991.

42 Ibid.

43 Diaz Infante. Juan Jose. Personal interview with the author. Mexico City, 17th March 2000.

44 Daphne, Spain. 'Excerpts from the Contemporary Workplace'. In Jane Rendell, Barbara Penner, and Iain Borden (eds.), *Gender Space Architecture*. London, Routledge, 2000, p. 119.

45 Colomina, Beatriz. 'The Split Wall: Domestic Voyeurism'. In Beatriz Colomina (ed.), *Sexuality and Space*. New York, Princeton Architectural Press, 1992.

46 Hartsock, N.C.M. 'The Feminist Standpoint: Developing the Ground for a Specifically Feminist Historical Materialism'. In Sandra Harding and Merrill B. Hintikka (eds.), *Discovering Reality*. Dordrecht, Reidel Publishing Company, 1983, p. 295.

47 Paz, Octavio. *The Labyrinth of Solitude*. Translated by Lysande Kemp, Yara Milos and Rachel Philips Belash. London, Penguin Books, 1990.

48 Kuhlmann, Dörte. *Gender Studies in Architecture: Space, Power and Difference*. London, Routledge, 2013, p. 204.

49 Colomina, Beatriz. 'The Split Wall: Domestic Voyeurism'. In Beatriz Colomina (ed.), *Sexuality and Space*. New York, Princeton Architectural Press, 1992.

50 'Women, Architecture and Identity' – Personal Details, Stuart Hall with others, interview with Denise Scott Brown, BBC Open University, 1992.

51 Lorenz, Clare. *Women in Architecture: A Contemporary Perspective*. New York, Rizzoli, 1990.

5

Mexican Architecture and Postcolonialism

DOI: 10.4324/9781003318934-6

Mexican Architecture and Postcolonialism

Architecture in Mexico, although often written as if it were a subsumed part of Western architectural culture, is, in fact, largely determined and defined by its postcolonial condition. In other words, it is regarded not as 'architecture', but as 'Mexican architecture' – the word 'Mexican' being used here as an adjective that defines its source as being non-Western, as part of the 'other'. The superiority of Western architecture where modernism originates and thus is considered an 'intellectual property', as stated by architecture professor Felipe Hernández, is 'achieved largely through strategies of disavowal which deny validity to the Other (Latin American modern architecture). That is why the non-western Other can only emerge in relation to European norm'.[1] Mexican architecture is thus seen as part of Mexico's postcolonial condition, a condition that affects, conforms and defines the ambivalence of its architecture, as somehow being similar to Western architecture, yet not quite Western. At the same time, it also represents Mexico's enduring struggle to become part of Western discourses. Hence, Mexico's postcolonial condition is at the very core of the nation's very existence; its past and present; its body and soul. For this reason, every architect in Mexico has had to face the existential dilemma and drama of conforming to a discipline whose standards are set by others, by the ideology of would-be colonizers. This intensifies the feelings of 'otherness' and prompts responses that form part of the postcolonial phenomenon. This chapter therefore addresses the elements that constitute the postcolonial discourse in architecture precisely to examine their contribution to the making of Mexican Modernist architecture in the twentieth century.

MEXICO'S POSTCOLONIAL IDENTITY

Mexico, as a modern nation, has its origins in Spanish colonialism that involved a practice of domination, involving the subjugation of one people (the colonized) over another (the coloniser) to gain material benefits and impose cultural values. Postcolonialism, as a branch of cultural theory, contends that colonialism continues to shape the relationship between the colonizer and the colonized even after former colonies have supposedly 'won' their freedom. Mexico's postcolonial history began with its creation as a nation after becoming independent from Spain in 1821, but soon turned instead to an economic and cultural dependency on the most important European nations in the nineteenth century, notably France. During the twentieth century, Mexico's dependency switched to the United States, the most powerful country after the Second World War, and this dependency is well-entrenched and still persists today. Within this evolving postcolonial

Mexican Architecture and Postcolonialism

condition, Mexico has had to develop and defined its identity constantly. During the twentieth century, as it entered a post-revolutionary, modernized world, Mexico developed a national identity conceived by its politicians and intellectuals as a project of cultural nationalism that enjoyed its days of splendour from the 1920s to the 50s.[2] A very important part of this cultural project was the creation of a sense of national identity based essentially on what was considered as '*Lo Mexicano*' – best translated as 'Mexican-ness'. This social-cultural construct was clearly derived from Mexico's sense of 'otherness'. To understand the key images and tropes that emerged from the nationalist movement and how they permeated into architecture, it is useful to mention the contributions made by four leading Mexican intellectuals; namely, José Vasconcelos in *The Cosmic Race*, Samuel Ramos in *Profile of Man and Culture in Mexico*, Edmundo O'Gorman's *The Invention of America* and Octavio Paz's *The Labyrinth of Solitude*. These nationalistic discourses also permeated into the artistic realm of Mexican muralism between 1920 and 1950, also known as the 'Mexican Renaissance'. José Villagrán recounts how he was very much impressed by that movement:

> I started to work with José Vasconcelos, in the Department of Conservation of Buildings, and there I had the opportunity of meeting Rivera, Montenegro and Orozco, who had started their campaign of mural painting. Each day, I would enter the Department of Public Education and I would find Diego [Rivera] painting upon scaffolding, and the same at San Pedro with Montenegro. We would frequently talk, and I started to feel the obligation that we, as future architects, should have in promoting a type of work similar to the Renaissance. In the Renaissance, they started to work in other areas, by using what was already there before them to create something new!! This meant to produce work that would really belong to their time. I considered that this was also needed in Mexico! But in relation to the economic conditions and the idiosyncrasy of what is Mexican.[3]

Mexico's nationalist project was comprised of three main elements residing in its 'otherness': ethnicity, place-identity and relationship to the United States. Mexico's ethnic composition became an important part of its postcolonial condition and of the definition of its identity, particularly after the Mexican Revolution. Mexico's major ethnic group is defined as 'mestizo', which refers to a person of combined European and Indigenous American descent. The concept of 'mestizo' thus became a cultural construction transformed by Mexican intellectuals into their discourse on 'national identity' in relation to the pursuit of modernity.[4] Hence, the myth of the cosmic 'mestizo' race occupied much of Mexico's twentieth-century

219

identity, becoming part of cultural and social manifestations to which architecture and art contributed greatly.

The second important element in Mexico's nationalist project was the concept of place-identity. This referred to notions of the past, of a nostalgic place that is essentially bounded and enclosed, and out of which emerges notions of nationalism and indeed stereotypical images of Mexico as a country. These images fix the meanings of place by constructing a singular, static identity based on a particular moment in time. Thus, the notion of place-identity idealizes a romantic view of Mexico, with its dusty landscape and quaint villages. This view was shared by many Mexican architects as a source of pride or inspiration, as in the case of Luis Barragán, who declared:

> My interest in architecture started to flourish through my visits to different Mexican villages and their homes. I found in the popular Mexican house an incredible beauty, particularly those from the state of Michoacán. This state has the prettiest popular architecture. You see here [referring to his library], this is Las Trojes [a village] in the state of Michoacán. These visits and excursions in Mexico developed my love for architecture, and my desire to express this in the modern house.[5]

Ricardo Legorreta, a follower of Barragán, whose architecture was therefore often classified as vernacular and regionalist, believed that it is Mexico's 'unchanging' towns and villages – where place and time have apparently stood still – that supplied the raw emotion and passion in his architecture:

> For me, the influence of Mexico as a country is definite. The influence of Mexican villages, the influence of Mexican music, Mexican landscape, has been definite. The scale that is used in Mexico is very particular. That is why I think that the environment is what makes a person.[6]

Mexican cultural identity in terms of the feeling of 'otherness' is also greatly determined by a third element, which is the relationship to the Western 'self' – in this case, the United States. Mexican intellectuals like Edmundo O'Gorman and Octavio Paz both addressed this issue as a key part of the construction of Mexican identity. O'Gorman presented the myth of the 'Two Americas' which establishes two possibilities of development for America as a new continent: one was to imitate Europe, replicating the latter's image; the other was to adapt the European model to its own circumstances by creating what he called a 'transformed model'. O'Gorman believed that Latin America, including Mexico, had chosen the second

Mexican Architecture and Postcolonialism

alternative of a transformed model, mainly due to the presence and activity of its indigenous population; whereas, in his view, the United States was clearly based on an imitation of the European model, copying the belief systems, institutions, hierarchical system of classes and their tendency to denigrate manual crafts.[7] Octavio Paz likewise explains the relationship between Mexico and the United States in terms of oppositions that went beyond economic dependency into something more complex and quite profound, which he described as 'irreconcilable attitudes'. According to Paz, Mexico and the United States are two neighbours who are condemned to live together, in adjacency, but will always be separated by their deep social, economic and psychic differences that extend further than their physical and political frontiers.[8]

Mexico – like the rest of Latin America – thus switched from dependency on Europe to the United States as part of its process of westernization.[9] Latin American intellectuals often used the plot of Shakespeare's *The Tempest*, such as the Uruguayan José Enrique Rodó in his book, *Ariel*, and especially the metaphor of Caliban and Ariel, to describe the connection with the United States. In this schema, the United States is Caliban, being rational, brutish, technically orientated and expressing pragmatic values, whereas Latin American is Ariel, with a tendency towards emotion, aesthetics, idealism and sacrifice.[10] These differences between the 'Two Americas' therefore were deep in their essence and idiosyncrasies, and as such created a distinct 'spirit' and way of life. Mexican contemporary architects echoed these ideas, particularly picking up on the 'Caliban' and 'Ariel' debate. Ricardo Legorreta for instance, described the 'Ariel' character of Mexico by stating:

> Mexicans are essentially romantic and essentially mysterious, and essentially desire a combination of private and public life. So, these are the emotions that I want to a search for in my architecture. We are very mysterious, but mysterious does not mean a complex building. Mystery is a deep refined emotion.[11]

In terms of the economics of construction, Enrique Norten explained the essential difference between 'Caliban' and 'Ariel' in cost terms by declaring:

> In the United States, it costs 70% labour and 30% materials whereas in Mexico it is 20% labour and 80% materials. This means they are diametrically opposed to us. So then, we must understand that Mexico is a country with a surplus of manual labour that requires work, and that it is our responsibility to design in such a fashion so that we may offer more work to more people.[12]

Mexican Architecture and Postcolonialism

Mexico's national identity thus became part of its Modernist architectural discourse for much of the twentieth century, influencing both the theoretical and ideological foundations of the discipline. By the late-1960s and early-70s, however, Mexican nationalism became increasingly questioned as part of the wider changes happening internationally during this period. From the 1980s, the influence of nationalism began to fade, and contemporary Mexican intellectuals such as Roger Bartra, Raúl Béjar and Carlos Monsiváis even abandoned the whole principle, and instead took up a critical position. Bartra, for example, sought to demystify Mexican nationalist culture and definitions of 'Mexican-ness', declaring it to be merely a fabrication of the hegemonic ruling group and a superficial meta-discourse used by Mexicans (and indeed many foreigners) to explain their national identity.[13] Béjar also questioned the validity of a Mexican national culture, calling for the abandonment of the idea of a singular overarching concept in favour of heterogeneity and contradiction. He argued that all cultures are a product of hybrid mixtures, some more than others, and that the hybrid nature of the 'mestizo' is not exclusive to Mexican culture.[14] Some of the 13 selected Mexican Modernist architects clearly share this view. Clara de Buen, for one, said, 'I do not believe that there is one identity. I think there are many. It is not the same thing here in Distrito Federal [Mexico City] than in Monterrey for example'.[15] Ricardo Legorreta expressed a similar idea in architectural terms:

> I think that in a certain way we make a mistake by talking about one Mexican architecture, or about Mexican architecture at all. For me, there must be hundreds of Mexican architectures. The architecture in Monterrey has nothing to do with the architecture in Chiapas, for example. And the architecture from Yucatán has nothing to do with the one in Baja California.[16]

Another leading intellectual critic of the concept of Mexican national identity was Carlos Monsiváis, who stated that the term is so diversified and elusive that it appears to be like Lacan's 'slippery signified': extremely difficult, if not impossible, to grasp. The majority of Mexican people did not even want to discuss the term 'national identity', according to Monsiváis, because they just wanted to see themselves simply as 'Mexicans'.[17] This stance also influenced ideas in architecture, particularly for the third- and fourth-generation Mexican Modernist architects. For instance, Carlos Mijares stated:

> One is what one is, independently of what one attempts to be or not to be. I was born Mexican. I was conceived in Mexico, and in this sense, there are many

Mexican Architecture and Postcolonialism

things that I do that are Mexican because they are; because they are here, be-
cause they are part of this era, because they belong to someone that is part of
this culture with all of its characteristics that for some may be positive and for oth-
ers negative. But to assume that there is the specific purpose of being Mexican,
well no. At least, personally, this does not interest me. I say I am not interested
because I am Mexican, and that's it. [18]

Clara de Buen, likewise, echoed this viewpoint:

I believe that you are Mexican if you want it or not. So, to try to be Mexican in
spite of it all, does not interest me. If you try to take in account the different
situations that surround you in the urban context, the economic context and the
opportunities you have to make buildings in Mexico, then your architecture will
be Mexican. [19]

And in relation to architecture's identity, Alberto Kalach pointed out:

I believe that I should not worry about cultural identity as such. If I worried as to
how to express myself, or as to how Mexican architecture should express itself,
then I would be committed to forms and I would have a preconceived notion,
instead of trying to solve the problem of space and construction in the correct
manner. [20]

As the sense of Mexican nationalist identity diminished during the twentieth century, so, too, did support for arguments based on ethnicity or on the relationship
to the United States. 'Mestizo' culture, once used as a nationalist element to
unite the heterogeneous composition of the Mexican nation, has proven to be
incapable of doing anything other than highlighting diversity among its ethnic
groups; hence, the differences were never resolved. Therefore, the issue of what
'Mexican-ness' might be remains open, and perhaps will always remain open.

From the 1990s, the process generally known as globalization became a contemporary challenge to ideas about place-identity. In many countries, there were
groups that now appealed to place-identity as the answer to globalization, which
they considered to be a dangerous and homogenizing force. Such reaction also
found voice in Mexico, with intellectuals such as Monsiváis articulating on behalf
of a threatened Mexican identity he felt was being endangered by an increasing
economic dependency on the United States – a worry triggered by the aforementioned NAFTA agreement in 1992. But in Mexico, as elsewhere, there were those

223

Mexican Architecture and Postcolonialism

who were in favour of globalization, and it appears that most of the selected Modernists architects for this book fell more into this latter camp. Ricardo Legorreta, for example, summed up the pros and cons of Mexico's position:

> I have always seen NAFTA as an opportunity. Unfortunately, the majority of Mexican architects have seen it as either an invasion or an opportunistic situation. The first group took drastic tactics to defend themselves, while the second group positioned themselves to become part of the foreign team of architects that were coming into Mexico. I see things quite the opposite. I see them as an opportunity for conquest and not as a chance of defeat. I think that it is here that Mexican architecture has not taken its full advantage.[21]

Due to the socio-economic changes brought about by globalization since the 1990s, especially in terms of the effect these are having on space-time compression, notions of place-identity clearly needed to be redefined not in terms of specificity and internalized history, but instead by social relationships. Sense of place was becoming something that was dynamic, with no boundaries, no unique identity, yet without denying its uniqueness as a place. Abraham Zabludovsky argued that what was needed was a changed appreciation of 'local' and 'global':

> This is essential since we now know in five minutes what is happening in another part of the world. There is no problem now in teaching something in Mexico that is being done in Madrid or any other place in the world. The conditions are particular to the place although the problem that is being addressed may be international. We must not think that everyone is 100% different, or that societies are totally different in our world today.[22]

Enrique Norten shared this desire to alter current notions of place and open up to new concepts:

> I believe that in this global world we live in, we all participate in a universal condition in every field of knowledge. So, architecture has different local shades, but not 'Mexican'. Probably in our culture, traditions and everything else, we could say that we may be closer to Tokyo, especially we here in Mexico City. Those in Monterrey are closer to Dallas than to Oaxaca. So, where does it start and where does it end, this idea of 'Mexicanidad' ['Mexican-ness'] in a global world? I believe this is a completely obsolete concept. What interests me now is how to explain my work at a local level, within the specific conditions of its settings, of where it is going to be built.[23]

Mexican Architecture and Postcolonialism

The views of these Mexican Modernists thus corresponded to a new and emerging concept of globalization in the final part of the twentieth century, seeing it not as a force that will homogenize economies and cultures worldwide, but which will produce another kind of uneven geographical development and uniqueness of place. Each place will thus retain a distinctive mixture of wider and more local social relations, producing a different set of linkages both local and worldwide.[24]

From this analysis, we can see that the notion of Mexican national culture and its myths were constructed as part of a historical process of identity formation during the twentieth century, and thus should not be judged harshly. More important is to realize that, behind all these elements argued to constitute Mexican identity, there is no moral or truth guaranteeing them. Following the Mexican Revolution of 1910–17, the discipline turned into a site for nationalistic struggles and soon after that, a flag-bearer for modernity. Then, from the mid-1920s through to the 1950s, architecture responded both to Mexico's project of cultural nationalism and to common ideals of 'International Style' Modernism. Later on – roughly from the mid-1960s to the 1980s – it became influenced by regionalist movements, and by the 1990s, it was clearly more pluralist and affected by growing patterns of globalization. In all these phases, however, Mexican architecture was always cast as the 'other' within architectural ideology: emotional, colourful, hand-made and low-cost, in contrast to Western architecture that was considered rational, costly and high-tech. The genealogy of representations shows that what lies beneath them is not a sense of authenticity or truth, but the will to represent something. And these representations are the result of negotiations and choices that Mexican Modernist architects have made in the past and present, as part of their postcolonial condition. The outcome is a mode of architecture that is westernized yet not Western.

Postcolonial theory indicates three different responses that people could take, and it is helpful to examine these concepts in relation to the approaches that Mexican Modernists did take, so as to explain their work further. Firstly, it is possible to identify tactics of subversion based on 'mimicry', which involved a direct imitation of westernized patterns. Secondly, there was the subversive tactic of 'hybridity', whereby Western elements were mixed in along with local or national patterns. Thirdly, there are elements in Mexican architecture that strove to be recognized as the 'other'; that is, as representing 'Mexican-ness' by use of emotional registers that resorted to magic, legend and naiveté, and thus to the simplicity of the forms and colours of vernacular architecture. In this way, Mexican Modernist architecture set out to confirm a sense of identity and difference by adopting an architectural style that could also assert its postcolonial condition, paralleling the

Mexican Architecture and Postcolonialism

approach that has become especially well explored in literature and literary studies in Latin America under the term 'Magical Realism'.[25] The following sections will discuss the kinds of architectural expressions used by the selection of Mexican Modernists that fall into these three categories.

Mimicry and Dissimulation

Postcolonial studies define 'mimicry' as a means of camouflage or a mimetic mode through which the colonized population establishes a deliberately partial and distorted representation that menaces the ideology of the colonizer. According to postcolonial theorist Homi Bhabha, mimicry always needs to be constructed around ambivalence in order to be effective; it imitates, and so appears to be the same but is never quite the same.[26] Mimicry is undoubtedly a key element in Mexican cultural identity in general, with many intellectuals like Samuel Ramos and Octavio Paz interpreting it as Mexico's need to imitate and to pretend as part of the postcolonial process of submission and domination. Ramos said that Mexico's obsession with Western culture was stronger than any interest in creating its own. For him, this explains why Mexicans look down on their own culture and compensate by imitating or mimicking what they believe to be a superior culture.[27] On the other hand, Paz argues that, instead of a feeling of inferiority, what Mexicans were really experiencing was a deep sentiment of solitude. This did not mean that you feel inferior, but that you always feel that you are different. Through what he calls 'dissimulation', Mexicans were able to become closer to the Western model in using dissimulation to change one's appearance rather than one's nature, and thus become transparent, as a means to become nobody.[28]

In Mexican architecture, mimicry can be found in the imitation of Western styles even prior to Modernism, in the twentieth century movement. Luis Barragán, for example, believed that earlier Mexican architects had imitated European countries, and France in particular, because of their inherent inferiority complex. He explained that he wanted his architecture to react:

> against all of the ostentatious decorations from France. The French influence has dominated, and had dominated in Mexico, and in my opinion, this is an inferiority complex that we have because the Mexican houses we see in our villages are beautiful, as are those in Mexico City. There is more beauty in a house like Sanborns and in Hotel Iturbide, and in all of the old houses we have here and in Puebla, than in those French houses located in Paseo de la Reforma.[29]

Mexican Architecture and Postcolonialism

Mimicry also corresponds to the trend to have the same cultural buildings as Western countries. Abraham Zabludovsky recalls that, when he was growing up in Mexico City in the 1920s and 30s, the fashion at that time was for opulent historically and culturally themed cinemas, which were similar to Grauman's Chinese Theatre in Los Angeles:

> Many movie houses of that time were inspired or were done in the manner of the grand styles. Near our home there was a cinema called 'El Cairo'. It was Plaster of Paris Byzantine; in the inside, taking you back to the Middle Eastern deserts. There was the 'Chinese Palace', and of course the great contribution of Cine Alameda located on Juarez Avenue.[30]

The use or not of mimicry within Mexican Modernist architecture divided those who were selected for this book; some architects rejected any form of mimicry, while others were proud to display Western influences in their design. Luis Barragán considered mimicry to be a lack of creativity and a weakness in thinking, as well as reflecting a return to the older model of Beaux-Arts education/architecture:

> My concept of current Mexican architecture done in the past 15 to 20 years is that it has fallen into an academicism. There is no imagination, and no new forms are invented. It is an incorrect interpretation of international architecture similar to what is being done everywhere. In my opinion, for our climate and for any other climates about 50% of the glass used is wasted. The windows are exaggerated, diminishing intimacy in homes and offices. The enormous glass panes used do not give a sense of shelter. The architect needs to think a bit more before designing glass facades that have become an academic standard, without acknowledging the amount of light needed in the interior spaces of houses, offices, clinics or any other building.[31]

Abraham Zabludovsky, on the other hand, confessed to have been very interested as a young architect in imitating Le Corbusier when designing his college projects for Mexico City:

> I was doing my thesis based in the information that we were getting about recent projects and on the books of Le Corbusier. This was (a project) of high-rise blocks of flats with gardens under the buildings. We believed then, in eliminating the small plots of the city. Of course, I wouldn't do this now, but that was part of the challenge of a group of young architects against the 'establishment'. We wanted to demonstrate then, that the future of the city was totally different.[32]

Mexican Architecture and Postcolonialism

The mimicking of western architecture became particularly strong in Mexican Modernism in the 1930s – perhaps not surprising, given that the 'International Style' was widely seen as a means to achieve the image of modernity that developed Western countries possessed. José Villagrán García's Hospital de Cardiología, as can be seen in the comparison below, thus followed the Paimio Sanatorium by Finland's Alvar Aalto in its formal composition and spatial distribution (Figures 5.1 and Figure 5.2).

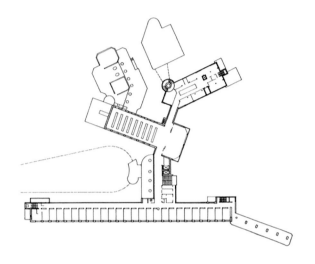

Figure 5.1 Alvar Aalto: Paimio Sanatorium Floor Plan, Finland, 1929.

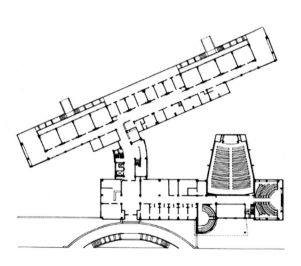

Figure 5.2 José Villagrán García: Hospital de Cardiología, Floor Plan, Mexico City, 1937.

Mexican Architecture and Postcolonialism

Also, among this first generation of Mexican architects, Juan O'Gorman was one of the most passionate embracers of Modernism (even if he later grew despondent about its ideology). In the pair of linked houses/studios that he designed for Diego Rivera and Frida Kahlo in 1930s, O'Gorman was overtly mimicking the slightly earlier Ozenfant Studio in homage to Le Corbusier (Figure 5.3 and Figure 5.4).

Figure 5.3 Le Corbusier: Studio Amédée Ozenfant, Paris, 1924.

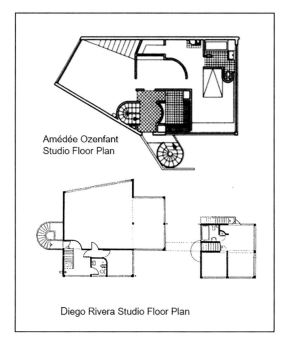

Figure 5.4 Studio Amédée Ozenfant and Studio Diego Rivera, Floor Plans. Public Domain.

Mexican Architecture and Postcolonialism

Figure 5.5 Juan O'Gorman: Casa Estudio de Diego Rivera y Frida Kalho, Mexico City, 1930.

Here, O'Gorman went beyond the formal usage of Le Corbusier's architecture to that of interpretating Modernism like a connoisseur. This is clear in the way he used the construction materials and elements like the exposed-concrete spiral staircase, serrated skylight roof and *fenêtre longueur* for the design of Rivera's house/studio (Figure 5.5).

Like O'Gorman, many of the Mexican Modernist architects were interested in the way that this new approach might help with the country's socio-economic development. From the third generation, Juan José Díaz Infante, for instance, believed that prefabrication methods and technological materials could solve Mexico's housing deficit if they could be taken further than what Archigram in Britain and the Metabolists in Japan were doing, when he stated that:

> *Archigram, Kurokawa and all their projects in the Expo in Osaka during the 1970s, only a few projects were actually built. We really need to do more because I believe it is not a wrong road to follow. Metabolism is not going to change neither is their utopia; someday it is going to happen. Now there are more membranes*

Mexican Architecture and Postcolonialism

and inflatable structures and they are not so utopian because all the things Archigram envisioned has now been done, and also all of (Kisho) Kurokawa's ideas. We have made 11,000 plastic houses in Saudi Arabia, and 5,500 throughout the world. They are all cellular and metabolic.[33]

Figure 5.6 Juan José Díaz Infante: Prefabricated Housing Prototype, Circa 1964.

In the design by Díaz Infante for his prefabricated house (Figure 5.6), we can also trace the influence of Buckminster Fuller and Paolo Soleri, especially the way in which he used the utopian theories of those figures to address Mexico's housing problems. Díaz Infante genuinely thought that he was adapting their ideas to suit Mexican reality.

Carlos Mijares is another who was proud of the influences he received from Western architects:

For me, influences are constant. I mean I have not yet finished studying and since one doesn't finish studying, we are always exposed to new influences we are attracted to. The architect that I was attracted to when I was a student was Le Corbusier. He was my idol as well as for some of my fellow classmates. Another was Mies van der Rohe, and even more after I visited some of his buildings, which for me is the correct way of understanding architecture. I still admire Le Corbusier, Louis Kahn and Jørn Utzon, to mention a few that I consider to be key.[34]

Mexican Architecture and Postcolonialism

Figure 5.7 Louis Kahn: Indian Institute of Management, Ahmedabad, 1962.

Figure 5.8 Carlos Mijares: Christ Church, Mexico City, 1989.

Mijares, however, consciously went beyond the formal mimicry of the architects that he admired, and instead tried to share their concepts, such as the importance of the site context and an appreciation of the intrinsic nature of each building material he used. Hence, the buildings by Mijares,

Mexican Architecture and Postcolonialism

like Christ Church in Mexico City, although they might resemble the work of Louis Kahn (Figure 5.7 and Figure 5.8), are also proof of the rational and systematic use of bricklaying techniques by Mijares out of his respect for craftsmanship.

Figure 5.9 I.M. Pei: John Hancock Tower, Boston, 1973.

Figure 5.10 Juan José Díaz Infante: Bolsa Mexicana de Valores, Mexico City, 1990.

233

Mexican Architecture and Postcolonialism

Mexican Modernist architecture was thus considered to be a universal language that initially reflected the pursuit of modernity, and which, by the 1990s, was being used to showcase Mexico's growing economic and political power. As iconic buildings designed in steel and glass attempted to achieve an international 'First World' image, Díaz Infante's Bolsa Mexicana de Valores (Figure 5.9) followed the influence of The John Hancock Tower in Boston (Figure 5.10) while Javier Sordo Madaleno's Edificio Reforma Lomas Altas (Figure 5.12) followed the trend set by The Regency Hyatt Hotel in Dallas (Figure 5. 11).

Figure 5.11 Welton Beckett: Regency Hyatt Hotel, Dallas, 1978.

Mexican Architecture and Postcolonialism

Figure 5.12 Javier Sordo Madaleno: Edificio Reforma Lomas Altas, Mexico City, 1995.

The need for strong, symbolic meaning in Mexican Modernist architecture was well captured by Abraham Zabludovsky and Teodoro González de León in the 1970s and 80s through their mimicry of the textures and tectonic elements of Brutalism pursued by the likes of Paul Rudolph in the USA and Denys Lasdun in Britain. Thus, the strong institutional style of the Colegio de México and Universidad Pedagógica (Figure 5.14) resemble the work of Kallmann, McKinnell & Knowles for Boston City Hall (Figure 5.13). In Mexico, however, these Brutalist contributions did not face the same severe critical backlash as in Europe or the USA.

Mexican Architecture and Postcolonialism

Figure 5.13 Kallmann, McKinnell & Knowles: Boston City Hall, 1968.

Figure 5.14 Abraham Zabludovsky and Teodoro González de León: Universidad Pedagógica, Mexico City, 1982.

Mexican Architecture and Postcolonialism

The adoption of Western building technologies played an important role in mimicry by Mexican Modernist architects. Ricardo Legorreta says that he initially 'meddled' in this type of advanced technology in his Torre Celanese in the mid-1960s, but quickly abandoned this trend because, as he explained:

> I did not find it to be a clear and positive tool for Mexican architecture. . . . To try to do this type of architecture is a bit against culture, and you get into lots of problems. The Celanese building, although it was an expression of the structure, was not something complicated. High-Technology is not a characteristic of buildings in Mexico.[35]

Nonetheless, Legorreta's Celanese Building (Figure 5.16) offers a good example of mimicry through its use of technology, given that the structure consists of a deck of slabs with large cantilevers around the corners of the ground floor.[36] In this, it clearly resembled Frank Lloyd Wright's Price Tower in Oklahoma City, as shown in Figure 5.15.

Unlike Legorreta, the selected architects from the fourth generation of Mexican Modernists are openly attracted to the use of advanced technology and construction materials. Indeed, they consider it a matter of great importance to be knowledgeable about up-to-date information on such aspects. Alberto Kalach, for one, acknowledged that he was influenced greatly by the impact of globalization on architecture:

> I think that in the 1990s there were a lot of publications that emphasized details, and since everybody nourishes on magazines and publications, well I think that many people thought that was the way to go.[37]

Another from that generation, Enrique Norten, feels that, although he uses advanced technological innovations in his projects, he has not abandoned the formal and material inheritance from older Mexican architecture:

> In order to understand the material, it is necessary to understand the socio-economic condition of our country and its political conditions, from which the constructive possibilities derived as well as the methods and techniques and eventually the selection of the materials . . . But for us it was very important, or we believed and were convinced that construction processes were linked to materials and these were the most adequate for certain specific circumstances, of the time and the place . . . I believe that the buildings we made could only be built in Mexico at that time . . . these are Mexican buildings.[38]

Mexican Architecture and Postcolonialism

Figure 5.15 Frank Lloyd Wright: Price Tower, Oklahoma City, 1956.

Figure 5.16 Ricardo Legorreta: Torre Celanese, Mexico City, 1968.

Mexican Architecture and Postcolonialism

Both these fourth-generation architects appear to be highly influenced by Tadao Ando and Renzo Piano. Kalach's use of exposed, reinforced concrete, wood and glass resembles Ando's architecture in the desire to be highly tactile and visually sensual. The Casa GGG, is an example of this influence as can be seen in the resemblance of this house with Ando's Vitra Conference Pavilion. (Figure 5.17 and Figure 5.18).

Figure 5.17 Tadao Ando: Vitra Conference Pavilion, Weil am Rhein, 1993.

Figure 5.18 Alberto Kalach: Casa GGG, Exterior. Mexico City, 2000.

Mexican Architecture and Postcolonialism

Norten, on the other hand, is more attracted to the technological use of structures to create large-span spaces, with his scheme for the Escuela National de las Artes being obviously akin to Renzo Piano's Bercy 2 Shopping Centre, on the outskirts of Paris (Figure 5.19 and 5.20).

From such architectural examples, we can see that the mimicry of Western architecture by Mexican Modernist architects varied from the appropriation of

Figure 5.19 Renzo Piano: Bercy 2 Comercial Centre, Renzo Piano, Paris, 1990.

Figure 5.20 Enrique Norten: Escuela Nacional de Arte Teatral, Mexico City, 1994

Mexican Architecture and Postcolonialism

Western forms, materials and technology, through to deeper theoretical paradigms and ideologies. These similarities went beyond superficial attributes, as shown by their sophisticated appearance in floor plans, open-plan layouts, atriums, shell structures and so on. Thus, there is evidence in these buildings of a refined mimicry that surpassed any cartoon-like imitation, and perhaps that suppleness, which Mexican Modernist architecture could achieve, is why mimicry still seems so prevalent today in Mexico's buildings.

Hybridity and Simulation

According to postcolonial theory – especially that of Homi Bhabha – hybridity is a negotiated condition produced by the continual interface and exchange between colonial and colonized, thus creating a 'hybrid' that is neither just the 'other' nor the 'self'. Hybridity is important because two original elements create a third expression that can be understood as something different and novel.[39] However, it needs to be pointed out that hybridity is not at all new to Mexican architecture. It can be found throughout the Mexican Historicist styles, in which Neoclassical, Baroque, Gothic and even Art Deco elements were mixed with pre-Hispanic elements to produce architecture with distinctive Mexican traits. Thus, during the twentieth century, Modernist architects were just following the same pattern in resorting to hybridity in the search for Mexican identity – especially due to the ideological influences after the Mexican Revolution that underpinned the project of cultural nationalism.

There are, of course, many variations in the levels of overtness and abstraction of Mexican and Western features present in a hybridized building. Pedro Ramírez Vázquez's celebrated Museo de Antropología (Figure 5.21) is a strong example of a building designed on Modernist premises but also employing the traditional Mexican patio, or quadrangle, as the main spatial organizer. In its three-dimensional proportions, the building is reminiscent of the pre-Hispanic Nunnery Quadrangle in the Mayan city of Uxmal (Figure 5.22), as Ramírez Vázquez openly acknowledged (Figure 5.23 and Figure 5.24):

> *The use of the lattice [brise-soliel] is related to Uxmal but the function it has is totally different. In Uxmal there is the intention of a chiaroscuro in the top part of the building, but it is not a lattice, it is a closed volume. In the museum, it is*

241

Mexican Architecture and Postcolonialism

totally open as a brise-soleil. *The lattices are prefabricated in both cases. You make the pieces the same size and later placed them in site. In Uxmal limestone is used, while in the museum it is aluminium and glass. There is an intention of keeping the same proportions in an environment with similar dimensions, as a consequence.*[40]

Figure 5.21 Pedro Ramírez Vázquez: Museo de Antropología, Mexico City, 1964.

Figure 5.22 Cuadrángulo de las Monjas, Uxmal, Yucatán, Circa Eighth Century CE.

Mexican Architecture and Postcolonialism

Figure 5.23 Nunnery Quadrangle, East Building Bas-Relief Detail.

Figure 5.24 Pedro Ramírez Vázquez: Museo de Antropología, Mexico City, 1964. Detail of the Brise-Soleil on the Upper Floor.

Museums and other public buildings, such as embassies, national pavilions and exhibition centres, are typologies through which Mexican Modernists explored ideas of hybridity. Museo Tamayo and the Mexican Embassy in Brazil are two instances by Abraham Zabludovsky and Teodoro González de León, as, while they are recognizable as governmental institutions of their time through their use of exposed concrete, they also contained overt references to pre-Hispanic architecture (Figure 5.25). In Chapter 2, we saw that the spatial arrangement of Museo

Mexican Architecture and Postcolonialism

Tamayo was focussed on the internal circulation of people using the building; whereas its external form, in an attempt to provide better daylighting, carried echoes of the ancient Mexican stepped pyramids.

Zabludovsky defended this use of pyramidal shapes by saying they were a result of the building programme in the Museo Tamayo, while, in the case of the Mexican Embassy in Brazil, it was because of specific local construction guidelines (Figure 5.25):

When we were designing in Brasilia, we were limited by the regulations that established that there could not be walls to separate the plots of one embassy from the next. So, we designed three platforms where the three main buildings were placed. As a result of the digging to create the platforms we had lateral slopes or incline planes that blocked the view of the neighbouring buildings. Afterwards, people found this similar to pyramids, Mexican pyramids. And they claimed that these were our influence. Well of course, I have seen the pyramids and so I cannot disclaim this. But there are also pyramids in Egypt, and I have seen pictures of them too![41]

Zabludovsky explained that he was thus not purposely trying to achieve hybridity in these designs, since he did not even believe that his buildings need be

Figure 5.25 Abraham Zabludovsky and Teodoro González de León: Museo Tamayo Exterior, Mexico City, 1981.

Mexican Architecture and Postcolonialism

recognized as 'Mexican'. A very different attitude is expressed by Agustín Hernández, who claimed, 'Since my professional exam, I tried to look for something authentic. To create something original that would represent what is Mexican. I wanted to do a national architecture'.[42]

Perhaps the clearest example of hybridity by Hernández is in the Heroico Colegio Militar in Mexico City (Figure 5.27).

Figure 5.26 Pre-Hispanic Archaeological Site at Monte Albán, Oaxaca, Seventh Century CE.

Figure 5.27 Agustín Hernández and Manuel González Rul: Heroico Colegio Militar, Mexico City, 1976.

Mexican Architecture and Postcolonialism

Here, he and Manuel González Rul designed a group of buildings that integrated Modernist and pre-Hispanic features at both the urban and architectural level, emulating those of Monte Albán in Oaxaca (Figure 5.26). Hernández explained:

> *The project was different because of its spatial conception using masses and voids, based on those used in pre-Hispanic ceremonial centres . . . the site's topography . . . served as a backdrop or background to the complex and to close off the plaza. The buildings and the whole compound faced the talud or natural inclined planes of the hill.*[43]

Another famous instance of hybridity, in being both 'modern' and 'native' at the same time, was the Mexico '68 emblem for the Olympic Games (Figure 5.28), attributed to Lance Wyman, who was working as part of a design team headed by Pedro Ramírez Vásquez. When Ramírez Vásquez was asked if the emblem was inspired by the crafts of the Huichol, one of Mexico's native Indian groups, he answered:

> *No, a Huichol Indian actually did it! I asked him to make the word Mexico on a piece of wood! Well, at that time in the Museum of Modern Art in New York, and in Europe, there was a trend called 'Op Art' which used concentric lines and parallel lines that vanished and focused in different places as part of an optical game. This was part of the contemporary language of art at that time. We believed we should address the world in this up-to-date language. When we saw this trend, we realized that it coincided with Huichol crafts.*

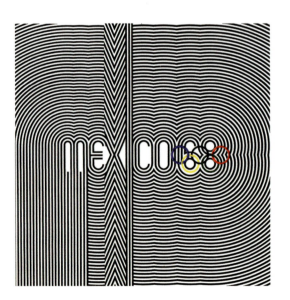

Figure 5.28 Mexico '68 Olympic Games Logo.

Mexican Architecture and Postcolonialism

> There is a very good anecdote involving Alfaro Siqueiros. I had a very good friendship with Alfaro Siqueiros, because his daughter was a good friend of my wife. When the logo of Mexico '68 came out, Siqueiros phoned me and said:
>
> > 'Pedro, I am sorry, but I am going to scold you and hard'. 'Why professor?', I asked. 'Because you are ignoring the great formal force of engravings from (José Guadalupe) Posadas or Leopoldo Méndez, in favour of the trendy Op Art', is what he told me. 'But Professor, it's a contemporary language too. Isn't Op Art, Huichol?', I said. He was quiet for a bit, and then he said: 'I am glad that I spoke to you, Pedro. It is OK'.
>
> So, this logo is Mexican, but it used the contemporary language of that [earlier] time.[44]

However, by far the best example of hybridity in twentieth-century Mexican Modernist architecture that truly challenged Western paradigms was La Ciudad Universitaria (CU), the main campus of the Universidad Nacional Autónoma de México (UNAM). This campus created what has been called a condition of 'plastic integration' given that all its buildings have murals with historical and educational narratives. It was proudly considered in Mexico as the height of nationalistic representation of those qualities that might be seen as 'Mexican-ness'. Yet, to the influential Italian architectural historian and critic, Bruno Zevi, it was instead a distortion of international Modernism, so much so that he called it *'Grottesseco Messicano'*,[45] perhaps in response to its unintended subversion of Western paradigms.

The strongest appearance of hybridity within La Ciudad Universitaria is in the Central Library designed by Juan O'Gorman (Figure 5.29). Here, O'Gorman returned to his trade as a painter via the murals he created to cover the entire surface of this prismatic building. These murals openly referenced Mexican muralism and served to represent UNAM's credo and its Mexican identity. This return to his roots by O'Gorman indicated his increasing disillusion with the ideals of 'International Style' Modernism and his growing appreciation of pre-Hispanic murals with their strong colours and vivid storytelling qualities. So hybrid was this building that the aforementioned Mexican painter, Alfaro Siquerios, referred to it disapprovingly as a *gringa* dressed in a typical Mexican costume called the *China Poblana*.[46] Despite such criticisms, it became the most internationally recognized icon of Mexican Modernist architecture, making famous this prestigious university.

Hence, it is obvious that hybridity was one of the most popular traits employed by the first and second generations of Mexican Modernists, and indeed is still being employed even today. Hybridized architectural expressions, however,

Mexican Architecture and Postcolonialism

Figure 5.29 Juan O'Gorman: Biblioteca Central, CU, Mexico City, 1953.

encountered serious competition in another approach that sought to introduce a more abstract form of Mexican elements in building designs. This deeper trend, based upon the Mexican vernacular and a nostalgic sense of the rural past, was initiated by Luis Barragán, through his so-called 'emotional architecture' of the 1940s, later gaining more popularity and recognition in the 1960s. It will thus be examined now as a third approach that Mexican Modernist architects tended to adopt as part of their postcolonial condition.

Emotional Architecture or Magical Realism

Mexican Modernist architecture, being rooted in the concept of place-identity, at times seemed to evoke the notion of the 'Subverted Eden' and a lost primitive innocence that had existed before the Spanish Conquest, creating an interest in a sense of a primitive time and mysticism. Architecture of this kind is often defined as 'emotional' or 'regionalist' or simply as 'Mexican' architecture. It appears to reflect feelings of stasis, nostalgia and legend. In this way, it may be compared to what is known in literature and literary studies as 'Magical Realism'. This term refers to the Latin-American novels and short stories of authors such as Jorge Luis Borges, Gabriel García Márquez, Juan Rulfo, Lezama Lima and Carlos Fuentes, to name a few. Magical Realism is considered as an eccentric, supernatural, mysterious and surreal form of literature, in explicit opposition to the rational, logical, technical, systematic and scientific culture of Western countries. In both architecture and literature or in films, its manifestations correspond to the clichéd view that Westerners have of Latin Americans, and in this case, Mexicans.

The 'logic' behind Magical Realism, according to Alejo Carpentier and Gabriel García Márquez, is a colonial one that affirms that the history of Latin America can only ever be understood as magical, and thus Magical Realism is a mode of writing that strives to depict this deeper reality. Carpentier argued that history is more fantastical than any fiction through his famous motto of 'Marvelous Real', under which he wrote his famous novel *The Kingdom of This World* in 1949. Similarly, García Márquez always claimed that, as an author, he has not invented anything, and that all he did was to register what he saw in the actual reality that surrounds him. One of his most pertinent quotes is: 'The first condition of magical realism, as the name suggests, is that it is a rigorously true fact that, however, seems fantastic'.[47] The concept of Magical Realism was first produced in the 1960s as a need to postulate a 'difference' to the 'other'. Magical Realism was viewed by Western cultural elites as being irrational, incomprehensible and nostalgic, and hence became used as an essentialist critique of international interpretations of Latin American literature. Magical Realism inscribes a telluric vision of Latin American people and their indomitable character, in order precisely to explain their lack of material progress in relation to Western, industrialized countries, placing them within a cosmic, magical vision with its own rules. It was given the seal of approval by European and North American writers and critics during the 1960s, 70s and 80s as part of the legitimization of the geo-political divisions between the so-called 'First World' and 'Third World' nations. Magical Realism has since become an established part of Western discourse, and as such it is no longer a discourse from the margins, nor does it speak for the subaltern or the subjugated anymore.

If we compare the phenomenon of Magical Realism in literature and films with what is classified as 'Mexican' architecture, we can see extremely close similarities in that all are interpreted by Western critics as emotional and surreal. Using Frederic Jameson's definition of Magical Realism within films, there are certain principal characteristics that are shared. These include the use of historical themes from the past; the use of colour as a source of pleasure; the use of dynamic narratives that are reduced, concentrated and simplified; and finally,

Mexican Architecture and Postcolonialism

and perhaps most importantly, their willingness be regarded as the 'other'.[48] It seems that what is classified as 'Mexican' architecture by Westerners suffers, like Magical Realism in literature and films, from the same stereotypical notions assigned to the 'other' in order to reinforce the Western 'self'. Hence, vernacular naiveté, traditional narratives and vivid colours were made famous in the architecture of Luis Barragán and Ricardo Legorreta and by the early work of Javier Sordo Madaleno, with these becoming manifestations of the 'other' that could be accepted because they posed no real threat to Western architectural paradigms.

Figure 5.30 Luis Barragán: Own House/Studio, Casa Tacubaya, 1947.

Mexican Architecture and Postcolonialism

Western critics have thus long detected in the work of Luis Barragán the manifestation of so-called 'Mexican' architecture, yet Barragán himself said that he never expected that sort of interpretation for his design of his own house/studio in Tacubaya:

> My house has represented for me a spontaneous thing, because I made it not looking for anything other than my own taste in popular architecture, to get the feeling of being in Mexico and in a house . . . This house was the one that has given me more recognition here and abroad.[49]

Barragán's own house/studio, like most of his oeuvre, was meant to remind us of past times in traditional Mexican villages, and therefore, indeed, a seemingly timeless and mystical place. Its enclosed spaces give intimacy through the controlled use of daylight and the way that they frame views of the garden. The rooftop (Figure 5.30) is another space that seems to borrow part of the sky to create an evocative environment. Barragán's magical sense is also felt in his landscape designs like those in the neighbourhood of Las Arboledas or the riding stables of Cuadra San Cristóbal in Los Clubes (Figure 5.31). Both examples drew upon strong tectonic elements like beams and walls painted in vibrant colours and at different scales and proportions to produce emotions of amazement, drama and the exotic.

Figure 5.31 Luis Barragán: Cuadra San Cristobal, Los Clubes, Mexico City, 1968.

251

Mexican Architecture and Postcolonialism

Ricardo Legorreta is another who considered emotion to be an essential characteristic of Mexican people and of Mexican architecture. He candidly claimed that he considered himself to be 'a very emotional person and extremely romantic, so I believe very much in emotional architecture, like Barragán'.[50] However, Legorreta's architecture, although influenced by Barragán, is very different in its scale and scope, as he was most successful when applying this type of architecture to building typologies other than housing. He used his own magical architectural language in a large manner for the Hotel Camino Real in Mexico City, as well as in Fábrica Automex, where the volumes produce a surreal landscape reminiscent of paintings by Giorgio de Chirico. As well as these alterations in scale and typology, Legorreta's understanding of emotional architecture diverges from Barragán's mysticism in the search for shock and surprise, as seen in the fountain of the Museo MARCO in Monterrey (Figure 5.32), where a peaceful courtyard is suddenly flooded by a loud gush of water that pours unexpectedly into the square. Legorreta fervently believed that Mexican Modernist architecture should have a

Figure 5.32 Ricardo Legorreta, Museo MARCO, Monterrey, 1992.

Mexican Architecture and Postcolonialism

Figure 5.33 Ricardo Legorreta: San Antonio Public Library, San Antonio, Texas, USA, 1993.

sense of humour and fun, and so he created witty elements like the gigantic balls that playfully roll down from San Antonio Public Library in the United States (Figure 5.33), producing an amusing scene for visitors.

Furthermore, Javier Sordo Madaleno is an architect who also searched from the beginning of his career for 'Mexican' architectural forms that could evoke what he believed to be an intrinsically Mexican identity:

> *This is one of the aspects for me that every time I have the opportunity to mention it, I do. I believe that architects should or must keep to their roots. You are a Mexican architect; you have certain roots that you need to express. I believe that this has made Mexico a very special country at an architectural level. So, I believe we should keep evolving. How are we to do this? Well, with the elements that you have identified and dissected through your experience; architectural elements that form spaces with noticeable Mexican roots, although these have since evolved.*[51]

Sordo Madaleno thus mastered the use of architectural features which contained Mexican referents in terms of juxtaposed scales, blank walls and geometrical

253

shapes, using these to create bizarre buildings and landscapes. Such details were typically designed in an overstated manner for large shopping centres or hotels. In the shopping centres in Mexico City at the Plaza Moliere (now El Palacio de Hierro Polanco) and at El Palacio de Hierro Santa Fe, for instance, he adorned the facades with enormous Mexican iron gates in evocation of these historical elements, while at the same time changing their very nature. Perhaps his most famous building is the Westin Los Cabos Resort Villas & Spa on the Baja California peninsula, where he exaggerated the building's tectonic elements by creating a huge cut-out that framed an immense view of the ocean beyond (Figure 5.34).

In terms of the 'emotional' qualities of certain Mexican buildings, publications and photography also can be credited for the great popularity that was gained, typified as such for its use of textures and colours. The relevant buildings are portrayed as mystical and enchanted environments, whether in written or photographed accounts. This 'Mexican' architecture, just like Magical Realism in literature and films, gained international recognition, and so, in that sense, it became a part of international merchandising – as if somehow in retribution from the hegemony of capitalism. 'Mexican' architecture could thus seem to be very alive and well within its postcolonial context, yet only receive compensatory recognition at international level. And, like in Magical Realism

Figure 5.34 Javier Sordo Madaleno: Westin Los Cabos Resort Villas & Spa, Los Cabos, Baja California Sur, México, 1993.

Mexican Architecture and Postcolonialism

in other fields, it did gain wider prestige for Mexican architecture – this being, however, the prestige of the marginal and of the eccentric.[52] Hence, it became, however regrettably, just part of the construction of the 'other' within Mexico's postcolonial condition.

According to the Indian philosopher, Aijaz Ahmad, there is a need within literature studies in North America to incorporate more seriously the work that is produced in other parts of the world and not just classify it as belonging to notional 'Third World'.[53] In this sense, Gayatri Chakravorty Spivak believes that this version of the 'other' has been assigned by Western countries simply in order to incorporate it into 'First World' academia, as part of an ongoing colonizing, discursive process that reduces 'Third World' to the 'other' – with a sense of other that does not bother or cause trouble and with whom you can easily live.[54] Perhaps we should also extend this viewpoint to the analysis of architecture. As such, 'Mexican' emotional architecture might potentially drift away from its point of origin to become something significant in other parts of the world. Otherwise, the phenomenon of 'Mexican' architecture would yet again be being constructed through Western academic intellectual discourses and marketing strategies.

It is a very real dilemma. Ricardo Legorreta, for example, noted that he thought his architecture had been so appreciated internationally because it had displayed 'Mexican' features:

> I think this is one of the reasons we have been successful in the United States. Contrary to what critics say, when we make our architecture, North Americans discover it and for them is a novelty. It's not a novelty in its use of walls or colour, but what is a novelty for them is the emotional part it arouses. They discover the emotion of having peace in their home as a wonderful thing, since their own architecture does not have this . . . Maybe it has been recognized internationally as such, and they talk about a Mexican architect that is doing this or that type of architecture. And of course, this can also be due to the emotions it arouses. Yes, it is because of this.[55]

More practically, Javier Sordo Madaleno added that this type of architecture not only reflects Mexican identity but also offers a commercial appeal:

> This is the only element that will give the Mexican architect an edge, or the possibility to defend [our] work and position in the architectural world. Often, we do not have within our hands the technology or the budget or many of the elements that are present in countries more industrialized than ours.[56]

Mexican Architecture and Postcolonialism

Yet there was trenchant criticism of those Mexican Modernist architects who chose to play that card. Enrique Norten said that he did not agree with the acceptance that this type of Mexican architecture was receiving. He argued that a similar problem had happened before in terms of painting, which had been categorised as a 'Mexican' style to be used for promotional and advertising campaigns:

> [It] has been a marketing device. I always compare this with painting. There is Mexican painting, but if you do not paint like (Rufino) Tamayo or Frida Kalho or (Francisco) Toledo, you cannot be considered a Mexican painter. So then, there are fabulous painters, abstract painters. I believe that we have to recognize that these are Mexican paintings. This is fair, isn't it? This is very common with stereotypes. I have colleagues, without mentioning names, that it is obvious that they go throughout the world selling their architecture as 'Mexican' architecture, and in this they have been very successful.[57]

Thus, while hybridity and mimicry are considered as common mechanisms of resistance towards domination in the postcolonial context, Magical Realism is unique in having become the direct expression of 'Mexican-ness' in a way that also romanticizes 'Mexican Architecture' – this being an entirely created identity. Here the question of identity is being negotiated and performed in the context of cultural transition. For this reason, Spivak is suspicious not so much by the acceptance given to Magical Realism by Western writers and critics, but as to what it comes to stand for in Latin American and why it covers such a vast cultural area, assigning it in a verdict that feels more like it wants to be a defining agenda.[58] What bothers Spivak, and perhaps what bothered many Mexican Modernist architects, is the way that this architecture has been typecast, implying that the subjugated or subaltern will never be allowed to speak, since they adapt their voices to what Westerners want to hear, rather than what they want to say. Yet, for those architects that promoted this architecture, this perhaps was the only way that they, as the subaltern, could achieve acceptance and even win in this global cultural and economic power game.

Out of the many subversive possibilities of resistance examined in this chapter, there were three strategies developed under postcolonial conditions that offered Mexican architects a form of resistance: mimicry and dissimulation; hybridity and simulation; or else an emotional sense of architecture, in the form of 'Magical Realism'. What this means, therefore, is that Mexican Modernist architecture needs to be questioned in terms of the apparent centrality

Mexican Architecture and Postcolonialism

of the universalist, westernized discourse that it still promotes. Postcolonial theory can be used to interrogate the nature of the architectural discipline, and in doing so, overcome the limitations of understanding Mexican architecture by bringing such issues in 'from the margins'. It also helps to reveal and question the nature of the prevailing 'canon', and the supposedly dominant notions of truth and knowledge which were imposed by Western intellectuals in places like Mexico.

In conclusion, this chapter has focussed upon the ways in which postcolonial politics played an important part in determining Mexican identity during the twentieth and early-twenty-first centuries, and how this then permeated the politics of space and place in relation to Modernist architecture. It also examined the subaltern condition, or subjugated status, of Mexican architects and their buildings, and how these ultimately portrayed Mexico as a nation and its buildings in terms of the 'other'. Modernist architecture in Mexico was thus absorbed by the wider Western discourse, and Mexican architects and academics served as partisan advocates of modernization and westernization. Postcolonial studies help to analyse architectural production in Mexico beyond its narrow, formal, spatial and technical attributes, thus challenging its ideological contents and cultural assumptions in order to start upon a real decolonizing process that can enable contemporary Mexican architects to represent themselves and their architecture differently from how it has been represented hitherto by westernized discourse. It is important to begin this process by refusing to conform to the logic of binary oppositions shaped by the 'canon', so that Mexico's architects can now reconceive of themselves – not as part of a fixed 'other' – but instead through their own architectural identity.

NOTES

1 Hernández, Felipe. *Beyond Modernist Masters: Contemporary Architecture in Latin American*. Basel, Birkhäuser, 2010, p. 19.

2 Monsiváis, Carlos. 'Lo Sagrado y lo Profano: Mexico Identidad y Cultura'. In *Identidad Nacional*. México, Universidad Autónoma Metropolitana, 1994.

3 Gómez, Lilia and Miguel Angel Quevedo. 'Entrevista con el arquitecto José Villagrán García'. In *Testimonios Vivos 20 arquitectos*. México, Cuadernos de arquitectura 15–16 INBA, Mayo–Agosto 1981.

4 Alcantara Mejia, Jose Ramon. 'La Transferencia de lo Colonial: El mestizaje y el contra del discurso literario en México'. In Alfonso Toro and Fernando de Toro (eds.), *El Debate de la postcolonialidad en Latinoamérica*. Madrid/Frankfurt, Vervuert, Iberoamérica, 1999, p. 309.

Mexican Architecture and Postcolonialism

5 Ramírez Ugarte. Alejandro. *Conversación con Luis Barragán*. Guadalajara, Arquitónica, 2015.

6 Legorreta, Ricardo. Personal interview with the author. Mexico City, October 16, 2000.

7 O'Gorman, Edmundo. *La Invención de América*. México, Fondo de Cultura Económica, 1993.

8 Paz, Octavio. *The Labyrinth of Solitude*. Translated by Lysande Kemp, Yara Milos, and Rachel Philips Belash, London, Penguin Books, 1990.

9 Carranza, Luis E. and Fernando Lara. *Modern Architecture in Latin America: Art, Technology, and Utopia*. Austin, University of Texas Press, 2015.

10 Castro-Gómez, Santiago and Eduardo Mendieta. *Teorías sin disciplina. Latinomericanismo poscolonialidad y globalización en debate*. San Francisco, University of San Francisco, 1998, p. 7.

11 Legorreta, Ricardo. Personal interview with the author. Mexico City, 16th October 2000.

12 Norten, Enrique. Personal interview with the author. Mexico City, 30th May 2000.

13 Bartra, Roger. *La Jaula de la Melancolía Identidad y Metamorfosis del Mexicano*. México, Ed Debolsillo, 2016.

14 Béjar, Raúl. *El Mexicano: Aspectos Culturales y Psicosociales*. México, UNAM, 1979.

15 de Buen, Clara. Personal interview with the author. Mexico City, 16th October 2000.

16 Legorreta, Ricardo. Personal interview with the author. Mexico City, 16th October 2000.

17 Monsiváis, Carlos. 'Lo Sagrado y lo Profano: México, Identidad y Cultura'.

18 Mijares, Carlos. Personal interview with the author. Mexico City, 30th May 2000.

19 de Buen, Clara. Personal interview with the author. Mexico City, 16th October 2000.

20 Kalach, Alberto. Personal interview with the author. Mexico City, 26th May 2000.

21 Legorreta, Ricardo. Personal interview with the author. Mexico City, 16th October 2000.

22 Zabludovsky, Abraham. Personal interview with the author. Mexico City, 31st May 2000.

23 Norten, Enrique. Personal interview with the author. Mexico City, 30th May 2000.

24 Massey, Doreen. *Space, Place and Gender*. Cambridge, Polity Press, 1994.

25 Richards, Nelly. 'Intersectando Latinoamérica con el latinoamericanismo: discurso académico y crítica cultural'. In Santiago Castro-Gómez and Eduardo Mendieta (eds.), *Teorías sin disciplina. Latinomericanismo, poscolonialidad y globalización en debate*. San Francisco, University of San Francisco, 1998.

26 Bhabha, Homi. *The Location of Culture*. London, Routledge, 1994, p. 85.

27 Ramos, Samuel. *El Perfil del Hombre y la Cultura en México*. México, UNAM, 1991.

28 Paz, Octavio. *The Labyrinth of Solitude*. Translated by Lysande Kemp, Yara Milos, and Rachel Philips Belash, London, Penguin Books, 1990.

29 Ramírez Ugarte, Alejandro. *Conversación con Luis Barragán*. Guadalajara, Arquitónica, 2015.

30 Zabludovsky, Abraham. Personal interview with the author. Mexico City, 31st May 2000.

31 Ramírez Ugarte, Alejandro. *Conversación con Luis Barragán*. Guadalajara, Arquitónica, 2015.

32 Zabludovsky, Abraham. Personal interview with the author. Mexico City, 31st May 2000.

33 Diaz Infante, Juan Jose. Personal interview with the author. Mexico City, 17th March 2000.

34 Mijares, Carlos. Personal interview with the author. Mexico City, 30th May 2000.

35 Legorreta, Ricardo. Personal interview with the author. Mexico City, 16th October 2000.

36 Bergdoll, Barry, Carlos Eduardo Comas, Jorge Francisco Liernur, and Patricio del Real. *Latin America in Construction: Architecture 1955–1980*. New York, Museum of Modern Art, 2015.

37 Kalach, Alberto. Personal interview with the author. Mexico City, 26th May 2000.

38 Norten, Enrique. Personal interview with the author. Mexico City, 30th May 2000.

39 Bhabha, Homi. 'The Third Space: Interview with Homi Bhabha'. In Jonathan Rutherford (ed.), *Identity, Community, Culture, Difference*. London, Lawrence and Wishart, 1990, p. 21.

40 Ramírez Vázquez, Pedro. Personal interview with the author. Mexico City, 20th March 2000.

41 Zabludovsky, Abraham. Personal interview with the author. Mexico City, 31st May 2000.

42 Hernández, Agustín. Personal interview with the author. Mexico City, 17th March 2000.

43 Ibid.

44 Ramírez Vázquez, Pedro. Personal interview with the author. Mexico City, 20th March 2000.

45 Zevi, Bruno, 'Grottesco Messicano'. In *L'Espresso*, Rome, December 29, 1957, p. 16. Also reproduced in *Arquitectura México* 62, 1958, p. 110. Also quoted in Celia Esther Arredondo Zambrano, 'Modernity in Mexico: The Case of the Ciudad Universitaria'. In *Modernity and the Architecture of Mexico*. Austin, University of Texas Press, 1997, p. 103.

46 Herner, Irene. 'David Alfaro Siqueiros: maquinas armónicas'. In Miguel Ángel Echegaray (ed.), *La Pintura Mural En Los Centros De Educación De México*. México City, SEP, 2003, p. 153.

47 CNN en Español. 'Las mejores frases de Gabriel García Márquez'. *Broadcast*, 17th April 2018. https://cnnespanol.cnn.com/2018/04/17/las-mejores-frases-de-gabriel-garcia-marquez/

48 Jameson, Frederic. 'On Magical Realism in Film'. In *Critical Inquiry*. Chicago, University of Chicago Press, Vol. 12. No. 2, Winter 1986, pp. 301–325.

49 Ramírez Ugarte, Alejandro. *Conversación con Luis Barragán*. Guadalajara, Arquitónica, 2015.

50 Legorreta, Ricardo. Personal interview with the author. Mexico City, 16th October 2000.

51 Sordo Madaleno, Javier. Personal interview with the author. Mexico City, 27th May 2000.

52 Zamora, Lois Parkinson and Wendy B. Faris (eds.). *Magical Realism: Theory, History, Community*. Durham NC, Duke University Press, 1995, p. 2.

53 Ahmad, Aijaz. *In Theory, Classes, Nations, Literatures*. London, Verso, 1992, p. 214.

54 Spivak, Gayatri Chakravorty. 'Poststructuralism, Marginality, Postcoloniality and Value'. In Peter Collier and Helga Geyer-Ryan (eds.), *Literary Theory Today*. New York, Cornell University Press, 1990.

55 Legorreta, Ricardo. Personal interview with the author. Mexico City, 16th October 2000.

56 Sordo Madaleno, Javier. Personal interview with the author. Mexico City, 27th May 2000.

57 Norten, Enrique. Personal interview with the author. Mexico City, 30th May 2000.

58 Spivak, Gayatri Chakravorty. 'Poststructuralism, Marginality, Postcoloniality and Value'. In Peter Collier and Helga Geyer-Ryan (eds.), *Literary Theory Today*. New York, Cornell University Press, 1990.

Epilogue

DOI: 10.4324/9781003318934-7

Epilogue

It is now 100 years since Modernist architecture first began to appear in Mexico and yet its presence can be felt now more than ever, in every new urban development, every new building and in the increasingly globalized character of Mexican cities and in the profile of their skylines. However, the importance and impact of Modernism as an architectural movement in Mexico goes beyond its formal character and its spatial qualities, as this book shows. Mexican Modernism's presence as a cultural phenomenon became an integral part of the transformation of everyday life in terms of beliefs, rituals and activities. Hence, Mexican Modernist architects became active participants in creating these new cultural values and patterns as part of Mexico's process of modernization/westernization, thereby altering not only its built spaces but, more importantly, the minds of its people. Mexican Modernism, once it was fulsomely adopted, remained remarkably consistent and dominant thereafter. For example, functionalism was still being proclaimed as a design principle in Mexico well into the 1990s; while there was little if any Mexican involvement in the critiques of 'International Style' Modernism, such as those made by Team X in the 1950s; there was virtually no Postmodernist design of the type found in the USA and Europe during the 1970s and 80s; practically no High-Tech movement as in Britain; very little interest in Deconstructivism and other US theoretical approaches in the 1990s; and so on. Mexican Modernist architecture thus stayed remarkably homogenous in its discourse up to the end of the twentieth century – and indeed is much the same today in the early years of the 2020s.

The point having been made, it does not necessarily mean that this is a positive situation. As this book also demonstrates, Mexican Modernist architecture as a cultural expression has always been the outcome of power relationships. Hence, the five identified power structures – academic, social status, economic/political, gender and postcolonial – were examined to see how they enforced power relationships through built form and inhabited space. What were revealed were the ways in which architecture can serve to marginalize and differentiate people – academically, socially, economically, sexually and even ethnically – by imposing novel cultural values and beliefs as if they are (relatively) fixed social constructs. By studying these kinds of issues behind the scenes, as it were, the book has unpacked the factors involved in the design of Mexican Modernist architecture with the hope of providing a contribution that can help the development of the architectural profession more broadly. As has been noted, any attempt to improve the architectural profession in such a way 'needs to operate within a collaborative framework, one offering equal opportunities according to talent rather than a particular social status, political affiliation, economic model, gender, geographic and economic location'.[1]

Epilogue

The value of this book is precisely that it heightens our awareness of Mexican architecture's paradigms, stereotypes and assumptions, precisely by studying these different kinds of power mechanisms. My aims in writing the book have thus been twofold. Firstly, I wanted to provoke within the Mexican architectural profession a loss of innocence – by revealing architecture's suppressed meaning, assumed authority and intrinsic nature – to trigger a reawakening of conscience and of accountability among practitioners today. To achieve this goal, Mexican architects will need to acknowledge their responsibilities in the production and reproduction of cultural patterns and power structures. Although Michel Foucault pointed out that 'architects are not figures of domination and they have no power over people',[2] they nonetheless participate directly – as this book clearly demonstrates – in creating the formal and spatial power structures that are contained in buildings. Mexican architects thus have to recognize this situation and instead adopt a more critical stance towards their profession, its teachings and practices, so that they can decide what they really want to endorse. My second aim in this book was to encourage new approaches that are able to resist and even defy existing paradigms in order to suggest kinds of architecture which exist outside these boundaries, thereby promoting a desire for social and cultural renewal. Hence, the purpose of disclosing the underlying mechanics of power within Mexican Modernist architecture is to go beyond those mechanics, to create alternative possibilities.

Thankfully, there are some very good examples now in twentieth-first century Mexico of how one might disavow at least some of the power structures. For instance, the university-based training system, whose order and control are required for the important task of legitimizing the profession, now has those who realize that architects need to recognize, as architecture, those buildings being created outside their realm. For example, recognizing that more than 65% of new houses in Mexico are, in fact, being self-built by their owners, some Mexican scholars as well as building material companies are now promoting the idea of 'architecture without architects' by writing manuals for how to construct one's own dwelling. Some of these manuals were displayed in the Mexican Pavilion at the 15th Venice Architecture Biennale in 2016, wherein more than 25 design construction manuals were exhibited to provide a starting point for how to rethink the past and future of architecture in Mexico.

In terms of economic and political power structures, there is, however, still very little being built in Mexico outside the power networks represented by the Mexican state, business corporations and Catholic Church. At the same time, today one can find some examples of architecture that is neither intended to be

Epilogue

financially viable nor likely to be built but which contributes instead to broader ideas about its socio-economic and cultural constraints. Simply stating these realities would be inadequate and ineffective, yet there is an honest attempt to push things on in, for example, the approach of Futura, a Mexican design firm founded in 2008 by Vicky González and Iván García. They have opted for a unique way of approaching projects that they claim offers a balance between compliance and rebellion. As such, they began their practice by setting out four basic rules by which they need to abide. Rules No.1 and No.4 acknowledge the role of economic and political power structures in the realm of design, but also establish the way in which Futura should be dealing with these power structures. Rule No.1 therefore declares, 'Never work for politicians, religious or gambling institutions' – whereas Rule No.4 states: 'Always choose nice people, great projects and experimentation above money'.[3] Through these two rules, they openly accept their accountability as part of Mexico's economic and political power structures, while at the same time they set limits to what kinds of compromises are acceptable by making it clear just what they will do or will not do for profit.

A growing number of architects and other professionals in Mexico are looking to elsewhere in Latin American for examples of how architecture might avoid perpetuating elitist cultural patterns that are rooted in social differentiation and marginalization. One such case was the policy devised by the former mayor of Medellin in Colombia, Sergio Fajardo Valderrama, which he called 'social urbanism'. His aim was to create, through built form, democratic spaces for education and cultural activities particularly in the most deprived and dangerous areas of that city once so riddled with drug-gangs. The model was hence later replicated in other cities in Latin America, such as Monterrey and Chihuahua in Mexico, where important buildings have been erected in poor and dangerous areas of the city. For instance, Centro Comunitario Independencia was built overlooking Monterrey's city centre by a leading local architect, Agustin Landa Vértiz, and La Cátedra Blanca in 2011. That same year, another community centre was also built in the periphery of the city of Chihuahua in Vistas del Cerro Grande by the firm Arquitectura en Proceso, for this very purpose.

As to the hope of creating innovative design beyond the branding techniques of the 'star-architect' system, this remains non-existent in Mexico. Currently, architecture plays an important role within the Mexican consumption system as both a financial investment and a desirable commodity which supports and maintains capital accumulation. Therefore, most Mexican architects assume that this is the game they have to play to be successful – especially now that numerous

Epilogue

international 'star-architects' are designing and building in the country. Mexican architects are not merely branding themselves and their work, but some even offer branding techniques to clients as part of their design package. Only a few architects who prefer to keep a low profile, and indeed are uninterested in any kind of official recognition other than from their clients, seem immune to these commercial pressures.

Although much has been accomplished in at least acknowledging Mexican architecture to be a highly gendered discipline and profession, it nonetheless remains a masculine field that continues to discriminate against women. Gender inequality is deeply rooted and difficult to change. In Mexico today, some 49.34% of university students in all subjects are female, and slightly over 50% of those studying architecture are women. Unfortunately, however, fewer of these women will join the workforce as practicing architects. According to the National Occupational and Employment Survey, carried out in 2019, there is a workforce of about 9 million professionals in Mexico. Only 227,000 are architects, urban designers and product designers – and from these, just 30.9% are women, while 69.1% are men.[4] Hence although the percentage of female architects and urban designers has risen in Mexico during the past two decades, these figures show that just three of every ten working architects and urban designers are women. So, despite the shift in gender understanding, there are still obviously cultural barriers that disincentivize women from practicing as architects. In a more positive vein, some female architects are now, in the twenty-first century, starting to compete toe-to-toe with their male counterparts, responding to what Sara Topelson, a leading Mexican architect, boldly called 'The Century of Women'. Thus, while a mere handful of female Mexican Modernist architects ever gained any recognition during the twentieth century, there are now around 30 women who are regularly receiving acknowledgement and winning awards. Some of these most distinguished women in Mexican architecture today are also well-known within the global scene, such as Tatiana Bilbao, Fernanda Canales, Frida Escobedo, Gabriela Carrillo, Gabriela Etchegaray and Rozana Montiel. It is important to point out, among these architects, the work of Frida Escobedo and her Serpentine Pavilion in London, designed in 2018 (Figure 6.1). Also notable is her recent appointment by the Metropolitan Museum of Art in New York to design the new Oscar L Tang and HM Agnes Hsu-Tang Wing, which was previously assigned to David Chipperfield Architects.

Although these leading female architects have reached global recognition, still up-and-coming young female architects in Mexico are unhappy that architecture

Epilogue

Figure 6.1 Frida Escobedo, Serpentine Pavilion, London. 2018.

Epilogue

remains such a gendered profession, yet often they do not want to turn gender into an issue. For instance, Paola Calzada claims:

> There have always been female architects, but their work has not usually been recognized by the leader of the firm, group or men. This is changing as more and more women are managing to balance their private life with their work life. For me, this balance is achieved as men also take housework and childcare with pride, allowing women to be released from this obligation. That is, there is now a distribution of work, although not fair yet, but more balanced.[5]

Jimena Fernández likewise states that:

> The role of women has always been important; it is just that before it was behind some male figure. Today, we are liberating ourselves a little more from that shadow. We are opening our own architecture and design studios and having more presence. We are the part that sees architecture with other eyes, that makes it more empathetic and that understands that architecture must be lived. Although I don't think it's a gender issue but a social (cultural) issue.[6]

Figure 6.2 Jimena Fernández, Casa de Los Árboles. Coatepec, Veracruz. 2022.

Epilogue

Lisa Beltrán backs up such views when she notes, 'In architecture as in any other aspect of life, women have the role they chose, because one thing is the role that society wants to impose on you and something else is what you chose to do with your life, knowledge and work'.[7] Saidee Springall agrees, in declaring, 'I believe that women architects must define and find their own ways to be successful and gain recognition; develop new battlefields that are not confrontational with the male gender. It should not be men who validate our work but ourselves and society as a whole, [we should be] making our way and building a new front'.[8] But, although progress is being gained slowly and steadily in terms of women participating in the architectural professional, there is still much to be done to understand the gendering mechanisms within built form and architectural space. In Mexico, there is little awareness of architecture as a gendering device and the ways in which it acts on the body by segregating, secluding, surveying and controlling – thereby upholding cultural patterns that perpetuate gender formation. Further studies therefore need to be undertaken and more problems examined to create greater recognition of the problem. Architects must become aware of their accountability in perpetuating gender patterns; instead, they should be proposing designs that go beyond these stereotypes.

Similarly, while there is growing understanding of Mexico's postcolonial condition more widely in relation to culture, politics, economics and so on, architects in the twenty-first century seem worryingly unconcerned. Indeed, they have lost all interest in trying to express a nationalist voice and identity, being instead more preoccupied with how to deal with the influx of international competition due to globalization. Signs of architectural globalization can be found in Mexico's major cities with new buildings by the likes of Norman Foster, Richard Rogers, Zaha Hadid, Cesar Pelli and Tadao Ando. Therefore, within a globalized market, Mexican architects are not worried about the status of 'otherness' but about how to compete against international firms. Mimicry and hybridity are very much present in contemporary Mexican architecture. Mimicry is perhaps more prevalent in this need to submit and pretend, to compensate for an underprivileged position by imitating or mimicking what is believed to be a superior architecture. This explains the increasing use of complex geometries or of eco-technologies or of daring technical solutions to create an architecture equal to their foreign counterparts. Excellent instances of this can be found in the work of Mauricio Rocha, Alberto Kalach, Tatiana Bilbao, Javier Sánchez, Fernanda Canales, Bernardo Gómez Pimienta and Javier Sordo Madaleno, to name but a few. Their architecture tries to create an internationalized character imbued with monumentality, diversity and contrast in an effort to produce experiences

Epilogue

rather than just spaces, as well, of course, as responding to global concerns and market conditions.

Despite the evident changes in Mexican architecture, it is plain to see that there are serious challenges that remain in the profession and which must be addressed. Consequently, there is much more that must be done. What is crucial is to produce a new way of thinking that goes beyond the constraints of the prevailing power structures and beyond the discipline as traditionally conceived. This book, therefore, hopes to help to free Mexican architecture from the myths of twentieth-century Modernism so that a new conceptualization of the profession can be created. The five power structures identified here through the cultural studies approach are intended to highlight ways to go beyond the profession's present discourse and to find ways to produce a new kind of practice – precisely by acknowledging that architecture can always be different to what it currently is.

Although this book seeks to go beyond an architectural profession governed by Western institutions and paradigms, it does so by using what are Western thought structures. It is impossible to oppose Western thought if you have not been subjected to it, either as a Westerner or as a westernized non-Westerner, as in my case. Therefore, my aim here is not to dismiss Western thought; only to oppose the tyranny of reason and certainty that represses and excludes that which is uncertain. This book hence does not reject the concept of reason; rather, it rejects reason's dogmatism and its efforts to represent itself as a timeless certainty. This, however, is not to declare that nothing is real, or else that everything is merely a cultural, linguistic or historical construct – but that nothing can be seen as less real for being culturally, linguistically or historically determined, especially when there is no universal or timeless models to which it can be compared. Furthermore, I do not believe that there are an infinite number of meanings, just that there is never only one – the Western one. Instead, I would like to argue, by using the words of the US social activist bell hooks, that:

> Contradictions reveal the mystery and magic of life. they remind us that everything cannot be understood by pure reason – that the world of intuition, dreams and folklore are all ways of knowing that shape and guide our work. To be open to those oppositional ways of knowing that teach us how to transgress we must free our imagination.[9]

In conclusion, this book reveals the power structures that determined Mexican Modernist architecture in the twentieth century and challenges its foundations

Epilogue

to obtain a fuller understanding of that which was outside its paradigms; that is, outside its margins. As the author, this book was carried out from the margins, established by my vantage point as a Mexican, and thus a non-Western person, as a member of a middle-class capitalist society in a developing nation within a neoliberal global economy, as well as a woman who inhabits all these realms. Therefore, it was written from the margins, from outside the predominate element of the dyad, not as a lesser place nor as a diminished condition but as a place of change that allows me to see beyond the so-called 'reality'; from a place that opens the door for the unexpected and the unforeseen to produce and intuit a new definition of architecture and of the world. Yes, we are a dream and the manipulation of others. We are constructed by the 'other' and in the image of their 'otherness'. But it is in the awareness of this condition that we achieve the possibility of change. We must teach how to free our imagination, because 'it is our imagination that lets us move beyond boundaries – without imagination we cannot reinvent and recreate the world – the space we live in so that justice and freedom for all can be realized in our lives – every day and always'.[10] It is in this awareness of the consciousness of our existence as a dream or as a construct that we are able to act, to subvert, to resist and to create. For it is far better to be aware that one is a dream than to continue to believe that we are 'real' without the possibility of questioning our existence.

NOTES

1 Toy, Maggie. *The Architect: Women in Contemporary Architecture*. New York, AD Publications, 2001, p. 9.

2 This was an important point made by Michel Foucault. See: Rabinow, Paul (ed.). *The Foucault Reader: An Introduction to Foucault's Thought*. Harmondsworth, Penguin Books, 1986, p. 245.

3 García, Ivan and Vicky Gonzalez. 'A Brand after All'. *Futura*. http://byfutura.com/who-we-are/, accessed 5th October 2020.

4 Secretaria Nacional de Empleo. 'Observatorio Laboral'. *Gob. Mx*, 1er trimestre 2019. www.observatoriolaboral.gob.mx/static/estudios-publicaciones/Tendencias_empleo.html, accessed 5th October 2020.

5 Glocal. '10 | Arquitectas Mexicanas Destacadas'. *Glocal Design Magazine*, 7th March 2017. https://glocal.mx/10-arquitectas-mexicanas-destacadas/, accessed 5th October 2020.

6 Ibid.

7 Ibid.

8 Ibid.

Epilogue

9 hooks, bell, Julie Eizenberg and Hank Koning. Quoted in Jane Rendell, Barbara Penner, and Iain Borden (eds.), *Gender, Space, Architecture*. London, Routledge, 2000, p. 397.

10 hooks, bell. 'Choosing the Margin as a Space of Radical Openness'. In Jane Rendell, Barbara Penner, and Iain Borden (eds.), *Gender, Space, Architecture*. London, Routledge, 2000, p. 398.

Acknowledgements

Acknowledgements

My sincere and profound thanks to Murray Fraser for urging me to write this book and for persuading me that it was indeed possible. In fact, I would like to thank all of my teachers who, like Murray, inspired and stimulated my love for architecture and for research. I must also recognize the participation of my many students who, throughout my years in teaching architecture at Tec de Monterrey, also motivated my love for my profession. These people are my inspiration.

In the actual making of this book, first and foremost, I must also record my indebtedness to Murray Fraser for kindly reading my draft version and offering his prompt comments, as well as for his constant advice and encouragement. My heartfelt gratitude also goes to my sister Estela, who supported me by proofreading my work. I am also greatly indebted to my friends and colleagues Ana Cecilia Cantú, Carsten Krohn, Diego Rodriquez, Julieta Cantú and Roberto Zuñiga, who gracefully gave me their beautiful photographs contributing to both enhancing and illustrating this book. My deepest thanks to them; for their photographs helped me express images, concepts and emotions. I am truly grateful, as well, to the various architecture studios like Legorreta Arquitectos, Sordo Madaleno Arquitectos, Taller de Arquitectura X Alberto Kalach, Archivo Arquitecto Pedro Ramirez Vazquez, Frida Escobedo Estudio and JF Studio Jimena Fernandez for providing photographs of their work and for giving me the permission for their publication.

This book is a reflection of my love for architecture and for architects. I love the special world architects live in, which, for me, is very different than the actual world. I am particularly thankful to the ten architects – Pedro Ramírez Vázquez, Agustín Hernández, Abraham Zabludovsky, Carlos Mijares, Ricardo Legorreta, Juan José Díaz Infante, Enrique Norten, Alberto Kalach, Javier Sordo Madaleno and Clara de Buen – who opened their studios and their offices to welcome me 20 years ago (Figure A.1). They allowed me to interview them, giving me their full attention and their honest answers. Without these interviews, this book would not have been possible. These interviews helped me better understand architecture and its complexities. I was also able to get a glimpse of their wonderful and fantastic personal world. In doing this, I also was able to understand and to convey how Mexican Modernist architecture was constructed and how it contributed to twentieth-century Mexico and to the world's architecture.

Acknowledgements

Figure A.1 Author with the Key Mexican Architects. Top Row: Pedro Ramírez Vázquez, Abraham Zabludovsky and Ricardo Legorreta. Middle row: Carlos Mijares, Juan José Díaz Infante and Enrique Norten. Bottom row: Clara de Buen, Alberto Kalach and Javier Sordo Madaleno.

Illustration Credits

Illustration Credits

COVER

Ricardo Legorreta: The Hotel Camino Real front patio and fountain, Mexico City, 1969. Image by Carsten Krohn.

BACKCOVER

Ricardo Legorreta: The Hotel Camino Real front patio and fountain, Mexico City, 1969. Image by Carsten Krohn. Permission to publish © Mathias Goeritz/ SOMAAP/México/2022.

CHAPTER 1

Chart 1.1 15 Main Schools of Architecture in Mexico During the Twentieth Century. Image created by the author.

Chart 1.2 Image created by the author.

Chart 1.3 Classifications of Mexican Modernist architecture used in the 36 key selected texts. Image created by the author.

Chart 1.4 Chronology of descriptions of Mexican Modernist architecture identified by Enrique X. de Anda. Image created by the author.

Chart 1.5 Top Ten Most Photographed Buildings in the Selected 36 Books. Image created by the author.

Fig. 1.1 Pedro Ramírez Vázquez: The Museo Nacional de Antropología, Main Façade, Mexico City, 1964. Image by Julieta Cantú.

Fig. 1.2 Juan O'Gorman: Biblioteca Central UNAM, Mexico City, 1952. Image by Carsten Krohn.

Fig. 1.3 Luis Barragán: Casa Estudio Tacubaya, Mexico City, 1948. Image by Julieta Cantú. Courtesy of © Barragán Foundation, Switzerland/ProLitteris.

Fig. 1.4 Luis Barragán and Mathias Goeritz: The Torres de Satélite, Mexico City, 1957. Image by Carsten Krohn. Permission to publish © Barragan Foundation, Switzerland/ProLitteris, Zurich/SOMAAP/2022. Permission to publish © Mathias Goeritz/SOMAAP/México/2022.

Fig. 1.5 First Generation, from left to right: José Villagrán García, Luis Barragán and Juan O'Gorman. Public Domain.

Fig. 1.6 Juan O'Gorman, Diego Rivera, Ruth Rivera Marín and Heriberto Pagelson: Museo Anahuacalli, Mexico City, 1955. Image by Julieta Cantú.

Fig1.7 Second Generation, from left to right: Pedro Ramírez Vazquez, Abraham Zabludovsky and Agustín Hernandez. Image by Julieta Cantú.

Fig. 1.8 Agustín Hernández: Calakmul, Mexico City, 1997. Image by Julieta Cantú.

Fig. 1.9 Third Generation, from left to right: Ricardo Legorreta, Carlos Mijares and Juan José Díaz Infante. Image by Julieta Cantú.

Illustration Credits

Fig. 1.10 Legorreta + Legorreta and Rogers Stirk Harbour + Partners: Torre BBVA, Mexico City, 2016. Image by Carsten Krohn.

Fig. 1.11 Fourth Generation, from left to right: Enrique Norten, Clara de Buen, Alberto Kalach and Javier Sordo Madaleno. Image by Julieta Cantú.

Fig. 1.12 Alberto Kalach: Biblioteca Vasconcelos, Mexico City, 2007. Image by Carsten Krohn.

Graph 1.1 Image created by the author.

Graph 1.2 Statistics for the main architectural texts about Mexican Modernist architecture written from 1920–2000. Image created by the author.

Graph 1.3 Locations/languages for the main architectural texts about Mexican Modernist architecture written from 1920–2000. Image created by the author.

Map 1.1 The Network Map of Abraham Zabludovsky. Image created by the author.

Map 1.2 The Network Map of Ricardo Legorreta. Image created by the author.

Map 1.3 The Network Map of Luis Barragán. Image created by the author.

Map 1.4 The Network Map of Clara de Buen. Image created by the author.

Map 1.5 The Network Map of All 13 Key Mexican Architects. Image created by the author.

Map 1.6 The Network Map of José Villagrán García. Image created by the author.

Map 1.7 The Network Map of Juan José Díaz Infante. Image created by the author.

CHAPTER 2

Fig. 2.1 Spatial Diagrams Taken From Kim Dovey, *Framing Places Mediating Power in Built Form,* 1999. London, Routledge.

Fig. 2.2 José Villagrán García: Sanatorio para Tuberculosos de Huipulco, Mexico City, 1929. Image Public Domain.

Fig. 2.3 Sanatorio para Tuberculosos de Huipulco, Floor Plan and Spatial Diagram. Image created by the author based on Born, Esther. *The New Architecture in Mexico*. New York, The Arquitectural Record, William Morrow & Company, 1937.

Fig. 2.4 José Villagrán García: Instituto Nacional de Cardiología, Mexico City, 1937. Image Public Domain.

Fig. 2.5 Instituto Nacional de Cardiología, Floor Plan and Spatial Diagram. Image created by the author based on Noelle, Louise and Carlos Tejeda. Catálogo Guía de Arquitectura Contemporánea. México, Ed. Fomento Cultural Banamex, 1993.

Fig. 2.6 Pedro Ramírez Vázquez: The Museo Nacional de Antropología, Interior Courtyard, Mexico City, 1964. Image by Julieta Cantú.

Fig. 2.7 The Museo Nacional de Antropología, Floor Plan and Spatial Diagram. Image created by the author based on Trueblood, B. *Ramírez Vázquez en la arquitectura, Realización y diseño*. Mexico City, Editorial Diana, 1989.

Fig. 2.8 Sala Mexica With the Aztec Calendar, Mexico City. Image by Julieta Cantú.

Fig. 2.9 Pedro Ramírez Vázquez: The Museo del Templo Mayor Main Façade, Mexico City, 1987. Image by Ana Cecilia Cantú.

Illustration Credits

Fig. 2.10 The Museo del Templo Mayor Interior With the Tlaltecuhtli as the Centrepiece of the Museum. Image by Ana Cecilia Cantú.

Fig. 2.11 Museo del Templo Mayor, Floor Plans Showing the Circulation Pattern in Red Arrows. Image created by the author based on Vargas Salguero, Ramón. *Historia de la arquitectura y el urbanismo mexicanos*. México, Fondo de Cultura Económica, 1998.

Fig. 2.12 Zabludovsky and González de León: Museo Tamayo Exterior, Mexico City, 1981. Image by Julieta Cantú.

Fig. 2.13 Zabludovsky and González de León: Museo Tamayo Interior, Mexico City, 1981. Image by Carsten Krohn.

Fig. 2.14 Museo Tamayo, Floor Plans, Section and Spatial Diagram. Image created by the author based on Glusberg, Jorge: *Abraham Zabludovsky, arquitecto*. México, Noriega Editores: Consejo Nacional para la Cultura y las Artes, 1998.

Fig. 2.15 José Villagrán Garcia, Juan Sordo Madaleno, Ricardo Legorreta and José Adolfo Wiechers: The Hotel Maria Isabel, Mexico City, 1963. Image by Julieta Cantú.

Fig. 2.16 The Hotel Maria Isabel, Floor Plan and Section. Image created by the author based on Toppelson, Sara. *50 Años de Arquitectura en Mexicana*. México, Ed. Plazola, 1999.

Fig. 2.17 Ricardo Legorreta: The Hotel Camino Real Front Patio and Fountain, Mexico City, 1969. Image by Carsten Krohn. Permission to publish © Mathias Goeritz/SOMAAP/México/2022.

Fig. 2.18 The Hotel Camino Real, Floor Plans and Spatial Diagram. Image created by the author based on Mutlow, John V. *Legorreta Arquitectos: Ricardo Legorreta, Víctor Legorreta, Noé Castro*. México, Gustavo Gili, 1997.

Fig. 2.19 Nuño, Mac Gregor and de Buen: The Estación del Metro Pantitlán Linea A, Mexico City, 1991. Image by Ana Cecilia Cantú.

Fig. 2.20 Juan José Díaz Infante: The Terminal de Autobuses de Oriente (TAPO), Mexico City, 1978. Image by Ana Cecilia Cantú.

Fig. 2.21 Juan José Díaz Infante: The Terminal de Autobuses de Oriente (TAPO), Mexico City, 1978. Image by Ana Cecilia Cantú.

Fig. 2.22 The TAPO Bus Station, Floor Plan and Spatial Diagram. Image created by the author based on Díaz Infante Núñez, Juan José. *Díaz Infante visto por Díaz Infante*. México, I. Maya Gómez, J. Torres Palacios, 1988.

Fig. 2.23 Zabludovsky and González de León: Citibanamex C.F. Lomas, Mexico City, 1989. Image by Julieta Cantu.

Fig. 2.24 Citibank C.F. Lomas, Floor Plans and Spatial Diagram. Image created by the author based on Glusberg, Jorge: *Abraham Zabludovsky, arquitecto*. México, Noriega Editores: Consejo Nacional para la Cultura y las Artes, 1998.

Fig. 2.25 Zabludovsky and González de León: Citibanamex Oficina Central, Mexico City, 1987. Image by Julieta Cantú.

Fig. 2.26 Citibanamex Oficina Central, Floor Plan and Elevation, Mexico City, 1987. Image from Glusberg, Jorge: *Abraham Zabludovsky, arquitecto*. México, Noriega Editores: Consejo Nacional para la Cultura y las Artes, 1998.

Fig. 2.27 Citibanamex Oficina Central, Spatial Diagram. Image created by the author based on Glusberg, Jorge: *Abraham Zabludovsky, arquitecto*. México, Noriega Editores: Consejo Nacional para la Cultura y las Artes, 1998.

Illustration Credits

Fig. 2.28 Pedro Ramírez Vázquez: Palacio Legislativo de San Lázaro, Mexico City, 1981. Image by Ana Cecilia Cantú.

Fig. 2.29 Zabludovsky and González de León: Delegación Cuauhtémoc Building, Mexico City, 1973. Image by Julieta Cantú.

Fig. 2.30 Delegación Cuauhtémoc Building, Floor Plan and Spatial Diagram. Image created by the author based on Glusberg, Jorge: *Abraham Zabludovsky, arquitecto*. México, Noriega Editores: Consejo Nacional para la Cultura y las Artes, 1998.

Fig. 2.31 Pedro Ramírez Vázquez: Torre de Tlatelolco, Mexico City, 1960. Image by Julieta Cantú.

Fig. 2.32 La Bolsa Mexicana de Valores, Site Plan. Image from Toppelson, Sara. *50 Años de Arquitectura en Mexicana*. México, Ed. Plazola, 1999.

Fig. 2.33 Juan José Díaz Infante: La Bolsa Mexicana de Valores Exterior, Mexico City, 1990. Image by Julieta Cantú.

Fig. 2.34 Juan José Díaz Infante: La Bolsa Mexicana de Valores Interior, Mexico City, 1990. Image by Julieta Cantú.

Fig. 2.35 Zabludovsky and González de León: INFONAVIT Building Main Entrance, Mexico City, 1975. Image by Ana Cecilia Cantú.

Fig. 2.36 INFONAVIT Building, Floor Plans and Spatial Diagram. Image created by the author based on Glusberg, Jorge: *Abraham Zabludovsky, arquitecto*. México, Noriega Editores: Consejo Nacional para la Cultura y las Artes, 1998.

Fig. 2.37 Nuño, Mac Gregor and de Buen: Corporativo IBM Santa Fe, Mexico City, 1997. Image by Julieta Cantú.

Fig. 2.38 Corporativo IBM Santa Fe, Floor Plan and Spatial Diagram. Image created by the author based on *Revista Enlace*, Year 10, Number 7, July 2000.

Fig. 2.39 Juan O'Gorman: Escuela Técnica Industrial, Mexico City, 1934. Image Public Domain.

Fig. 2.40 Escuela Técnica Industrial and Spatial Diagram. Image created by the author based on Born, Esther. *The New Architecture in Mexico*. New York, The Arquitectural Record William Morrow & Company, 1937.

Fig. 2.41 Nuño Mac Gregor de Buen: Colegio Alexander Von Humboldt, Mexico City, 1990. Image by Julieta Cantú.

Fig. 2.42 Abraham Zabludovsky: Colegio Monte Sinai Complex, Mexico City, 1994. Image by Ana Cecilia Cantú.

Fig. 2.43 Colegio Monte Sinai, 1994. Drawing taken from Organizaciones Espaciales https://slideplayer.es/slide/10303483/ Published by Ramona Rojo Calderón.

Fig. 2.44 Zabludovsky and González de León: El Colegio de México, Mexico City, 1975. Image by Julieta Cantú.

Fig. 2.45 Zabludovsky and González de León: El Colegio de México Patio, Mexico City, 1975. Image by Julieta Cantú.

Fig. 2.46 El Colegio de México, Floor Plans and Spatial Diagram. Image created by the author based on Glusberg, Jorge: *Abraham Zabludovsky, arquitecto*. México, Noriega Editores: Consejo Nacional para la Cultura y las Artes, 1998.

Fig. 2.47 Christ Church, Floor Plan, Section and Spatial Diagram. Image created by the author based on *Revista Obras* Vol. 24, Number 238, Octubre 1992.

Illustration Credits

Fig. 2.48 Carlos Mijares: Christ Church exterior, Mexico City, 1989. Image by Julieta Cantú.

Fig. 2.49 Carlos Mijares: Christ Church Interior, Mexico City, 1989. Image by Julieta Cantú.

Fig. 2.50 Pedro Ramírez Vázquez: Basílica de la Virgen de Guadalupe Exterior, Mexico City, 1976. Image by Julieta Cantú.

Fig. 2.51 Floor Plan, Section and Spatial Diagram of the Basílica de la Virgin de Guadalupe. Image created by the author based on Trueblood, B. *Ramírez Vázquez en la arquitectura, Realización y diseño*. Mexico City, Editorial Diana, 1989.

Fig. 2.52 Pedro Ramírez Vázquez: Basílica de la Virgen de Guadalupe Interior, Mexico City, 1976. Image by Julieta Cantú.

Graph 2.1 Image created by the author.

Graph 2.2 Image created by the author.

Graph 2.3 Image created by the author.

Graph 2.4 Image created by the author.

CHAPTER 3

Fig. 3.1 Jardines del Pedregal, Mexico City, Urban Layout, Mid-1940s. Image created by the author.

Fig. 3.2 Mathias Goeritz: Plaza 'El Animal del Pedregal' at Jardines del Pedregal. Image by Julieta Cantú. Permission to publish © © Mathias Goeritz/SOMAAP/México/2022.

Fig. 3.3 Clara Porset, Comissioned by Luis Barragán: Silla Miguelito. Image created by the author.

Fig. 3.4 Ricardo Legorreta: Silla Vallarta, 1973. Image courtesy of Clásicos Mexicanos.

Fig. 3.5 Pedro Ramírez Vázquez: Equipal Moderno. Image courtesy of Archivo Arquitecto Pedro Ramírez Vásquez.

Fig. 3.6 Agustín Hernández: Silla Gala Chair, 1997. Image, Courtesy of Clásicos Mexicanos.

Fig. 3.7 Ricardo Legorreta: Museo MARCO, Monterrey, Mexico, 1991. Image courtesy of Julieta Cantú.

Fig. 3.8 Javier Sordo Madaleno: Plaza Moliere; Now Palacio de Hierro Plaza Moliere, Mexico City, 1997. Image by Julieta Cantú.

Fig. 3.9 Luis Barragán in His House/Studio. Permission to publish © Barragan Foundation, Switzerland/ProLitteris, Zurich/SOMAAP/2022.

Fig. 3.10 José Villagrán García. Image public domain.

Fig. 3.11 Juan O'Gorman. Image from on Born, Esther. *The New Architecture in Mexico*. New York, The Arquitectural Record William Morrow & Company, 1937.

Fig. 3.12 Pedro Ramírez Vázquez in His Office. Image Courtesy of Archivo Arquitecto Ramírez Vázquez.

Illustration Credits

Fig. 3.13 Agustín Hernández in His Studio. Image published in Hernández, Agustín. *Agustín Hernández Arquitecto*, México, Grupo Noriega Editores, 1998.

Fig. 3.14 Abraham Zabludovsky in One of His Buildings. Image published in Larrosa Irigoyen, Manuel. *Abraham Zabludosky Espacios para la Cultura*, 2000.

Fig. 3.15 Carlos Mijares in His Office. Image published in *Revista Obras* Vol. 24 Numero 238, octubre 1992.

Fig. 3.16 Ricardo Legorreta in His Office. Image published in Legorreta Vilchis, Ricardo. *Ricardo Legorreta* Tokyo, ADA Edita Tokyo, 2000.

Fig. 3.17 Juan José Díaz Infante in His Office. Image by Díaz Infante Casasus in Díaz Infante Núñez, Juan José. *Díaz Infante visto por Díaz Infante*. México, I. Maya Gómez, J. Torres Palacios, 1988.

Fig. 3.18 Enrique Norten. Image published, Banamex Master Magazine, año 3, número 28 agosto 02.

Fig. 3.19 Alberto Kalach. Detail of image published in León, Adriana. *Kalach + Alvarez*. Mexico, Gustavo Gili, 1998.

Fig. 3.20 Clara de Buen in the Earlier Part of Her Career. Image published, *Revista Enlace* Año 12 Número 7, 2002.

Fig. 3.21 Javier Sordo Madaleno in the Late 1990s. Image by Ignacio Urquiza, Courtesy of © Sordo Madaleno Arquitectos.

Fig. 3.22 Abraham Zabludovsky: La Templaza, Avenida Las Fuentes #34. Mexico City, 1971. Image by Ana Cecilia Cantú.

Fig. 3.23 La Templanza, Floor Plan (Maids' Quarters in Red) and Spatial Diagram. Image created by the author based on Glusberg, Jorge: *Abraham Zabludovsky, arquitecto*. México, Noriega Editores: Consejo Nacional para la Cultura y las Artes, 1998.

Fig. 3.24 Abraham Zabludovsky: Casa Zabludovsky; Now Museo de la Intervención Arquitectónica, Palacio Versalles 235, Colonia Lomas de Reforma, Mexico City, 1969. Image by Ana Cecilia Cantú.

Fig. 3.25 Zabludovsky House, Floor Plans (Maids' Quarters and Master-Bedroom in Red) and Spatial Diagram. Image created by the author based on Glusberg, Jorge: *Abraham Zabludovsky, arquitecto*. México, Noriega Editores: Consejo Nacional para la Cultura y las Artes, 1998.

Fig. 3.26 Ricardo Legorreta: Casa Monte Tauro in Monte Tauro #270, Lomas de Chapultepec, Mexico City, 1995. Image by Ana Cecilia Cantú.

Fig. 3.27 Legorreta's House, Floor Plans (Maids' Quarters and Master-Bedroom in Red) and Spatial Diagram. Image created by the author based on Legorreta Vilchis, Ricardo. *Ricardo Legorreta*. Tokyo: A.D.A. Edita Tokyo, 2000.

Fig. 3.28 Luis Barragán: Casa Estudio Tacubaya, Floor Plan (Maids' Quarters and Master-Bedroom in Red) and Spatial Diagram. Image created by the author based on Riggen Martínez, Antonio. *Luis Barragán: Mexico's modern master, 1902–1988*. New York, The Monacelli Press, 1996.

Fig. 3.29 Casa GGG, Floor Plans (Maids' Quarters in Red), Section and Spatial Diagram. Image created by the author based on *Revista Arquine*. Revista Internacional de Arquitectura. Num. 11, Mexico, Spring, 2000.

Illustration Credits

Fig. 3.30 Alberto Kalach: Casa GGG, Side view, Mexico City, 2000. Image by Julieta Cantú.

Fig. 3.31 Torre Citibank Reforma, Floor Plan (Service Areas in Red). Image created by the author based on Díaz Infante Núñez, Juan José. *Díaz Infante visto por Díaz Infante*. México, I. Maya Gómez, J. Torres Palacios, 1988.

Fig. 3.32 Juan José Díaz Infante: Torre Citibank Reforma, Mexico City, 1989. Image by Julieta Cantú.

Fig. 3.33 The Hotel Camino Real, Floor Plan (Service Areas in Red). Image created by the author based on Toppelson, Sara. *50 Años de Arquitectura en Mexicana*. México, Ed. Plazola, 1999. Graph 3.1 Image created by the author.

Fig. 3.34 Ricardo Legorreta: The Hotel Camino Real Lobby Showing the Entrance to the Ballroom to the Right and the Front Desk to the Left, Mexico City, 1968. Image by Carsten Krohn.

Graph 3.1 Image created by the author.

Map 3.1. Key Architects' Houses, Studios and House/Studios in Mexico City. Image created by the author.

Map 3.2 Map of Mexico City With Jardines del Pedregal (left) and Pedregal de Santo Domingo (right). Image created by the author.

Map 3.3 Key Buildings by the Four Generations of Modernist Architects in Mexico City. Image created by the author.

CHAPTER 4

Chart 4.1 Mexican Women's Participation in Undergraduate Studies. Source: INEGI.

Chart 4.2 Source: INEGI, 1999.

Fig. 4.1 Kalach + Álvarez Studio Staff in the 1990s: Daniel Alvarez on the Far Right, Alberto Kalach in the Centre and Adriana León Standing on His Right Side. Image published in León, Adriana. *Kalach + Alvarez*. Mexico, Gustavo Gili, 1998.

Fig. 4.2 Luis Barragán: Family Holiday House, Chapala, Altered in 1931. Image created by the author.

Fig. 4.3 Casa Efraín González Luna, Floor Plan and Spatial Diagram. Image created by the author based on Riggen Martínez, Antonio. *Luis Barragán: Mexico's modern master, 1902–1988*. New York, The Monacelli Press, 1996.

Fig. 4.4 Luis Barragán: Casa Efraín González Luna, Guadalajara, 1928. Image by Carsten Krohn. Permission to publish © Barragan Foundation, Switzerland/ProLitteris, Zurich/SOMAAP/2022.

Fig. 4.5 Luis Barragán: Gilardi House, Mexico City, 1976. Image by Diego Rodríguez. Permission to publish © Barragan Foundation, Switzerland/ProLitteris, Zurich/SOMAAP/2022.

Fig. 4.6 Luis Barragán: Gilardi House, Swimming Pool, Mexico City, 1976. Image by Carsten Krohn. Permission to publish © Barragan Foundation, Switzerland/ProLitteris, Zurich/SOMAAP/2022.

Fig. 4.7 Casa Gilardi, Floor Plans (Bedrooms in Blue and Maid's Quarters in Red) and Spatial Diagram. Image created by the author based on Riggen Martínez,

Illustration Credits

Antonio. *Luis Barragán: Mexico's modern master, 1902–1988*. New York, The Monacelli Press, 1996.

Fig. 4.8 Barragán's Casa Estudio Tacubaya, Floor Plans (Master-Bedroom in Blue and the Kitchen and Maid's Quarters in Red) and Spatial Diagram. Image created by the author based on Riggen Martínez, Antonio. *Luis Barragán: Mexico's modern master, 1902–1988*. New York, The Monacelli Press, 1996.

Fig. 4.9 Luis Barragán: Casa Estudio Tacubaya, Mexico City, 1947. Image by Carsten Krohn. Permission to publish © Barragan Foundation, Switzerland/ProLitteris, Zurich/SOMAAP/2022.

Fig. 4.10 Enrique Norten: Casa LE, Mexico City, 1996. Image by Julieta Cantú.

Fig. 4.11 Casa LE, Floor Plans (Bedrooms in Blue and Kitchen in Red) of the Spatial Diagram. Image created by the author based on Woods, Lebbeus. *TEN Arquitectos: Taller de Enrique Norten Arquitectos, S.C.* Barcelona, Gustavo Gili, 1995.

Fig. 4.12 Abraham Zabludovsky: Torres de Mixcoac, Mexico City, 1971. Image by Ana Cecilia Cantú.

Fig. 4.13 Abraham Zabludovsky: Torres de Mixcoac, Mexico City, 1971. Image by Ana Cecilia Cantú.

Fig. 4.14 Torres de Mixcoac, Floor Plan (Master-Bedroom in Blue and Kitchen in Red) and Spatial Diagram. Image created by the author, based González de León Teodoro and Abraham Zabludovsky. *Ocho conjuntos de habitación: arquitectura contemporánea mexicana = Mexican contemporany architecture*. México, Arquitectura y Sociedad, 1976.

Fig. 4.15 Alberto Kalach: Edificio Rodin, Mexico City, 1993. Image by Julieta Cantú

Fig. 4.16 Edificio Rodin, Detail. Image by Julieta Cantú.

Fig. 4.17 Edificio Rodin, Section (Bedroom in Blue and Kitchen/Dining in Red). Image created by the author based on León, Adriana. *Kalach + Alvarez*. Mexico, Gustavo Gili, 1998.

Fig. 4.18 Ricardo Legorreta: Plaza Reforma Offices, Mexico City, 1993. This Axial Entrance Places the Secretary as the Focal Point. Image by Lourdes Legorreta, courtesy of LEGORRETA®.

Fig. 4.19 Bufete Industrial, Floor Plan and Section (Private Areas in Blue and Public Areas in Red). Image created by the author based on Díaz Infante Núñez, Juan José. *Díaz Infante visto por Díaz Infante*. México, I. Maya Gómez, J. Torres Palacios, 1988.

Fig. 4.20 Juan José Díaz Infante: Bufete Industrial, Mexico City, 1979. Image by Julieta Cantú.

Fig. 4.21 A Low Wall is Used to Divide and Provide Privacy. Luis Barragán: Casa Estudio Tacubaya, Mexico City, 1947. Image by Diego Rodríguez. Permission to publish © Barragan Foundation, Switzerland/ProLitteris, Zurich/SOMAAP/2022.

Fig. 4.22 A Low Wall and Door Allow Surveillance From the Top Floor. Luis Barragán: Casa Estudio Tacubaya, Mexico City, 1948. Image by Diego Rodriguez. Permission to publish © Barragan Foundation, Switzerland/ProLitteris, Zurich/SOMAAP/2022.

Illustration Credits

Fig. 4.23 An Open Staircase with No Banister Provides Easy Surveillance From Top Floors. Luis Barragán: Casa Gilardi, Mexico City, 1976. Image by Diego Rodríguez. Permission to publish © Barragan Foundation, Switzerland/ProLitteris, Zurich/SOMAAP/2022.

Fig. 4.24 Agustín Hernández House, Side Elevation. Image created by the author based on Hernández, Agustín. *Agustín Hernández Arquitecto*, México, Grupo Noriega Editores, 1998.

Fig. 4.25 Agustín Hernández: His House, Mexico City, 1989. Image by Ana Cecilia Cantú.

Fig. 4.26 The Chimney is Used to Block the Direct View of the Studio. Luis Barragán's studio. Image by Diego Rodriguez. Permission to publish © Barragan Foundation, Switzerland/ProLitteris, Zurich/SOMAAP/2022.

Fig. 4.27 Luis Barragán: Casa Estudio Tacubaya, Exterior Studio Entrance. Image by Carsten Krohn. Permission to publish © Barragan Foundation, Switzerland/ProLitteris, Zurich/SOMAAP/2022.

Fig.4.28 Luis Barragán's Studio, Spatial Diagram of Ground Floor Showing the Entrance to the House on the Left and the Entrance to the Studio on the Right. Image created by the author based on Riggen Martínez, Antonio. Luis Barragán: Mexico's modern master, 1902–1988. New York, The Monacelli Press, 1996.

Fig. 4.29 Entrance to Ricardo Legorreta's Office. Image by Ana Cecilia Cantú.

Fig. 4.30 Reception Area of Ricardo Legorreta's Studio. To the Left and on a Lower Level, his Private Secretary and Office. To the Right, the Stairs That Lead to the Studio. Image by Ana Cecilia Cantú.

Fig. 4.31 Ricardo Legorreta's Studio, Floor Plan (Reception in Red and Legorreta's Office in Blue) and Section (Reception Area in Red and Legorreta's Office in Blue). Image created by the author based on an image courtesy of Legorreta Arquitectos

Fig. 4.32 Abraham Zabludovsky: His Studio, Mexico City, 1992. Image by Ana Cecilia Cantú.

Fig. 4.33 Abraham Zabludovsky's Studio, Floor Plan, Section (Reception Area in Red and Zabludovsky's Office in Blue) and Spatial Diagram. Image created by the author based on Díaz Infante Núñez, Juan José. *Díaz Infante visto por Díaz Infante*. México, I. Maya Gómez, J. Torres Palacios, 1988.

Fig. 4.34 Juan José Díaz Infante: His Studio, Inside the Geodesic Sphere, Mexico City, 1990. Image by Julieta Cantú.

Fig. 4.35 Juan José Díaz Infante: His House and Studio, Mexico City, 1990. Image by Julieta Cantú.

Fig. 4.36 Agustín Hernández: His Studio, Mexico City, 1976. Image by Julieta Cantú.

Fig. 4.37 The Daring Entrance to Agustín Hernández Studio. Image by Julieta Cantú.

Fig. 4.38 Agustín Hernández Office, Section and Spatial Diagram. Image created by the author based on Hernández, Agustín. *Agustín Hernández Arquitecto*, México, Grupo Noriega Editores, 1998.

Fig. 4.39 Nuño, Mac Gregor and de Buen's studio, Mexico City, Floor Plan and Spatial Diagram. Image created by the author.

Illustration Credits

CHAPTER 5

Fig. 5.1 Alvar Aalto: Paimio Sanatorium Floor Plan, Finland, 1929. Public Domain.

Fig. 5.2 José Villagrán García: Hospital de Cardiología, Floor Plan, Mexico City, 1937. Public Domain.

Fig. 5.3 Le Corbusier: Studio Amédée Ozenfant, Paris, 1924. Public Domain.

Fig. 5.4 Studio Amédée Ozenfant and Studio Diego Rivera, Floor Plans. Public Domain.

Fig. 5.5 Juan O'Gorman: Casa Estudio de Diego Rivera y Frida Kalho, Mexico City, 1930. Image by Julieta Cantú.

Fig. 5.6 Juan José Díaz Infante: Prefabricated Housing Prototype, Circa 1964. Image by Julieta Cantú.

Fig. 5.7 Louis Kahn: Indian Institute of Management, Ahmedabad, 1962. Image used under licence from Shutterstock.com.

Fig. 5.8 Carlos Mijares: Christ Church, Mexico City, 1989. Image by Julieta Cantú.

Fig. 5.9 I.M. Pei: John Hancock Tower, Boston, 1973. Image by Julieta Cantú.

Fig. 5.10 Juan José Díaz Infante: Bolsa Mexicana de Valores, Mexico City, 1990. Image used under licence from Shutterstock.com.

Fig. 5.11 Welton Beckett: Regency Hyatt Hotel, Dallas, 1978. Image by Roberto Zúñiga.

Fig. 5.12 Javier Sordo Madaleno: Edificio Reforma Lomas Altas, Mexico City, 1995. Image by Ana Cecilia Cantú.

Fig. 5.13 Abraham Zabludovsky and Teodoro González de León: Universidad Pedagógica, Mexico City, 1982. Image by Julieta Cantü.

Fig. 5.14 Kallmann, McKinnell & Knowles: Boston City Hall, 1968. Image by Julieta Cantú.

Fig. 5.15 Frank Lloyd Wright: Price Tower, Oklahoma City, 1956. Image used under licence from Shutterstock.com.

Fig. 5.16 Ricardo Legorreta: Torre Celanese, Mexico City, 1968. Image by Ana Cecilia Cantú.

Fig. 5.17 Tadao Ando: Vitra Conference Pavilion, Weil am Rhein, 1993. Image used under licence from Shutterstock.com.

Fig. 5.18 Alberto Kalach: Casa GGG, Exterior, Mexico City, 2000. Image by Julieta Cantú.

Fig. 5.19 Renzo Piano: Bercy 2 Comercial Centre, Renzo Piano, Paris, 1990. Image by Julieta Cantú.

Fig. 5.20 Enrique Norten: Escuela Nacional de Arte Teatral, Mexico City, 1994. Image by Julieta Cantú.

Fig. 5.21 Pedro Ramírez Vázquez: Museo de Antropología, Mexico City, 1964. Image by Julieta Cantú.

Fig. 5.22 Cuadrángulo de las Monjas, Uxmal, Yucatán, Circa Eighth Century CE. Image by Julieta Cantú.

Fig. 5.23 Nunnery Quadrangle, East Building Bas-Relief Detail. Image by Julieta Cantú.

Fig. 5.24 Pedro Ramírez Vázquez: Museo de Antropología, Mexico City, 1964. Detail of the Brise-Soleil on the Upper Floor. Image by Julieta Cantú.

Fig. 5.25 Abraham Zabludovsky and Teodoro González de León: Museo Tamayo Exterior, Mexico City, 1981. Image by Carsten Krohn.

Illustration Credits

Fig. 5.26 Pre-Hispanic Archaeological Site at Monte Albán, Oaxaca, Seventh Century CE. Image by Julieta Cantú.

Fig. 5.27 Agustín Hernández and Manuel González Rul: Heroico Colegio Militar, Mexico City, 1976. Image by Julieta Cantú.

Fig. 5.28 Mexico '68 Olympic Games Logo. Image Courtesy of Archivo Arquitecto Pedro Ramírez Vásquez.

Fig. 5.29 Juan O'Gorman: Biblioteca Central, CU, Mexico City, 1953. Image used under licence from Shutterstock.com

Fig. 5.30 Luis Barragán: Own House/Studio, Casa Tacubaya, 1947. Image by Julieta Cantú. Permission to publish © Barragan Foundation, Switzerland/ProLitteris, Zurich/SOMAAP/2022.

Fig. 5.31 Luis Barragán: Cuadra San Cristobal, Los Clubes, Mexico City, 1968. Image by Diego Rodríguez. Permission to publish © Barragan Foundation, Switzerland/ProLitteris, Zurich/SOMAAP/2022.

Fig. 5.32 Ricardo Legorreta, Museo MARCO, Monterrey, 1992. Image by Lourdes Legorreta, courtesy of LEGORRETA®.

Fig. 5.33 Ricardo Legorreta: San Antonio Public Library, San Antonio, Texas, USA, 1993. Image by Celia Esther Arredondo.

Fig. 5.34 Javier Sordo Madaleno: Westin Los Cabos Resort Villas & Spa, Los Cabos, Baja California Sur, México, 1993. Image by Ignacio Urquiza, courtesy of © Sordo Madaleno Arquitectos.

EPILOGUE

Fig. 6.1 Frida Escobedo, Serpentine Pavilion, London. 2018. Courtesy of Frida Escobedo.

Fig. 6.2 Jimena Fernández, Casa de Los Árboles. Coatepec, Veracruz. 2022. Render courtesy of JF Studio.

ACKNOWLEDGEMENTS

Figure A.1 Author with the Key Mexican Architects. Top row: Pedro Ramirez Vázquez, Abraham Zabludovsky and Ricardo Legorreta. Middle row: Carlos Mijares, Juan José Díaz Infante and Enrique Norten. Bottom row: Clara de Buen, Alberto Kalach and Javier Sordo Madaleno. Photos by Julieta Cantú.

ILLUSTRATIONS

Substantial efforts have been made to track down the copyright holders of images used in this book. The author and publishers apologize for any mistakes and omissions made inadvertently and, if notified, will correct them as soon as possible.

Bibliography

Bibliography

Adrià, Miquel. *Mexico 90s a Contemporary Architecture*. México, Gustavo Gili, 1996.

Ahmad, Aijaz. *In Theory, Classes, Nations, Literatures*. London, Verso, 1992.

Ambasz, Emilio. *The Architecture of Luis Barragán*. New York, Museum of Modern Art, 1976.

Arango Cardinal, Silvia. *Ciudad y Arquitectura. Seis Generaciones que Construyeron La América Latina Moderna*. México, Fondo de Cultura Económica, 2012.

Banamex Master Magazine, año 3, número 28, agosto 02.

Barthes, Roland. *Elements of Semiology*. Translated by Annette Lavers and Colin Smith, New York, Hill & Wang, 1973.

Barthes, Roland. *The Fashion System*. London, Jonathan Cape Ltd., The Trinity Press, 1985.

Bartra, Roger. *La Jaula de la Melancolía Identidad y Metamorfosis del Mexicano*. México, Ed Debolsillo, 2016.

Baudrillard, Jean. *The Consumer Society: Myths and Structures*. London, Sage Publications, 1998.

Baudrillard, Jean. *For a Critique of the Political Economy of the Sign*. Translated by Charles Levin, London, Verso, 2019.

Baudrillard, Jean. *Jean Baudrillard Selected Writings*. Edited by Mark Poster, London, Polity Press, 1998.

Baudrillard, Jean. *The System of Objects*. Translated by James Benedict, London, Verso, 2006.

Beauvoir, Simone. *The Second Sex*. Translated by Constance Borde and Sheila Malvonay-Chevallier, New York, Vintage Books, Random House, 2011.

Béjar, Raúl. *El Mexicano: Aspectos Culturales y Psicosociales*. México, UNAM, 1979.

Benévolo, Leonardo. *Historia de la Arquitectura Moderna*. 5th Edición, Barcelona, Gustavo Gili, 1982.

Bergdoll, Barry, Carlos Eduardo Comas, Jorge Francisco Liernur, and Patricio del Real. *Latin America in Construction: Architecture 1955–1980*. New York, Museum of Modern Art, 2015.

Berman, Marshall. *All That Is Solid Melts into Air: The Experience of Modernity*. New York, Penguin Books, 1988.

Bhabha, Homi. *Location of Culture*. London, Routledge, 1994.

Borges, Jorge Luis. *Collected Fictions*. Translated by Andrew Hurley, New York, Viking Books, 1998.

Born, Esther. *The New Architecture in Mexico*. New York, The Architectural Record William Morrow & Company, 1937.

Browne, Enrique. *La Otra Arquitectura en Latinoamérica*. México, Gustavo Gili, 1988.

Bullrich, Francisco. *Nuevos Caminos de la Arquitectura Latinoamericana*. Barcelona, Ed. Blume, 1969.

Burain, Edward R. (ed.), *Modernity and the Architecture of Mexico*. Austin, University of Texas Press, 1997, p. 103.

Canales, Fernanda. *Arquitectura en México, 1900–2010: la construcción de la modernidad, obras, diseño, arte y pensamiento*. México, Fomento Cultural Banamex, 2013.

Carranza, Luis E. and Fernando Lara. *Modern Architecture in Latin America: Art, Technology, and Utopia*. Austin, University of Texas Press, 2015.

Bibliography

Castañeda, Luis M. *Spectacular Mexico: Design, Propaganda, and the 1968 Olympics*. México, Grupo Financiero Banamex, 2014.

Castañeda, Luis M. *Spectacular Mexico: Design, Propaganda, and the 1968 Olympics*. Minneapolis, University of Minnesota Press, 2014.

Castro-Gómez, Santiago and Eduardo Mendieta (eds.). *Teorías sin disciplina. Latinomericanismo, poscolonialidad y globalización en debate*. San Francisco, University of San Francisco, 1998.

Cetto, Max. *Modern Architecture in Mexico*. New York, Praeger, 1961.

Chance, Julia and Torsten Schmiedeknecht (eds.). *Fame + Architecture (Architectural Design)*. Vol. 71. No. 6. London, Wiley-Academy, November 2001.

Choay, Françoise. *The Rule and the Model on the Theory of Architecture and Urbanism*. Edited by Denise Bratton, London, MIT Press, 1997.

CNN en Español. 'Las mejores frases de Gabriel García Márquez.' *Broadcast*, 17th April 2018. https://cnnespanol.cnn.com/2018/04/17/las-mejores-frases-de-gabriel-garcia-marquez/

Colle Corcuera, Marie-Pierre. *Sordo Madaleno: arquitectura en cuatro elementos*. México, Reverte Ed. 1998.

Collier, Peter and Helga Geyer-Ryan (eds.). *Literary Theory Today*. New York, Cornell University Press, 1990.

Colomina, Beatriz (ed.). *Sexuality and Space*. New York, Princeton Architectural Press, 1992.

Cruickshank, Dan. (ed.). *Sir Banister Fletcher's A History of Architecture (20th Edition)*. Architectural Press/RIBA, London. 1996.

Cuff, Dana. *Architecture: The Story of Practice*. Cambridge, MIT Press, 1991.

de Anda, Enrique X. *El Arte Mexicano*. Vol. 14, México, Salvat, 1986.

de Anda, Enrique X. *Historia de la arquitectura Mexicana*. México, Gustavo Gili, 1995.

de Buen, Clara. Personal interview with the author. Mexico City, 16th October 2000.

de Garay, Graciela. *Historia Oral de la Ciudad de México Testimonios de sus arquitectos (1940 90) Abraham Zabludovsky Investigación y entrevista*. México City, Instituto Mora, 1995.

Derrida, Jacques. *On Grammatology*. Translated by Gayatri Chakravoty, John Hopkins University Press, Baltimore, 2016.

Derrida, Jacques. *Writing and Difference*. Translated by Alan Bass, Chicago, University of Chicago Press, 1978.

Díaz Infante Núñez, Juan José. *Del dolmen a la kalikosmia*. México, I. Maya Gómez, J. Torres Palacios, 1988.

Díaz Infante Núñez, Juan José. *Díaz Infante visto por Díaz Infante*. México, I. Maya Gómez, J. Torres Palacios, 1988.

Diaz Infante Núñez, Juan Jose. Personal interview with the author. Mexico City, 17th March 2000.

Donald, P. 'The relationship between college grades and achievement: A review of literature'. *American College Testing Research Reports*. No. 7. Iowa City, Research Development Division, 1965.

Doubilet, Susan. 'P/A reader poll: Women in architecture'. *Progressive Architecture*. Vol. 70. No. 10, 1989.

Dovey, Kim. *Framing Places Mediating Power in Built Form*. London, Routledge, 1999.

Bibliography

Dovey, Kim, Elek Pafka, and Mirjana Ristic. *Mapping Urbanities Morphologies, Flows, Possibilities*. New York, Routledge, 2017.

Durning, Louise and Richard Wrigley. *Gender and Architecture*. Chichester, John Wiley and Sons, 2000.

Echegaray, Miguel Ángel (ed.). *La Pintura Mural En Los Centros De Educación De México*. México City, SEP., 2003.

Eggener, Keith. *Luis Barragán's Gardens of El Pedregal*. New York, Princeton Architectural Press, 2001.

Enciclopedia de México. In CD Rom. Copyright. Sabeca International Investment Corporation, 1998.

Ferguson, Russell. *At the End of the Century One Hundred Years of Architecture*. London, Abrams Pub., 1998.

Fernández, Justino. *Arte Moderno Contemporáneo*. México, Ed. UNAM, 1952.

Fernández Cox, Christian. *América Latina: Nueva Arquitectura una Modernidad posracionalista*. México, Ed. Gustavo Gili, 1998.

Fleming, John, Hugh Honour, and Nikolaus Pevsner. *The Penguin Dictionary of Architecture and Landscape Architecture*. 5th Edition, London, Penguin Books, 1998.

Foucault, Michel. *The Archaeology of Knowledge and the Discourse on Language*. Translated by A. M. Sheridan Smith, New York, Pantheon Books, 1970.

Foucault, Michel. *Discipline and Punish: The Birth of the Prison*. Translated by Alan Sheridan, New York, Vintage, 1979.

Foucault, Michel. *On Power*. Edited by L. Kritzman, New York, Routledge, 1988.

Foucault, Michel. *Power/Knowledge, Selected Interviews and Other Writings 1972–1977*. Edited by Colin Gordon, Brighton, The Harvester Press, 1980.

Foucault, Michel. *The Order of Things: An Archaeology of the Human Sciences*. New York, Vintage Books, 1994.

Frampton, Kenneth. *Modern Architecture a Critical History*. London, Thames & Hudson, 1980–92.

Fraser, Valerie. *Building the New World: Studies in the Modern Architecture of Latin America 1930 1960*. London, Verso, 2000.

García Bringas, Graciela. *Agustín Hernández, arquitecto*. México, Grupo Noriega Editores, 1998.

García, Ivan and Vicky González. 'A brand after all'. *Futura*. http://byfutura.com/who-we-are/, accessed 5th October 2020.

Glocal, '10 | arquitectas Mexicanas destacadas'. *Glocal Design Magazine*, 7th March 2017. https://glocal.mx/10-arquitectas-mexicanas-destacadas/, accessed 5th October 2020.

Glusberg, Jorge. *Abraham Zabludovsky, arquitecto*. México, Noriega Editores: Consejo Nacional para la Cultura y las Artes, 1998.

Gómez, Lilia and Miguel Ángel Quevedo. 'Entrevista con el arquitecto José Villagrán García'. In *Testimonios Vivos 20 arquitectos*. México, Cuadernos de arquitectura. 15–16 INBA, Mayo-Agosto, 1981.

Gómez, Lilia and Miguel Ángel Quevedo. 'Entrevista con el arquitecto Juan O'Gorman'. In *Testimonios Vivos 20 arquitectos*. México, Cuadernos de arquitectura 15–16 INBA, Mayo-Agosto, 1981.

Bibliography

González de León Teodoro and Abraham Zabludovsky. *Ocho conjuntos de habitación: arquitectura contemporánea mexicana = Mexican contemporany architecture*. México, Arquitectura y Sociedad, 1976.

González Gortázar, Fernando. *La arquitectura mexicana del siglo XX*. México, Consejo Nacional para la Cultura y las Artes, 1994.

Gropius, Walter. *Scope of Total Architecture*. New York, Collier Books, 1962.

Grosz, Elizabeth. *Volatile Bodies: Towards a Corporeal Feminism*. eBook, London, Routledge, 2020.

Gutiérrez, Ramón, Eladio Dieste, and Graciela María Viñuales. *Arquitectura Latinoamericana en el Siglo XX*. Barcelona, Lunwerg Editores, 1998.

Harding, Sandra and Merrill B. Hintikka (eds.). *Discovering Reality*. Dordrecht, Reidel Publishing Company, 1983.

Hernández, Agustín. *Agustín Hernández Arquitecto*. México, Grupo Noriega Editores, 1998.

Hernández, Agustín. Personal interview with the author. Mexico City, 17th March 2000.

Hernández, Felipe. *Beyond Modernist Masters: Contemporary Architecture in Latin America*. Basel, Birkhäuser, 2010.

Hernández, Felipe. 'Central and South America, 1920–Present Day'. In Murray Fraser (ed.). *Sir Banister Fletcher's Global History of Architecture*. 21st Edition, London, Bloomsbury.

Hillier, Bill. *Space Is the Machine*. Cambridge, University Press, 1999.

Hitchcock, Henry-Russell. *Latin American Architecture since 1945*. New York, Museum of Modern Art, 1955.

Hubert L. Dreyfus and Paul Rabinow. *Michel Foucault: Beyond Structuralism and Hermeneutics*. Chicago, The University of Chicago Press, 1982.

Hughes, Francesca. *The Architect Reconstructing Her Practice*. Cambridge, MIT Press, 1996.

Hurtado Azpeitia, Maria Eugenia. 'Mujeres en la Arquitectura'. In *Enlace*. México, Colegio de Arquitectos de la Cd. de México A.C., 2013.

Jameson, Frederic. 'On Magical Realism in Film'. *Critical Inquiry*. Vol. 12. No. 2. Chicago, University of Chicago Press, Winter 1986.

Jencks, Charles. *Architecture Today*. London, Academy Editors, 1988.

Kalach, Alberto. Personal interview with the author. Mexico City, 26th May 2000.

Katzman, Israel. *La arquitectura contemporánea mexicana: Precedentes y desarrollo*. México, INAH, 1963.

Kuhlmann, Dörte. *Gender Studies in Architecture Space, Power and Difference*. London, Routledge, 2013.

Larson, Magali Sarfatti. *'The Rise of Professionalism:' A Sociological Analysis*. Berkeley, University of California Press, 1977.

Larrosa Irigoyen, Manuel. *Abraham Zabludosky, Espacios para la Cultura*. México, Conaculta, 2000.

Legorreta, Ricardo. Personal interview with the author. Mexico City, 16th October 2000.

Legorreta Vilchis, Ricardo. *Ricardo Legorreta*. Tokyo, ADA Edita Tokyo, 2000.

León, Adriana. *Kalach + Alvarez*. México, Gustavo Gili, 1998.

Lorenz, Clare. *Women in Architecture: A Contemporary Perspective*. New York, Rizzoli, 1990.

Bibliography

Massey, Doreen. *Space, Place and Gender*. Cambridge, Polity Press, 1994.

McDowell, Linda. *Gender, Identity and Place*. Cambridge, Polity Press, 1999.

Mijares, Carlos. Personal interview with the author. Mexico City, 30th May 2000.

Miquel, Adriá. *México Arquitectura de los 90s*. México, Gustavo Gili, 1998.

Monsiváis, Carlos. 'Lo Sagrado y lo Profano: México Identidad y Cultura'. In *Identidad Nacional*. México, Universidad Autónoma Metropolitana, 1994.

Mutlow, John V. *Legorreta Arquitectos: Ricardo Legorreta, Víctor Legorreta, Noé Castro*. México, Gustavo Gili, 1997.

Myers, I.E. *Mexico's Modern Architecture*. New York, Cornwell Press, 1952.

Noelle, Louise. *Arquitectos contemporáneos de México*. México, Editorial Trillas, 1989.

Noelle, Louise and Carlos Tejeda. *Catálogo Guía de Arquitectura Contemporánea*. México, Ed. Fomento Cultural Banamex, 1993.

Norten, Enrique. Personal interview with the author. Mexico City, 30th May 2000.

Obregón Santacilia, Carlos. *Cincuenta Años de Arquitectura Mexicana (1900–1950)*. México, Editorial Patria, 1952.

O'Gorman, Edmundo. *La Invención de América*. México, Fondo de Cultura Económica, 1993.

Olsen, Patrice. *Artifacts of Revolution: Architecture, Society, and Politics in Mexico City, 1920–1940*. Lanham, MD, Rowman & Littlefield Publishers, 2008.

O'Rourke, Kathryn. *Modern Architecture in Mexico City: History, Representation, and the Shaping of a Capital*. Pittsburgh, University of Pittsburgh Press, 2017.

Ortega y Gasset, José. *El Tema de Nuestro Tiempo*. Madrid, Espasa-Calpe, 1975.

Ortiz, Cecilia and María Rosenberg. *Las Pieles del Espacio: Space, Speed and Skin*. México, Díaz Infante Editorial, 1999.

Paz, Octavio. *The Labyrinth of Solitude*. Translated by Lysande Kemp, Yara Milos, and Rachel Philips Belash, London, Penguin Books, 1990.

Placzek, Adolf K. *Macmillan Encyclopedia of Architects*. New York, Free Press, 1982.

Porter, E. *Women and Moral Identity*. Sydney, Allen & Unwin, 1991.

Probyn, Elspeth. 'The Body Which Is Not One: Speaking an Embodied Self'. *Hypatia*. Vol. 6. No. 3, Fall 1991.

Progressive Architecture. Tokyo, Japan, No. 39, 1983.

Rabinow, Paul. *The Foucault Reader: An Introduction to Foucault's Thought*. Harmondsworth, Penguin Books, 1986.

Ramírez Ugarte, Alejandro. *Conversación con Luis Barragán*. Guadalajara, Arquitónica, 2015.

Ramírez Vázquez, Pedro. Personal interview with the author. Mexico City, 20th March 2000.

Ramos, Samuel. *EL Perfil del Hombre y la Cultura en México*. Mexico, UNAM, 1991.

Rendell, Jane, Barbara Penner, and Iain Borden (eds.). *Gender, Space, Architecture*. London, Routledge, 2000.

Revista Enlace, *Año 10, No. 7, Julio 2000*.

Revista Enlace, *Año 12, No. 7, 2002*.

Revista Obras, Vol. 24, No. 238, Octubre 1992.

Riggen Martínez, Antonio. *Luis Barragán: Mexico's modern master, 1902–1988*. New York, The Monacelli Press, 1996.

Bibliography

Rittel, Horst. 'Evaluating evaluators'. *Accreditation Evaluation Conference of the National Architectural Accrediting Board*. New Orleans, March 1976.

Rutherford, Jonathan (ed.). *Identity, Community, Culture, Difference*. London, Lawrence and Wishart, 1990.

Salvat, Juan, José Luis Rosas, et al. *Historia del arte mexicano: Arte contemporáneo*. vols. 13–16, México, Editorial Salvat, 1986.

Schor, Nahomi. *Reading in Detail: Aesthetics and the Feminine*. London/New York, Routledge, 2007.

Secretaria Nacional de Empleo. 'Observatorio Laboral'. *Gob. Mx*, 1er trimestre 2019. www.observatoriolaboral.gob.mx/static/estudios-publicaciones/Tendencias_empleo.html, accessed 5th October 2020.

Sordo Madaleno, Javier. Personal interview with the author. Mexico City, 27th May 2000.

Stevens, Garry. *The Favoured Circle: The Social Foundations of Architectural Distinction*. London, MIT Press, 1998.

Toca, Antonio and Aníbal Figueroa. *México Nueva Arquitectura*. México, Ed. Gustavo Gili, 1991–1995.

Toppelson, Sara. *50 Años de Arquitectura en Mexicana*. México, Ed. Plazola, 1999.

Toro, Alfonso and Fernando de Toro (eds.). *El Debate de la postcolonialidad en Latinoamérica*. Madrid/Frankfurt, Vervuert, Iberoamérica, 1999.

Toy, Maggie. *The Architect: Women in Contemporary Architecture*. New York, Watson-Guptill, 2001.

Trueblood, Beatriz. *Ramírez Vázquez en la arquitectura: Realización y diseño*. México, Editorial Diana, 1989.

Villagrán, García. *Panorama de 62 Años de Arquitectura Mexicana Contemporánea*. México, Cuadernos de Arquitectura, 1963.

Williamson, Roxanne Kuter. *American Architects and the Mechanics of Fame*. Austin, University of Texas Press, 1991.

Wilson, Elizabeth. *The Sphinx in the City: Urban life, the Control of Disorder and Women*. London, Virago, 1991.

'Women, Architecture and Identity': Personal Details, Stuart Hall with others, interview with Denise Scott Brown, BBC Open University, 1992. www2.bfi.org.uk/films-tv-people/4ce2b7bf6411e 2020, pp. 1228–1263.

Woods, Lebbeus. *TEN Arquitectos: Taller de Enrique Norten Arquitectos, S.C.* Barcelona, Gustavo Gili, 1995.

Zabludovsky, Abraham. Personal interview with the author. Mexico City, 31st May 2000.

Zamora, Lois Parkinson and Wendy B. Faris (eds.). *Magical Realism: Theory, History, Community*. Durham NC, Duke University Press, 1995.

Zevi, Bruno. 'Grottesco Messicano'. In *L'Espresso*, Rome, BFC Media, 29 December 1957, p. 16. Also reproduced in *Arquitectura México* 62, 1958, p. 110.

Zevi, Bruno. *History of Modern Architecture*. London, Faber and Faber, 1950.

INDEX

Aalto, Alvar 18–9, 61, 228
Abraham Zabludosky Studio 206–07
Academia Nacional de Arquitectura 25
Adrià, Miquel 32
Agustín Hernández Studio 208–11
Ahmad, Aijaz 255
Aja, Maritza 23, 24
Albin, Enrique 24
Alessio, Jorge 24
Alfaro Siqueiros, David 3, 247
Álvarez García, Augusto H. 24
Álvarez, Daniel 24, 177
Ambasz, Emilio 50
Amédée Ozenfant Studio 229
Anahuacalli 52, 53
Ando, Tadao 239, 268
Archigram 37, 61, 230–31
Arquitectura en Proceso 264
Art Deco 33–4, 49, 241
Azcáraga Milmo, Emilio 150
Aztec Calendar 88

Ballina, Jorge 23–4
BAM South Site or 300 Ashland 63
Barthes, Roland 26, 14
Bartra, Roger 222
Barragán, Luis 7–8, 16, 22–4, 31, 35,
    42–3, 48–51, 54, 58, 60, 116, 127,
    129, 131–32, 137–38, 149, 153–54,
    160, 162, 182–84, 187–88, 197–99,
    202, 204, 220, 226–27, 248, 250–52
Barragán Schwartz, Rodolfo 23, 24
Basílica de la Virgen de Guadalupe 116,
    119–22
Bassols, Narciso 149
Baudrillard, Jean 126
Béjar, Raúl 222
Beltrán, Lisa 268
Benemérita Universidad Autónoma de
    Puebla 17
Benévolo, Leonardo 32

Benlliure, José Luis 24
Bercy 2 Shopping Centre 240
Bergdoll, Barry 32
Bhabha, Homi 6, 226, 241
Biblioteca Central Universidad Nacional
    Autónoma de México (UNAM) 43, 45,
    53, 80, 248
Biblioteca Vasconcelos 64–5
Bilbao, Tatiana 265, 268
Bolsa Mexicana de Valores (Mexican Stock
    Market) building 40, 61,107–09,
    233–34
Borges, Jorge Luis
Born, Esther 137
Boston City Hall 235–36
Bourdieu, Pierre 136
Broid, Isaac 23–4
Browne, Enrique 32
Brutalism or Brutalist style 56, 90, 102,
    206, 235
Bufete Industrial 195–96
Bullrich, Francisco 32
Bustamante, José Alberto 128

Cacho, Raúl 24
Calakmul building 57
Calzada, Paola 267
Campos, Mauricio 21, 24, 38
Campuzano, Jorge 24
Canales, Fernanda 265, 268
Candela, Félix 24, 116
Canesi, Federico 148
Capilla del Panteón 61
Carpentier, Alejo 249
Carranza, Luis E. 32
Carrillo, Gabriela 265
Casa Agustín Hernández 198, 201
Casa Barragán in Chapala a town in Jalisco
    located by Lake Chapala, the largest
    lake in Mexico 182
Casa Efraín González Luna 183–84

297

Index

Casa Estudio Diego Rivera also known as Casa Estudio Diego Rivera y Frida Kalho 43, 52, 229–30

Casa Estudio Tacubaya or Luis Barragán's house/studio 43, 46, 50, 51, 137, 160, 162, 187, 197–99, 203, 250–51

Casa GGG 163–64, 239

Casa Gilardi 51, 184–86, 197, 199–200

Casa LE 188–89, 192

Casa Monte Tauro or Legorreta's house in Monte Tauro 160–61

Casa-Cueva O'Gorman or grotto house 53

Casillas, Andrés 22, 24

Castañeda, Luis 32

Castro, Noé 22, 24, 60

Centro Comunitario Independencia 264

Centro Cultural Arte Contemporáneo 150

Centro Financiero Banamex Lomas (now Citibanamex C.F. Lomas) 98–100

Cetto, Max 22, 24, 129

Chakravorty Spivak, Gayatri 255–56

Chance, Julia 137

Chavez Morado, José 102

Choay, Françoise 36

Christ Church 61, 117–18, 232

Citibanamex Oficina Central Las Capuchinas 99–101

Ciudad Universitaria or (CU) also known as Universidad Nacional Autónoma de México UNAM 17, 53, 80, 247

Colegio Alemán Alexander Von Humboldt or simply Colegio Von Humboldt 63, 113–14

Colegio de Arquitectos 25

Colegio Monte Sinai 113–14

Comas, Carlos Eduardo 32

Comité Administrador del Programa Federal de Construcción de Escuelas (CAPCE) 148

Commodity 126–27, 130–31, 136, 150–51, 154, 166, 264

Convento de las Capuchinas 116

Corporativo IBM Santa Fe 111

Cosanti Foundation 68

Creixell del Moral, José Luis 24

Creixell Diaque, José 24

Critical Regionalism 30, 33, 35, 61

Cuadra San Cristóbal 51, 251

Cuadrángulo de las Monjas in Uxmal 87, 241–43

Cueto, Alejandro 24

Cuevas, José A. 24

Cuff, Dana 15

de Anda, Enrique X. 30–2, 34–6

de Buen, Clara 7, 18, 23–5, 35, 48, 62–4, 95–6, 111, 113, 131, 133, 144, 149, 152, 177–79, 211–12, 222–23, 274–75

de Buen, Oscar 149

de Chirico, Giorgio 252

de la Mora y Palomar, Enrique 24, 40

de Yturbe, José 24

Deconstructivism or Deconstruction 2, 5–6, 262

Dehesa Gómez Farias, María Luisa 173

Del Dolmen a la Kalikosmia 37

del Moral, Enrique 21, 24, 38

del Real, Patricio 32

Delegación Cuauhtémoc 55, 81, 103–05

Deterioration of the Economic Model 80–1

Devaluation Crisis 78, 81

Díaz Infante, Juan José 7, 24, 37–41, 48, 58, 61, 82, 95, 97, 105, 107–08, 131, 142–43, 164, 194–95, 207, 230–31, 234, 274–75

Díaz Morales, Ignacio 22, 24

Dieste, Eladio 32

Discourse analysis 5, 6

Discursive author 48, 53, 55–7, 61, 65–6

Dissimulation 226, 256

Dovey, Kim 74–6

Dunster, David 136

Edificio Reforma Lomas Altas 234–35

Edificio Rodin or Departamentos Rodin 65, 192–93

298

Eggener, Keith 42, 129
El Animal del Pedregal or simple 'El Animal' 128, 129
El Colegio de México 56, 104, 113, 115–16, 235
El Palacio de Hierro Polanco also Plaza Moliere 134, 254
El Palacio de Hierro Santa Fe 254
El Pedregal 43, 51, 127–29, 154–55
Elizondo, Alejandro 24
Emotional architecture 31, 34–5, 131, 248, 252, 255
End of the Century Stage 82
Equipal Moderno 132–33
Escobedo, Frida 265–66, 274
Escuela Nacional de Arte Teatral 63, 240
Escuela Técnica Industrial 112–13
Estación del Metro de Pantitlán Línea A 95–6, 98, 149
Estadio Azteca 55
Etchegaray, Gabriela 265
Exchange-value 126–27, 130
Export-Led-Growth Economic Model 77, 79

Fábrica Automex 252
Fajardo Valderrama, Sergio 264
Ferguson, Russell 32
Fernández Cox, Christian 30, 32
Fernández, Jimena 267, 274
Fernández, Justino 32
Figueroa, Aníbal 32
Fleming, John 32
Fletcher, Banister, Sir 32
Foster, Norman 268
Foucault, Michel 14, 48, 74, 263
Framing Places 74–5
Frampton, Kenneth 30, 32
Fraser, Murray 32, 274
Fraser, Valerie 32
Fuente de los Patos 129
Fuentes, Carlos 249
Fuller, Buckminster 37, 61, 207, 231
Functionalist or functional 3, 18–9, 27, 30–1, 37–8, 40, 49–50, 52, 54, 56–8, 62, 65, 67, 86, 117, 126–27, 131, 137, 158, 173, 262
Futura 264

Gamboa de Buen, Jorge 24
García Márquez, Gabriel 249
García, Iván 264
García, Susana 23–4
García, Xavier 32
Giedion, Siegfried 136
Globalization 4, 223–25, 237, 268
Goeritz, Mathias 22, 24, 31, 38, 47, 128–29
Gómez Pimienta, Bernardo 24, 268
González de León, Teodoro 21, 24, 55, 88, 98–9, 103, 109, 113, 148, 190, 235, 243
González Gortazar, Fernando 32
González Rul, Manuel 24, 245, 246
González, Vicky 264
Govela, Alfonso 24
Governmentality 15–6
Grauman's Chinese Theatre 227
Gropius, Walter 3, 136
Grotesseco Messicano 247
Gutiérrez, Ramón 32

Hadid, Zaha 268
Hanson, Julienne 75
Hernández, Agustín 7, 18, 21, 24, 48, 54, 56–7, 132, 137, 140, 147, 174, 201, 209–11, 245–46, 274
Hernández, Felipe 218
Heroico Colegio Militar 43, 56, 245
High-Tech 57, 62, 225, 237, 262
Hillier, Bill 75
Hitchcock, Henry-Russell 32
Honour, Hugh 32
hooks, bell 269
Hospital Manuel Gea González 37
Hotel Camino Real Ixtapa 43
Hotel Camino Real or Hotel Camino Real Mexico City is the first hotel of this franchise. 43, 58, 81, 93–5, 150, 164, 166–67, 252

299

Index

Hotel Iturbide 226
Hotel María Isabel Sheraton 81, 92–4
Huichol 246–47
Hybridity 225, 241–42, 244–47, 256, 268

ICA (Ingenieros Civiles Asociados) 50, 149
Iglesia de La Medalla Milagrosa 116
Iglesia del Perpetuo Socorro 61
Import-Substitution Economic Growth
    Strategy Model 77, 80
Indian Institute of Management in
    Ahmedabad 232
Ingersoll, Richard 62
Instituto del Fomento Nacional de Vivienda,
    also known as INFONAVIT 81,
    109–10, 148
Instituto Nacional de Cardiología also
    Hospital Nacional de Cardiología 50,
    83, 85–6, 228
Instituto Politécnico Nacional 17
Instituto Tecnológico y de Estudios
    Superiores de Occidente 17
International Style 3, 34, 127, 225, 228,
    247, 262

Jameson, Frederic 249
Jardines del Pedregal also known as
    Jardines del Pedregal de San Ángel or
    simply El Pedregal 43, 51, 127–29,
    154–55
Jencks, Charles 32
John Hancock Tower 233, 234
Juan Jose Diaz Infante´s house/studio in
    Amsterdam Street 40, 61, 207–08

Kahn, Louis 18, 61, 231–33
Kalach, Alberto 7, 24, 36, 48, 62, 64,
    135, 142, 144, 147, 163, 177, 190,
    192, 223, 237, 239, 268, 274–75
Kalach+Alvarez 177
Kalho, Frida 230, 256
Kalikosmia 37–40, 61, 97, 131
Kallmann, McKinnell & Knowles 235–36

Katzman, Israel 32
Kurokawa, Kisho 230–31

La Geoda 207
La Patera 81
La Templanza 157–9
Landa Verdugo, Agustín 24
Landa Vertiz, Agustín 24, 264
Lara, Fernando 32
Las Arboledas 251
Late-Modernist 57
Lazo Barreiro, Carlos 24
Lazo Pino, Carlos 24, 38
Le Corbusier 3, 18–9, 37, 190, 227,
    229–31
Legarreta, Juan 24
Legorreta, Ricardo 7, 21–22, 24, 31, 38,
    43, 48, 58, 60, 66, 92–3, 131–32,
    142, 149–50, 152–54, 158, 160, 164,
    166, 176, 179, 204, 206, 220–22,
    224, 237, 250, 252, 255, 274–75
Legorreta, Víctor 22, 24
León, Adriana 24, 177
Liernur, Jorge Francisco 32
Lima, Lezama 249
López Carmona, Fernando 24, 40
López Mateos, Adolfo 54, 105, 148

Mac Gregor, Carlos 23–4, 63, 95–6, 111,
    144, 177, 211–12
Magical Realism 226, 248–50, 254, 256
Magritte, René 41
Mariscal, Francisco 24, 38
Martínez Velasco, Juan 24
Marvelous Real 249
Mary St. Albans 129
Méndez, Leopoldo 247
Mercedes House 63
Mestizo 219, 222–23
Metabolism is an architectural movement
    also known as Japanese Metabolists
    37, 61, 230–31
Mexican Colonial 49

Index

Mexican Embassy in Brazil 243–44
Mexican muralism 219, 247
Mexican Olympic Games or Mexico City
    1968 Olympic Games also simply
    1968 Olympic Games 3, 78, 93, 246
Mexican Pavilion at the 15th Venice
    Architecture Biennale 263
Mexican Renaissance, or The Mexican
    Mural Renaissance 219
Mexican Revolution 2, 37, 49, 77, 83, 98,
    112, 219, 225, 241
Mexican-ness 5, 51, 62, 219, 222–25,
    247, 256
Mexicas 89
Mexico '68 emblem for the Olympic Games
    246
Mex-Tech Creole 63
Michelangelo 136
Mies van der Rohe, Ludwig 18, 61, 231
Mijares, Carlos 7, 18, 22–4, 35, 41, 48,
    58, 60, 61, 63, 117, 131, 135, 138,
    141, 147, 174–75, 222, 231–33,
    274–75
Mijares, Rafael 24
Mimicry 225–27, 232, 235, 237,
    240–41, 256, 268
Moctezuma, Pedro 24
Modern 8, 18, 27, 31, 32, 33, 34, 39,
    49, 52–3, 61, 66, 87, 94, 129,
    131–32, 136, 151, 164, 178,
    188–89, 218, 220, 246
Modernism 2–4, 6–8, 28, 38, 43, 49,
    52–3, 56, 58, 62, 67, 76, 83, 85,
    173, 181, 189, 218, 225–26,
    228–30, 247, 262, 269
Modernity 2–3, 32, 63, 77, 219, 225,
    228, 234
Modernization 2, 4–5, 68, 78, 80, 257,
    262
Monsiváis, Carlos 193, 222
Montalbán, Ricardo 150
Monte Albán 245
Montiel, Rozana 265

Multibanco Mercantil (now Actinver M.
    Lomas de Chapultepec) 98
Mumford, Lewis 136
Muñoz, David 24
Museo de Arte e Historia de Guanajuato 64
Museo de Arte Moderno 86
Museo de Historia de México 86
Museo del Templo Mayor 55, 88–90
Museo MARCO 134, 252
Museo Nacional de Antropología o Museo
    de Antropología 43–4, 55, 80, 86–7,
    89, 103, 241–43
Museo Tamayo 55, 88, 90–2,104,
    243–44
Museum of Modern Art in New York 246
Myers, Irving Evan 32

Neoliberal Model or Neoliberal Economy 3,
    77–78, 82, 98, 121, 270
Neo-Prehispanic 33
Noelle, Louise 32
Norten, Enrique 7, 21, 24, 48, 62–3,
    131, 132, 142, 143, 147, 188,
    192, 221, 224, 237, 240, 256,
    274–75
North American Free Trade Agreement
    (NAFTA) 3, 78, 223–24
Nuño, Aurelio 23–4, 63, 95–6, 111, 144,
    177–78, 211–12
Nuño, Mac Gregor de Buen Studio or NMB
    Studio 212–13
Nuño, Mac Gregor, de Buen (NMB) 23–4,
    63, 95, 111, 144, 177, 212–13

O´Gorman, Juan 7, 24, 38, 43, 48–9,
    52–3, 80, 112–13, 131, 137, 139,
    149, 176, 229–30, 247
O'Gorman, Edmundo 219–20
O'Rourke, Kathryn 32
Obregón Santacilia, Carlos 24
Oficinas de ICA (Ingenieros Civiles
    Asociados) 50
Olsen, Patrice 32

301

Index

Ondarza, Fernando 23–4
Op Art 246–47
Organic Architecture 18
Orozco, José Clemente 3, 219
Ortega y Gasset, José 6–7
Ortiz Monasterio, Manuel 24, 38
Ortiz, Cecilia 40
'Other', Otherness 5, 218–20, 225, 241,
    249–50, 255, 257, 268, 270

Pabellón de México in the 1992 Seville
    Exposition 55
Paimio Sanatorium 228
Palacio Legislativo de San Lázaro 102
Palladio, Andrea 136
Pani, Mario 21, 24, 105, 151
Partido Revolucionario Institucional (PRI)
    77–8, 82
Paz, Octavio 3, 197, 219–21, 226
Pedregal de Santo Domingo 154–55
Pei, I.M. 233
Pelli, Cesar 42, 268
Pérez Palacios, Augusto 24, 56
Pérez-Gómez, Alberto 38
Pevsner, Nikolaus 32, 136
Piano, Renzo 239–40
Place-identity 219–20, 223–24, 248
Placzek, Adolf K. 32
'Plastic Integration' or visual arts integration,
    emerged in Mexico in the late 1940s,
    as a movement that promoted
    interdisciplinary work between
    architecture, painting and sculpture
    with the desire to turn it into a single
    aesthetic expression 247
Plaza 'El Animal' or Plaza 'El Animal del
    Pedregal' 128–29
Plaza Artz Pedregal 66
Plaza Moliere (now El Palacio de Hierro
    Polanco) 134, 254
Porfirio Díaz 2
Porset, Clara 131–32
Posadas, José Guadalupe 247

Postcolonial 4–6, 218–19, 225–26, 241,
    248, 254–57, 262, 268
Postcolonialism 218
Postmodernism 2
Postmodernist 19, 262
Price Tower 237–38
Pritzker Prize 42, 50

Ramírez Vázquez, Pedro 7, 24, 38, 40,
    42–3, 48, 54–5, 86, 88–9, 102–3, 105,
    107, 117, 119–22, 131–32, 137, 140,
    147, 153–54, 241–42, 244, 274–75
Ramírez, Ugarte Alejandro 8
Ramos, Samuel 219, 226
Rational 30–1, 50, 53, 55, 84, 221, 225,
    233, 249
Rationalism 18, 49
Rationalist 14
Real Academia de San Carlos 17–8, 37
Regency Hyatt Hotel, Dallas 234
Ricardo Legorreta Studio or
    Legorreta+Legorreta Studio 204–06
Rivera, Diego 3, 43, 51–3, 129, 148,
    219, 229–30
Rivera, Lupe 148
Rivera, Ruth 51
Rocha, Mauricio 268
Rodó José, Enrique 221
Rogers, Richard 59, 268
Rosenberg, María 40
Rossell de la Lama, Guillermo 21, 24, 148
Rulfo, Juan 249

Saarinen, Eero 18
Sáenz Viteri, Francisco 23–4
Sala Mexica 87–8
Salas Portugal, Armando 42
Salinas de Gortari, Carlos 55
Salmerón, Raúl 24
Sanatorio para Tuberculosos de Huipulco
    50, 83–4
Sánchez, Javier 268
Segura, Juan 24

Index

Serrano, Francisco J. 24
Serrano Cacho, Francisco 23–4, 63, 66
Shakespeare, William 221
Shared Development 78
Silla Gala 132–33
Silla Miguelito 131–32
Silla Vallarta 132
Silva-Herzog Flores, Jesús 148
Silvia Arango 6
Soleri, Paolo 68
Sordo Madaleno, Javier 7, 19, 22, 24, 35,
    38, 48, 62, 66, 130–32, 135, 145,
    149–50, 174–77, 234, 250, 253–55,
    268, 274–75
Sordo Madaleno, Juan 22, 24, 66, 93, 149
Space Syntax 6, 75
Spatial diagram 6–7, 75, 83–8, 88, 92,
    94–5, 98–101, 105, 110–13, 116,
    121, 157–63, 182–3, 186–88, 190–91,
    202, 204, 208, 210, 212–13
Springall, Saidee 268
Subverted Eden 248
Surrealist 30, 33
Symbolic-exchange 126, 130, 165

Tamayo, Rufino 256
TAPO (Terminal de Autobuses de Oriente)
    bus station 40, 61, 95–8
Team X 262
Tec de Monterrey 17, 274
Tejeda, Carlos 23–4, 32
Televisa mixed-use building 63
Teoría de la Arquitectura 36–7
The Circular Ruins 8
The Fountainhead is a 1943 novel by
    Russian-born American author Ayn
    Rand 136
The Invention of America 219
The Kingdom of This World 249
The Labyrinth of Solitude 219
The Rule and the Model 36
The Tempest 221
Third World 249, 255

Tlaltecuhtli 89–90
Tlaltelolco 105–06
Toca, Antonio 19
Toledo, Francisco 256
Topelson, Sara 265
Torre BBVA 59
Torre Celanese 237–38
Torre Citibank Reforma 164–66
Torre de Mexicana de Aviación 55
Torre de Tlatelolco 81, 105–06
Torres de Mixcoac 81, 148, 158, 190–91
Torres de Satélite 43, 47
Torres, Ramon 24
Trans-discursive author 48, 52–3
Treib, Marc 42

Universidad Anáhuac 17, 40, 174
Universidad Autónoma de Guadalajara 17
Universidad Autónoma de Nuevo León 17
Universidad Autónoma de Veracruz 17
Universidad Autónoma Metropolitana 17
Universidad de Guanajuato 17
Universidad de Las Américas 17
Universidad Iberoamericana 'Ibero' 17, 19,
    23, 35, 63
Universidad La Salle 17
Universidad Nacional Autónoma de México
    (UNAM) 17, 37, 43, 53, 80, 154, 247
Universidad Pedagógica Nacional 55, 113,
    235–36
Use-value 126–27, 130
Utzon, Jørn 18, 231
Uxmal 87, 241–43

Valparaiso School 68
Vasconcelos, Fernando 24
Vasconcelos, José 219
*Vers Une Architecture (Towards a New
    Architecture)* 38
Villagrán García, José 7, 18, 21–2, 24,
    36–8, 40–2, 48–50, 52, 54, 56, 80,
    83–5, 92, 131, 137, 139, 151, 173,
    219, 228

303

Index

Viñuales, Graciela María 32
Vistas del Cerro Grande (Community
    Centre) 264
Vitra Conference Pavilion 239

Welton Beckett & Associates 234
Western, Westerner, Westernized 2–3, 5–6,
    8, 14–15, 17, 19, 25, 31, 37, 40, 41,
    49, 58, 67, 76–7, 147, 154–55, 196,
    218, 220, 225–28, 231, 237, 240–41,
    247, 249–51, 255–57, 269–70
Westernization 2, 4–5, 68, 221, 257, 262
Westin Los Cabos Resort Villas & Spa or
    Westin Regina Los Cabos Hotel 66, 254

Wigley, Mark 180
Williamson, Roxanne Kuter 136
Wilson, Elizabeth 194
Wright, Frank Lloyd 68, 237–38

Yáñez, Enrique 24, 38

Zabludovsky, Abraham 7, 21, 24–5, 48,
    54–6, 88, 98–9, 103, 109, 113, 115,
    121, 127, 131–33, 138, 141, 147–48,
    151, 157–58, 160, 190, 206, 224,
    227, 235, 243–44, 274–75
Zárate, Guillermo 24, 38
Zevi, Bruno 18, 247